John R. Pescosolido
Professor Emeritus
Central Connecticut State University
New Britain, Connecticut

Reviewers

Maria Driend
Literacy Coordinator
Cooperative Education Services
Trumbull, Connecticut

Terese D'Amico
Gifted Education Specialist for Grades 3–6
Thomas Jefferson Magnet School
Euclid City Schools
Euclid, Ohio

Patricia D'Amore
Assistant Literacy Coordinator
Cooperative Educational Services
Trumbull, Connecticut

Dr. Donna Ronzone
Principal and Director of Special Education
Briggs Elementary School District
Santa Paula, California

STECK-VAUGHN
ELEMENTARY · SECONDARY · ADULT · LIBRARY
A Harcourt Company

www.steck-vaughn.com

Acknowledgments

Editorial Director Stephanie Muller
Senior Editor Amanda Sperry
Assistant Editor Julie M. Smith
Associate Director of Design Cynthia Ellis
Senior Design Manager Cynthia Hannon
Designer Deborah Diver
Media Researcher Sarah Fraser
Editorial Development, Design, and Production The Quarasan Group, Inc.
Cover Illustration Ken Joudrey
Senior Technical Advisor Alan Klemp

PHOTO CREDITS 3 ©Tim Flach/Stone; 5 ©Stuart Westmorland/Stone; 6 ©John Henley/The Stock Market; 8 ©Laurie Campbell/Stone; 14 ©Charles Gupton/The Stock Market; 19-20 ©PhotoDisc, Inc.; 21 ©Barbara Penoyar/PhotoDisc, Inc.; 26 ©John Chard/Stone; 27 ©PhotoDisc, Inc.; 30 ©A. Ramey/PhotoEdit, Inc.; 32 ©Digital Studios; 33 ©Kevin R. Morris/Corbis; 34 left (l) ©AFP/Corbis; right (r) ©Nicole Duplaix/Corbis; 35-36 ©PhotoDisc, Inc.; 38 ©Corbis; 39 top (t) ©PhotoDisc, Inc.; bottom (b) ©Dennis Galante/FPG International; 41 ©PhotoDisc, Inc.; 42 ©EyeWire, Inc.; 43 ©Pictor International, Ltd./PictureQuest; 48 ©Esben Hardt/International Stock; 54 ©Corbis; 56 ©PhotoDisc, Inc.; 57 ©FPG International; 58 ©PhotoDisc, Inc.; 60 ©Corbis; 62 (basket) ©Joe Atlas/Artville; (bread) ©PhotoDisc, Inc.; 62-63 (ant) ©MetaTools; 63 (t) ©Tim Flach/Stone; (b) ©Jagdish Agarwal/Stock Connection/PictureQuest; 64 ©Tim Flach/Stone; 66 ©Corbis; 67 (t) middle (m) ©Comstock, Inc.; (b) ©MetaTools; 68 (t) ©PhotoDisc, Inc.; (m)(b) ©Corbis; 69-70 ©Corbis; 72 ©Dan McCoy/Rainbow/PictureQuest; 73 ©Karl Weatherly/Corbis; 74 ©PhotoDisc, Inc.; 75 ©EyeWire, Inc.; 76 ©Craig Tuttle/The Stock Market; 77 ©SuperStock, Inc.; 82 ©Richard Stockton/Southern Stock/PictureQuest; 83 ©Corbis; 88 ©C Squared Studios/PhotoDisc, Inc.; 89 ©SuperStock, Inc.; 94 ©Alan R. Moller/Stone; 95 (hat) ©Digital Studios; (shirt) ©Siede Preis/PhotoDisc, Inc.; (pants) ©Digital Studios; (shoes) ©PhotoDisc, Inc.; 100 ©Digital Studio; 101 ©Dusty Willison/International Stock; 106 (t) ©Corbis; (b) ©PhotoDisc, Inc.; 108 ©MetaTools; 109 ©Morton Beebe, S.F./Corbis; 110 ©Comstock, Inc.; 111 ©Jose L. Pelaez/The Stock Market; 114 ©PhotoDisc, Inc.; 116 ©Bob Firth/International Stock; 117 ©Corel Corporation; 122 ©SuperStock, Inc.; 123 ©Artville; 127 ©PhotoDisc, Inc.; 128 ©Peter Langone/International Stock; 130 (l) ©MetaTools; (m) ©SuperStock, Inc.; (r) ©David Young-Wolff/PhotoEdit, Inc.; 131 (l) ©Brownie Harris/The Stock Market; (r) ©Corbis; 132 ©SuperStock, Inc.; 133 ©PhotoDisc, Inc.; 134 ©Corbis; 136 (t) ©PhotoDisc, Inc.; (b) ©MetaTools; 137 (t) ©Reuters NewMedia Inc./Corbis; (bl) ©John Terence Turner/FPG International; (br) ©MetaTools; 138 ©PhotoDisc, Inc.; 140 ©Rolf Bruderer/The Stock Market; 141 ©Pete Saloutos/The Stock Market; 142 ©MetaTools; 143 ©Roy Morsch/The Stock Market; 144 ©Phil Degginger/Stone; 145 ©Tony Freeman/PhotoEdit, Inc.; 150 ©Jon Feingersh/The Stock Market; 151 ©Dennis O'Clair/Stone; 156 ©Mitch Kezar/Stone; 158 (l) ©BENELUX PRESS/H. Armstrong Roberts; (r) ©Lee Snider/Corbis; 159 (t) ©C.P. Cushing/H. Armstrong Roberts; (b) ©Archive Photos; 160 ©Archive Photos; 162 ©Pal Hermansen/Stone; 168 ©Mark Cooper/The Stock Market; 169 ©Greg Voight/International Stock; 170 (t) ©Frank Rossotto/The Stock Market; (bl)(br) ©Corbis; 171 (t) ©Joel Simon/Stone; (b) ©Palazzo del Bo, Padua, Italy/Mauro Magliani/SuperStock, Inc.; 172 ©Joel Simon/Stone; 174 ©Corbis; 175 ©Joe Atlas/Artville; 176-177 ©Corbis; 178 ©SuperStock, Inc.; 179 ©David Young-Wolff/PhotoEdit, Inc.; 180 ©Stuart Westmorland/Stone; 181 (l) ©Kennan Ward/Corbis; (m) ©Tom Brakefield/Corbis; (r) ©PhotoDisc, Inc.; 182 (t) ©Kennan Ward/Corbis; (b) ©Kunio Owaki/The Stock Market; 184 ©Cartesia/PhotoDisc/PictureQuest; 190 ©Comstock, Inc.; 191 (bowl) ©Felicia Martinez/PhotoEdit, Inc.; (cubes) ©Comstock, Inc.; 196 ©Telegraph Colour Library/FPG International; 198-199 ©Bob Daemmrich/Stock Boston; 200 ©Park Street Photography; 202 ©PhotoDisc, Inc.; 203 ©Comstock, Inc., ©PhotoDisc, Inc.; 207 ©PhotoDisc, Inc.; 208 ©PhotoDisc/PictureQuest; 209-210 ©Corbis; 211 ©Tony Freeman/PhotoEdit, Inc. Dictionary photos: 216 ©Rudi Von Briel/PhotoEdit, Inc.; 218 ©Nancy Dudley/Stock Boston; 225 ©Photo Edit, Inc.; 226 ©Yann Arthus-Bertrand/Corbis; 232 ©Duomo/Corbis; 234 Courtesy NASA; 235 ©Lowell Georgia/Corbis; 238 ©Jonathan Daniel/Allsport USA; 240 Courtesy NASA. Additional dictionary photos by: Corbis, Corel, PhotoDisc, Steck-Vaughn Collection.

ART CREDITS Ann Barrow 22-24, 73, 204-206; Anthony Carnabuci 112-114; Roger Chandler 15, 72 (b); Randy Chewning 107 (t); Doris Ettlinger 16-18; Eldon Doty 78-80, 129, 174; Drew-Brook-Cormack Associates 102-104, 193-194; Peter Fasolino 9, 84-86; Ruth Flanigan 5, 38, 107 (b), 140 (b), 152-154; John Steven Gurney 140 (t), 186-188, 209; Joseph Hammond 208 (b); Susan Jaekel 4, 61, 90-92; Cheryl Kirk-Noll 96-98; John Lund 28-30, 72 (t), 146-148, 157, 175 (b), 197, 208 (t); Erin Mauterer 44-46, 118-120, 141; Kathleen O'Malley 55, 185; Kevin O'Malley 3, 10-12; Daniel Powers 135, 163, 175 (t); Ilene Robinette 50-52; Neecy Twinem 164-166; Jason Wolff 124-126

Pronunciation key and diacritical marks copyright © 1998 by Houghton Mifflin Company. Adapted and reproduced by permission from *The American Heritage Student Dictionary*.

Steck-Vaughn Spelling: Linking Words to Meaning is a registered trademark of Steck-Vaughn Company.

Softcover ISBN 0-7398-3613-7   Hardcover ISBN 0-7398-5057-1

Printed in the United States of America
5 6 7 8 9 10 WC 08 07 06 05 04

The words *grasshopper, kangaroo, rabbit, snake,* and *tracks* are hidden on the cover. Can you find them?

Contents

Unit 5

Unit 6

Study Steps to Learn a Word

1 **Say** the word. What consonant sounds do you hear? What vowel sounds do you hear? How many syllables do you hear?

2 **Look** at the letters in the word. Think about how each sound is spelled. Find any spelling patterns or parts that you know. Close your eyes. Picture the word in your mind.

3 **Spell** the word aloud.

4 **Write** the word. Say each letter as you write it.

5 **Check** the spelling. If you did not spell the word correctly, use the study steps again.

Use the steps on this page to study words that are hard for you.

Spelling Strategies

What can you do when you aren't sure how to spell a word?

Say the word aloud. Make sure you say it correctly. Listen to the sounds in the word. Think about letters and patterns that might spell the sounds.

Look in the Spelling Table to find common spellings for sounds in the word.

Think about related words. They may help you spell the word you're not sure of.

instruction—instruct

Guess the spelling of the word and check it in a dictionary.

Write the word in different ways. Compare the spellings and choose the one that looks correct.

tuch   toch   (touch)   tooch

Think about any spelling rules you know that can help you spell the word.

To form the plural of a singular word ending in a consonant and y, change the y to i and add -es.

Listen for a common word part, such as a prefix, suffix, or ending.

appoint<u>ment</u>
<u>per</u>sonal

Break the word into syllables and think about how each syllable might be spelled.

an i ma tion

Create a memory clue to help you remember the spelling of the word.

<u>Cloth</u>ing is made of <u>cloth</u>.

Words with /ă/

rabbit

1. *a* Words

_____
_____
_____
_____
_____
_____
_____
_____
_____
_____
_____
_____
_____
_____
_____
_____
_____
_____

2. *au* Words

_____
_____

act
sandwich
traffic
magic
chapter
rabbit
snack
rapid
plastic
laughter
calf
program
planet
crash
salad
aunt
factory
magnet
half
crack

Say and Listen

Say each spelling word. Listen for the /ă/ sound you hear in *act*.

Think and Sort

Look at the letters in each word. Think about how /ă/ is spelled. Spell each word aloud.

How many spelling patterns for /ă/ do you see?

1. Write the **eighteen** spelling words that have the *a* pattern.

2. Write the **two** spelling words that have the *au* pattern.

Use the steps on page 6 to study words that are hard for you.

Spelling Patterns

a	au
act	laughter

Spelling and Meaning

Definitions   Write the spelling word for each definition. Use the Spelling Dictionary if you need to.

1. a heavenly body that circles the sun   _____

2. a place where things are made   _____

3. the movement of cars and trucks   _____

4. a young cow or bull   _____

5. a sound that shows amusement   _____

6. a ceremony or presentation   _____

7. a substance made from chemicals   _____

Analogies   An analogy states that two words go together in the same way as two others. Write the spelling word that completes each analogy.

8. *Perform* is to _____ as *exercise* is to *jog*.

9. *Big* is to *large* as *fast* is to _____.

10. *Third* is to *three* as _____ is to *two*.

11. *Bear* is to *honey* as *nail* is to _____.

12. *Feast* is to _____ as *mansion* is to *cottage*.

13. *Correct* is to *right* as *smash* is to _____.

14. *Hire* is to *employ* as *split* is to _____.

15. *Man* is to *woman* as *uncle* is to _____.

16. *Lettuce* is to _____ as *flour* is to *bread*.

17. *Kitty* is to *cat* as *bunny* is to _____.

18. *Room* is to *house* as _____ is to *book*.

19. *Artist* is to *art* as *magician* is to _____.

Word Story   In the 18th century, an English earl loved games so much that he didn't stop for meals. He would eat a slice of meat between two slices of bread. The food became popular and was named after the earl. Write the spelling word that names the food.

20. _____

Family Tree: *magnet* Compare the spellings, meanings, and pronunciations of the *magnet* words. Then add another *magnet* word to the tree.

magnetically

magnetic

magnetize

magnets

21.

magnet

Use each spelling word once to complete the story.

How Not to Buy Skis

George Ira Shore handed the fare to the bus driver and jumped aboard. Because there was little _____ 1 late in the evening, the bus was able to make _____ 2 progress to the hotel. "If I get there soon, maybe I'll have time to eat a _____ 3 in the restaurant," he told himself. "Maybe I'll have a ham _____ 4 or some pasta _____ 5 ."

When George was checking in at the hotel, a tall stranger spoke to him. "Skiing the North Slope tomorrow?" the stranger asked.

George was flattered to be taken for an experienced skier. The North Slope was hard. He forgot all about finding a snack.

"Allow me to introduce myself," the stranger said. "My name is Yul B. Sawrey. Here's my card."

"Oh, you sell ski equipment," said George.

"That's right. Maybe you've seen my skis advertised on TV while you were watching your favorite _____ 6 ," Sawrey said. "My skis are the only ones on the _____ 7 that won't break. They are crash-proof."

"That's amazing!" said George. "They sound too good to be true."

"Yes, they do," said Sawrey slyly. "Every pair of my skis is made in my own _____ 8 from a light new _____ 9 . Together they _____ 10 like a reverse _____ 11 . They push you away from anything into which you might _____ 12 . I call them my _____ 13 skis," Sawrey said.

"I'll buy a pair!" George shouted. "I can certainly use magic skis."

That night George decided he didn't need skiing lessons. He didn't even finish reading the first _____ in his
14
book, *How to Ski.*

The next morning George headed to the ski slopes and began skiing down the North Slope as fast as a _____.
15
CRASH! He hit a rock. Each of his brand-new skis broke in

_____ with a loud _____. The next
1617
thing he knew, he was in the hospital, wearing a cast from his

_____ to his hip.
18
George's _____ came to see him in the hospital.
19
She felt sorry for George.

"I made a big mistake, Aunt Ida," George told her. "I should have known better than to buy a pair of skis from a man named Yul B. Sawrey."

His aunt answered, "Well, now we can call you G. I. Shore Was!"

Their _____ could be heard down the hall.
20

act

sandwich

traffic

magic

chapter

rabbit

snack

rapid

plastic

laughter

calf

program

planet

crash

salad

aunt

factory

magnet

half

crack

Spelling and Writing

act
sandwich
traffic
magic
chapter
rabbit
snack
rapid
plastic
laughter
calf
program
planet
crash
salad
aunt
factory
magnet
half
crack

Write to the Point

Have you ever made a mistake that seems funny now when you think about it? Maybe you took some bad advice or tried to do something that was just too hard. Write a story that tells what happened. Try to use spelling words from this lesson.

Use the strategies on page 7 when you are not sure how to spell a word.

Proofreading

Proofread the e-mail message below. Use proofreading marks to correct five spelling mistakes, three capitalization mistakes, and two punctuation mistakes.

Proofreading Marks
◯ spell correctly
≡ capitalize
⊙ add period

e-mail

Address Book | Attachment | Check Spelling | Send | Save Draft | Cancel

Hi, andy,

This weekend I went skiing with my dad I was coming down a hill at a rapud speed when a calf ran out in front of me. I managed to avoid hitting it, but i tripped and landed with a krash. Nothing was hurt but the egg salad sanwitch I had brought along as a snak. it was squashed flat in its plastic wrapper I burst into laugter at the sight! What did you do this weekend? Let's talk later!

Bailey

Dictionary Skills

Alphabetical Order Words are listed in alphabetical order in a dictionary. When two letters are the same, the next letter is used to alphabetize them.

about around	able about	aboard about

Write each group of words in alphabetical order.

1. traffic   half   rabbit   plastic

_____

_____

_____

_____

2. program   aunt   planet   act

_____

_____

_____

_____

3. chapter   calf   crack   factory

_____

_____

_____

_____

4. salad   sandwich   magic   magnet

_____

_____

_____

_____

5. loose   laughter   library   length

_____

_____

_____

_____

6. raw   raccoon   rabbit   rapid

_____

_____

_____

_____

Challenge Yourself

What do you think each Challenge Word means? Check the Spelling Dictionary to see if you are right. Then use separate paper to write sentences showing that you understand the meaning of each Challenge Word.

Challenge Words	
candid	landslide
javelin	jabber

7. Because she had nothing to hide, the girl gave **candid** answers to her teacher.

8. Heavy rains on the steep mountain resulted in a **landslide.**

9. The athlete threw the **javelin** so that the point landed in the ground.

10. When I'm nervous, I **jabber** about unimportant things.

Words with /ā/

bakery

1. a-consonant-e Words

_____
_____
_____
_____
_____
_____

2. a Word

_____

3. ai, ay Words

_____
_____
_____
_____
_____
_____
_____
_____
_____

4. eigh Words

_____
_____
_____

5. ea Word

_____

paid
brain
scale
parade
raise
weigh
explain
escape
snake
holiday
remain
male
complain
weight
break
container
bakery
delay
neighbor
female

Say and Listen

Say each spelling word. Listen for the /ā/ sound you hear in _paid_.

Think and Sort

Look at the letters in each word. Think about how /ā/ is spelled. Spell each word aloud.

How many spelling patterns for /ā/ do you see?

1. Write the **six** spelling words that have the _a-consonant-e_ pattern.

2. Write the **one** spelling word that has the _a_ pattern.

3. Write the **nine** spelling words that have the _ai_ or _ay_ pattern.

4. Write the **three** spelling words that have the _eigh_ pattern.

5. Write the **one** spelling word that has the _ea_ pattern.

Use the steps on page 6 to study words that are hard for you.

Spelling Patterns

a-consonant-e	a	ai	ay	eigh	ea
m**a**l**e**	b**a**kery	p**ai**d	del**ay**	w**eigh**	br**ea**k

Spelling and Meaning

Clues   Write the spelling word for each clue.

1. This is a kind of reptile.   _____

2. People use a scale to do this.   _____

3. This word is the opposite of *fix*.   _____

4. People do this to tell why.   _____

5. This word is the opposite of *leave*.   _____

6. A band might march in one of these.   _____

7. A jar is one kind of this.   _____

8. This word is the opposite of *lower*.   _____

9. People may do this when they don't like something.   _____

10. This is a special day.   _____

Hink Pinks   Hink pinks are pairs of rhyming words that have a funny meaning.
Read each meaning. Write the spelling word that completes each hink pink.

11. a locomotive carrying geniuses   _____ train

12. a hotel worker on pay day   _____ maid

13. a light-colored weighing device   pale _____

14. something that is very heavy   great _____

15. a story told by a woman   _____ tale

16. what is used to build a community garden   _____ labor

17. plastic cakes and pies   _____ fakery

18. a story about a man   _____ tale

19. why the employees were paid late   pay _____

Word Story   One spelling word comes from the Latin word *excappare*, which meant "to leave a pursuer with just one's cape." The spelling word means "to get free." Write the word.

20. _____

Family Tree: *break*   Compare the spellings, meanings, and pronunciations of the *break* words. Then add another *break* word to the tree.

breaks

breakable

unbreakable

21.

rebreak

break

Use each spelling word once to complete the story.

The Parade That Almost Wasn't

The trouble started with the _____ 1 of Mr. Muller's pet snake.

Mr. Muller was our upstairs _____ 2. He lived in the apartment above

our shop, but on that day, he was away on a short _____ 3. The snake

got out through a _____ 4 in its cage. Then it crawled under the door,

down the hall, and into the freight elevator. When the elevator stopped, the snake

crawled into our busy _____ 5.

There were two customers at the counter, one _____ 6 and one

_____ 7. The woman had just _____ 8 for a big

birthday cake. The man was holding a loaf of bread and watching my mother

_____ 9 out a pound of Swiss cheese on the _____ 10.

Outside, a big noisy _____ 11 was passing. As Mom handed the man

the cheese, he looked down and saw the snake. The man screamed and ran out the

door. He ran right into the trumpet player, who dropped his trumpet and fell down. The

man from the bakery fell on top of him. Then the flute player tripped and fell on top of

them. The parade stopped.

Meanwhile the lady in our bakery dropped her cake and grabbed what she thought was an empty bucket to catch the snake. But it was a large _____ full of sugar. The heavy _____

12 · 13

of the full bucket was too much. She dropped it, spilling all the sugar. She

tried to get the _____ into the empty bucket, but she

14

slipped on the sugar and fell. The snake crawled out the door and into

the parade.

The saxophone player was the first to see the snake. He began to yell

so loudly that a vein stood out on his forehead. Finally the drum major

saw the snake. She used her _____. She told everyone

15

to _____ in line. Then she picked up the snake. "Let's

16

not _____the parade any longer," she said. "Start

17

marching when I _____ my baton." Holding the snake

18

and her baton high in the air, she began to march.

The flute player stood up and began to _____ about

19

an ache in his back. The trumpet player got up and picked up his

trumpet. The man from the bakery left and got lost in the crowd. The

parade began to move.

The next day a picture of the drum major

holding the snake was in all the papers.

Everyone said how brave she was. She said,

"Let me _____. My dad

20

works in the snake house at the zoo. He

took me to work with him a lot when I was

young. No silly old milk snake will ever

scare me!"

Drum Major Saves Parade

paid
brain
scale
parade
raise
weigh
explain
escape
snake
holiday
remain
male
complain
weight
break
container
bakery
delay
neighbor
female

Write to the Point

In "The Parade That Almost Wasn't," people said the drum major was brave because she wasn't afraid to pick up a snake. What is the bravest thing you ever did? Write a paragraph telling what you did and how you felt before and after you did it. Try to use spelling words from this lesson.

> Use the strategies on page 7 when you are not sure how to spell a word.

Proofreading

Proofread the journal entry below. Use proofreading marks to correct five spelling mistakes, three capitalization mistakes, and two punctuation mistakes.

Proofreading Marks
- ◯ spell correctly
- ≡ capitalize
- ⊙ add period

paid
brain
scale
parade
raise
weigh
explain
escape
snake
holiday
remain
male
complain
weight
break
container
bakery
delay
neighbor
female

March 9

I found out today that our nayber, pete, has a pet snake. he named the snake Toby Toby is a mayle garter snake, and he has beautiful stripes on his back. He sleeps in a cage that Pete made out of a wooden apple contayner. He spends the rest of his time watching Pete's pet mice. They look a little nervous to me.

I like Toby, but I hope he will remane at Pete's house He had better not excape and decide to visit my house. having him next door is just fine with me!

Language Connection

Sentences   A sentence begins with a capital letter and ends with a punctuation mark. A sentence that tells something ends with a period.

> I like chicken soup.

A sentence that asks a question ends with a question mark.

> Do you like chicken soup?

A sentence that shows strong feeling or surprise ends with an exclamation point.

> Don't spill the chicken soup!

The following sentences contain errors in capitalization and punctuation. Write each sentence correctly.

1. our class planned a holiday vacation

_____

2. mr. Peterson bought fresh bread at the bakery

_____

3. watch out for that snake by your foot

_____

4. what did you do on your break from school

_____

Challenge Yourself

Write the Challenge Word for each clue. Check the Spelling Dictionary to see if you are right. Then use separate paper to write sentences showing that you understand the meaning of each Challenge Word.

Challenge Words	
ailment	surveyor
fray	weightless

5. Astronauts do flips in their ships because everything is this in outer space. _____

6. People hire this person to measure their land. _____

7. Shoelaces do this when they are worn out. _____

8. When you have this, you don't feel very well. _____

Lesson 3

Words with /ĕ/

treasure

1. e Words

_____
_____
_____
_____
_____
_____
_____

2. ea Words

_____
_____
_____
_____
_____
_____
_____
_____
_____
_____

3. ie Word

_____

bench
healthy
thread
intend
invent
wealth
sentence
weather
self
instead
friendly
questions
measure
address
breath
pleasure
checkers
sweater
depth
treasure

Say and Listen

Say each spelling word. Listen for the /ĕ/ sound you hear in _bench_.

Think and Sort

Look at the letters in each word. Think about how /ĕ/ is spelled. Spell each word aloud.

How many spelling patterns for /ĕ/ do you see?

1. Write the **nine** spelling words that have the _e_ pattern.

2. Write the **ten** spelling words that have the _ea_ pattern.

3. Write the **one** spelling word that has the _ie_ pattern.

> Use the steps on page 6 to study words that are hard for you.

Spelling Patterns

e	ea	ie
bench	**thread**	**friendly**

Spelling and Meaning

Classifying   Write the spelling word that belongs in each group.

1. coat, jacket, _____
2. pins, needle, _____
3. name, phone number, _____
4. pirate, map, _____
5. width, height, _____
6. well, fit, _____
7. warm, kind, _____
8. statements, exclamations, _____

Rhymes   Write the spelling word that completes each sentence and rhymes with the underlined word.

9. Mr. Beckers and I enjoy playing _____ together.
10. Did you _____ the distance to the hidden treasure?
11. I sat on the _____ to study my French.
12. Good health is better than all the _____ in the world.
13. Heather doesn't like rainy _____.
14. On cold mornings, Seth can see his _____.
15. The sick elf did not feel like her normal _____.
16. Maria and Jonas _____ to send letters to the editor.
17. Henry wants to _____ a lightweight tent.
18. Dave will go with us _____ of Ted.
19. It is impossible to measure my _____.

Word Story   One of the spelling words comes from the Latin word *sententia*. *Sententia* meant a "thought, opinion, or idea." Write the spelling word.

20. _____

Family Tree: *breath*   Compare the spellings, meanings, and pronunciations of the *breath* words. Then add another *breath* word to the tree.

breathing
breathed
breathless
21.
breathe
breath
breaths

Use each spelling word once to complete the story.

The Chess Game

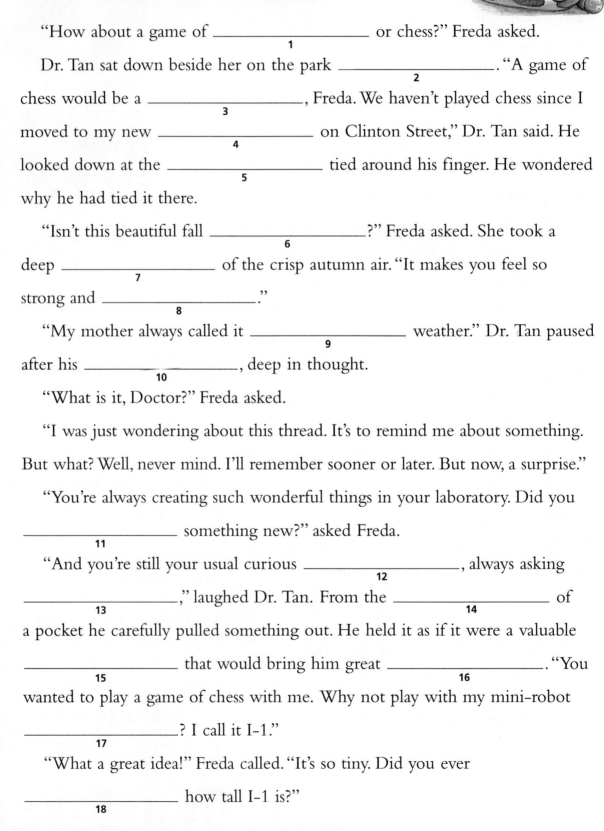

"How about a game of _____ or chess?" Freda asked.

Dr. Tan sat down beside her on the park _____. "A game of
                                                    2

chess would be a _____, Freda. We haven't played chess since I
                          3

moved to my new _____ on Clinton Street," Dr. Tan said. He
                              4

looked down at the _____ tied around his finger. He wondered
                                5

why he had tied it there.

"Isn't this beautiful fall _____?" Freda asked. She took a
                                      6

deep _____ of the crisp autumn air. "It makes you feel so
            7

strong and _____."
                    8

"My mother always called it _____ weather." Dr. Tan paused
                                          9

after his _____, deep in thought.
                  10

"What is it, Doctor?" Freda asked.

"I was just wondering about this thread. It's to remind me about something.
But what? Well, never mind. I'll remember sooner or later. But now, a surprise."

"You're always creating such wonderful things in your laboratory. Did you

_____ something new?" asked Freda.
        11

"And you're still your usual curious _____, always asking
                                                      12

_____," laughed Dr. Tan. From the _____ of
        13   14

a pocket he carefully pulled something out. He held it as if it were a valuable

_____ that would bring him great _____. "You
        15   16

wanted to play a game of chess with me. Why not play with my mini-robot

_____? I call it I-1."
        17

"What a great idea!" Freda called. "It's so tiny. Did you ever

_____ how tall I-1 is?"
        18

"I did, but I can't remember," Dr. Tan answered.

"Trying to beat a robot is going to be quite difficult. But I

_____ to do it," Freda said.

   19

"Pawn to Knight 4," said I-1 as it moved a pawn.

"Pawn to Queen 3," countered Freda.

"About this thread . . . ," wondered Dr. Tan.

An hour later Freda yelled, "Checkmate. I won!"

FIZZ! FIM!! FOOSH!!! I-1 bounced up and down, and sparks

flew everywhere. "I-1 won! I-1 won!" it screamed.

"I-1 certainly isn't very _____, Dr. Tan,"

                           20

said Freda.

Dr. Tan said, "I remember now! There was something

important I was supposed to tell you! I-1 must always be

allowed to win!"

FIZZ! FIM!! FOOSH!!!

bench
healthy
thread
intend
invent
wealth
sentence
weather
self
instead
friendly
questions
measure
address
breath
pleasure
checkers
sweater
depth
treasure

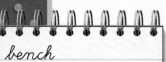

Write to the Point

Imagine that you want to teach a friend a game. Choose a game that is fun and easy to play. Write instructions telling how to play it. Explain each part of the game clearly and in the correct order. Try to use spelling words from this lesson in your instructions.

> **Use the strategies on page 7 when you are not sure how to spell a word.**

Proofreading

Proofread the newspaper article below. Use proofreading marks to correct five spelling mistakes, two capitalization mistakes, and three missing words.

> **Proofreading Marks**
> ◯ spell correctly
> ≡ capitalize
> ∧ add

Spelling Word List (cursive):

bench
healthy
thread
intend
invent
wealth
sentence
weather
self
instead
friendly
questions
measure
address
breath
pleasure
checkers
sweater
depth
treasure

All the Right Moves

A huge crowd was on hand for annual cheakers tournament last weekend. because the wethar was bad, the contest took place in the school gymnasium insted of at the park. The mood was frendly as players took their places and qestions were answered. Spectators held their breath as they watched play after play. beth Meadows was finally named champion. She will compete in the state meet Memphis next month. Runner-up was Ben Treasure, who also took home trophy.

Dictionary Skills

Guide Words Guide words are the two words in dark type at the top of each dictionary page. The first guide word is the first word on the page. The second guide word is the last word on the page.

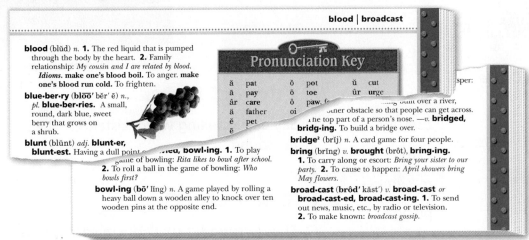

Write the following words in alphabetical order. Then look up each word in the Spelling Dictionary and write the guide words for the page on which it appears.

bench   **address**   **measure**   **intend**   **sentence**   **wealth**

Word	Guide Words
1. _____	_____ _____
2. _____	_____ _____
3. _____	_____ _____
4. _____	_____ _____
5. _____	_____ _____
6. _____	_____ _____

Challenge Yourself

What do you think each Challenge Word means? Check the Spelling Dictionary to see if you are right. Then use separate paper to write sentences showing that you understand the meaning of each Challenge Word.

Challenge Words

endeavor   concept
identical   meddle

7. Because of the team's **endeavor** to improve, they now have a trophy.

8. A democratic government is based on the **concept** that all people are equal.

9. It was no surprise that the **identical** twins looked exactly alike.

10. I'd give her advice, but I don't want to **meddle**.

Lesson 4

More Words with /ĕ/

desert

1. Words with One e

_____
_____
_____
_____
_____
_____
_____
_____
_____

2. Words with More Than One e

_____
_____
_____
_____
_____
_____
_____
_____
_____
_____
_____

else
century
extra
remember
pledge
selfish
petal
exercise
elephant
energy
desert
length
expert
metal
excellent
vegetable
metric
wreck
gentle
special

Say and Listen

Say each spelling word. Listen for the /ĕ/ sound.

Think and Sort

The /ĕ/ sound is spelled e in each of the spelling words. Some of the spelling words have one e. Others have more than one e, but only one is pronounced /ĕ/. Look at the letters in each word. Spell each word aloud.

1. Write the **nine** spelling words that have one *e*.

2. Write the **eleven** spelling words that have more than one *e*. Circle the *e* that has the /ĕ/ sound.

Use the steps on page 6 to study words that are hard for you.

Spelling Patterns

One e	More Than One e
century	pledge, elephant

Analogies   Write the spelling word that completes each analogy.

1. *Pineapple* is to *fruit* as *squash* is to _____.

2. *Wet* is to *dry* as *ocean* is to _____.

3. *Weak* is to *powerful* as _____ is to *generous*.

4. *Annoying* is to *irritating* as *wonderful* is to _____.

5. *Branch* is to *tree* as _____ is to *rose*.

6. *Construct* is to *build* as _____ is to *destroy*.

7. *Penny* is to *dollar* as *year* is to _____.

8. *Width* is to *wide* as _____ is to *long*.

9. *Recall* is to _____ as *border* is to *edge*.

10. *Oak* is to *wood* as *copper* is to _____.

Definitions   Write the spelling word for each definition.

11. relating to the system of weights and
    measures based on meters and grams   _____

12. mild   _____

13. more than what is usual or expected   _____

14. besides; in addition   _____

15. different from others   _____

16. physical activity that improves the body   _____

17. ability to do work   _____

18. a serious promise   _____

19. someone with special skill or knowledge   _____

Word Story   One spelling word is the name of an animal. It comes from the Greek word *elephas,* which was used to name the animal as well as its ivory. Long ago the spelling word was spelled *olyfaunt* in English. Write the spelling we use today.

20. _____

Family Tree: excellent   *Excellent* is a form of *excel.* Compare the spellings, meanings, and pronunciations of the *excel* words. Then add another *excel* word to the tree.

excellent

excels

21.

excelled

excel

excellently

Use each word once to complete the story.

Flower in the Garden

Carlo's whole family had been with the circus for more than a

_____. They all loved the circus. Carlo's mom was an
₁

_____ animal trainer. Carlo's job was to feed the animals and
₂

walk them around to give them their _____. But Carlo wanted
₃

to do something _____. He made a _____ that
₄ ₅

soon he would show everyone he was ready to learn to train animals himself.

One night the circus train was speeding across the _____.
₆

The train was making _____ time. If things went smoothly, the
₇

circus would arrive in Los Angeles by dawn. But things did not go smoothly.

The train hit something on the track, and tons of _____
₈

screeched to a halt. The train shook along its entire _____, and
₉

a door flew open. A frightened _____ headed quickly through
₁₀

this exit. She ran across a bare stretch of desert and disappeared.

Flower, as she was called, was no ordinary elephant. She always had plenty of

_____ for raising the huge circus tent. She gladly shared her
₁₁

food with the other elephants because she wasn't _____. Carlo
₁₂

would always _____ to give Flower water and food. And even
₁₃

though Flower weighed three _____ tons, she was very
₁₄

_____ with Carlo and sometimes
₁₅

tickled him with her trunk.

When Carlo saw that Flower was gone, he started to

look for her. He saw only a trail of large footprints leading

off into the darkness. Carlo asked the clowns if they had an

_____ motorcycle he could borrow. He
₁₆

pointed it in the direction of the footprints and turned up the throttle.

Carlo drove across the desert, looking for Flower. He followed Flower's footprints until he came to a little town. He saw Flower sitting in a _____ garden, quietly eating some

₁₇

carrots. The rest of the garden was a _____. Flower

₁₈

had even destroyed all the rose bushes at the edge of the garden. A bright red rose _____ was still stuck to her trunk.

₁₉

Just then the police arrived, and Carlo explained what had happened. The police helped Carlo get Flower out of the garden.

When Carlo returned to the circus train with Flower, everyone cheered. With Carlo's encouragement, Flower led all the other elephants in pulling the train back onto the tracks.

As the train was starting again, Carlo overheard the circus manager say that Carlo was _____. Carlo smiled as

₂₀

his mom said that her son was ready to learn to be an animal trainer.

else
century
extra
remember
pledge
selfish
petal
exercise
elephant
energy
desert
length
expert
metal
excellent
vegetable
metric
wreck
gentle
special

else
century
extra
remember
pledge
selfish
petal
exercise
elephant
energy
desert
length
expert
metal
excellent
vegetable
metric
wreck
gentle
special

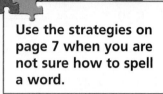

Write to the Point

Imagine that you are a newspaper reporter in the town where Flower went. Write a news article telling what happened after the circus train wrecked. Start with the headline "Elephant Escapes from Circus Train!" Include the most important details. Try to use spelling words from this lesson.

Use the strategies on page 7 when you are not sure how to spell a word.

Proofreading

Proofread the news article below. Use proofreading marks to correct five spelling mistakes, two punctuation mistakes, and three unnecessary words.

Proofreading Marks
◯ spell correctly
⊙ add period
ℓ take out

Master of the Air

Anna Chung is is an expurt circus acrobat visiting Cedar Rapids this month. In an interview for the Daily News, Ms. Chung told us about her work

"I remeber to practice every day. I also get plenty of of rest and exerize. If I didn't, I wouldn't have the enerjy to give a an excellant performance."

To see Chung in a performance this weekend, call 555-6262

Language Connection

Nouns   A noun is a word that names a person, place, thing, or idea. Proper nouns are capitalized. Common nouns are not.

Person	Place	Thing	Idea
teenager	desert	pumpkin	happiness
Cody	Utah	Lee Street	

Unscramble each sentence and write it correctly. Then circle the nouns.

1. drove desert week We the last through.

_____

2. the down swam wreck The to divers.

_____

3. Elephants Africa large are from animals.

_____

4. ran field length Andy the of the.

_____

5. vegetable Jill on ate plate every her.

_____

6. pen can't where I remember put and I paper my.

_____

7. globe to circle Explorers the seventeenth began century the in.

_____

Challenge Yourself

Use the Spelling Dictionary to answer these questions. Then use separate paper to write sentences showing that you understand the meaning of each Challenge Word.

Challenge Words

compel	dedication
condemn	pendulum

8. Do schools **compel** you to wear clown make-up?

_____

9. Should laws **condemn** cruel and unjust actions?   _____

10. Does someone who naps during school hours show great **dedication**?

_____

11. Is a **pendulum** a part on some clocks?   _____

Capitalized Words

June

1. **One-Syllable Words**

_____

_____

_____

2. **Two-Syllable Words**

_____

_____

_____

_____

_____

_____

_____

_____

_____

3. **Three-Syllable Words**

_____

_____

_____

_____

_____

4. **Four-Syllable Words**

_____

_____

5. **Abbreviation**

_____

October

Thursday

January

February

Monday

March

April

November

June

Wednesday

August

September

Tuesday

Sunday

July

Friday

December

May

Saturday

St.

Say and Listen

Say each spelling word. Listen for the vowel sounds.

Think and Sort

A **syllable** is a word part or word with one vowel sound. *Thursday* has two syllables. *October* has three syllables.

Look at the letters in each word. Think about the number of syllables in the word. Spell each word aloud.

1. Write the **three** spelling words that have one syllable.

2. Write the **nine** spelling words that have two syllables.

3. Write the **five** spelling words that have three syllables.

4. Write the **two** spelling words that have four syllables.

5. **One** of the spelling words is an abbreviation for *Street* and *Saint*. Write the word.

Use the steps on page 6 to study words that are hard for you.

Spelling Patterns

One Syllable	Two Syllables	Three Syllables	Four Syllables
March	A·pril	Oc·to·ber	Jan·u·ar·y

Spelling and Meaning

Hink Pinks   Read each meaning. Write the spelling word that completes each hink pink.

1. a doorway to spring   _____ arch

2. a song sung in a summer month   _____ tune

3. a day in the fifth month   _____ day

4. to recall the first month of fall   remember _____

Clues   Write the spelling word for each clue.

5. the first day of the school week   _____

6. the day after Monday   _____

7. the day after Saturday   _____

8. a short way of writing *Street*   _____

9. the month in which many people celebrate the new year   _____

10. the last day of the school week   _____

11. the eleventh month of the year   _____

12. the day before Friday   _____

13. the month after September   _____

14. the fourth month of the year   _____

15. the day before Sunday   _____

16. the day that begins with *W*   _____

17. the shortest month of the year   _____

18. the last month of the year   _____

19. the month that is the middle of summer   _____

Word Story   One spelling word comes from the name of the first Roman emperor. He was called Augustus Caesar, meaning "majestic Caesar." Write the spelling word that comes from *Augustus*.

20. _____

Family Tree: *Sunday*   *Sunday* comes from the word *sun*. Compare the spellings, meanings, and pronunciations of the *sun* words. Then add another *sun* word to the tree.

Sunday		sunnier
sunnily	21.	
sunless		sunny
	sun	

Use each spelling word once to complete the selection.

Let's Celebrate!

People in countries all over the world celebrate special days. Some countries have the same holidays. Here are a year's worth of special days around the world.

Most people cheer the day that begins each new year. In the United States and Canada, for example, this day is the first of _____. The beginning of

1
the Chinese new year depends on the cycle of the moon. New Year's Day in China can fall in January or during the next month, _____.

2

The rainy spring months of _____ and _____

3   4
bring the flowers that bloom in _____. These spring months also

5
have special days. Women's International Day is March 8. The Irish people celebrate

_____ Patrick's Day on March 17. In April people all over the world

6
plant trees on Arbor Day. It is a day for remembering to take care of our trees.

In May people in Japan honor children on Children's Day. In the United States, people honor mothers on Mother's Day. It falls on the second _____

7
in May. They honor fathers on Father's Day, which falls in the following month,

_____.

8

Fireworks announce celebrations of freedom during the summer. People in the United States have picnics and parades on the Fourth of _____. People in France celebrate Bastille Day on
₉
July 14. They use fireworks to remember the beginning of the French Revolution. Then the lazy days of summer roll into the month of _____. It's the last month for a summer vacation.
₁₀
In _____ summer ends. By that time almost
₁₁
everyone is back to work or school. A late summer holiday called Labor Day honors working people. With the fall comes the harvest. Some countries have set aside a special day to give thanks for the harvest. People in Canada celebrate Thanksgiving Day in _____.
₁₂
This is a month earlier than their neighbors in the United States. Families there get together for turkey dinners in _____.
₁₃
Thanksgiving Day in the United States is always on the fourth _____ of November. _____ is full of
₁₄ ₁₅
holiday festivities. People get together with friends and family. They eat holiday meals and often give gifts.

Of course, people have birthdays to celebrate. They also have graduations and anniversaries. Pick any day. Think about _____, the first day of the school and work week.
₁₆
Follow with _____ and _____.
₁₇ ₁₈
Someone is celebrating something somewhere. Some people wait to celebrate at the end of the week, especially on a _____ night or a
₁₉
_____. It doesn't matter,
₂₀
though, when you celebrate. You'll find others celebrating, too!

October
Thursday
January
February
Monday
March
April
November
June
Wednesday
August
September
Tuesday
Sunday
July
Friday
December
May
Saturday
St.

Spelling and Writing

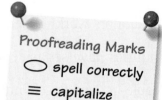

Write to the Point

What is your favorite holiday? What colors, sounds, tastes, and smells does it bring to mind? What are some special ways you celebrate the holiday? Write a description of a holiday you enjoy. Try to use spelling words from this lesson.

Use the strategies on page 7 when you are not sure how to spell a word.

Proofreading

Proofread the letter below. Use proofreading marks to correct five spelling mistakes, three capitalization mistakes, and two punctuation mistakes.

Proofreading Marks
- ⬭ spell correctly
- ≡ capitalize
- ⊙ add period

October
Thursday
January
February
Monday
March
April
November
June
Wednesday
August
September
Tuesday
Sunday
July
Friday
December
May
Saturday
St.

618 Hickory Court

Madison, WI 55705

October 5, 2002

dear Grandma,

Thank you so much for the new flute! It sounds great Every Wednesday I take lessons at mr. han's house on Forest Ste. On Munday, Octobre 10, I give my first recital. Our school band will play for the Veterans Day parade on Teusday, Novumber 11 Will you come to hear me play?

Love,

Jeremy

Using the Spelling Table

If you need to look up a word in a dictionary but aren't sure how to spell it, a spelling table can help. A spelling table lists common spellings for sounds. Suppose you are not sure how the first vowel sound in *August* is spelled. First, look in the table to find the pronunciation symbol for the sound. Then read the first spelling listed for /ô/, and look up *Agust* in the dictionary. Look for each spelling in the dictionary until you find the correct one.

Sound	Spellings	Example Words
/ô/	a au aw o ough o_e ou oa	already, autumn, raw, often, thought, score, court, roar

The following words contain boldfaced letters that represent sounds. Write each word correctly, using the Spelling Table on page 213 and the Spelling Dictionary.

1. rec**e**d _____
2. **a**lment _____
3. **e**sel _____
4. b**i**lt _____
5. myster**e** _____
6. l**a**ghter _____
7. l**oo**nar _____
8. **k**omet _____
9. c**u**sin _____
10. br**e**th _____
11. fr**e**ndly _____
12. bu**s**e _____
13. bri**j** _____
14. r**i**lax _____
15. sk**e** _____
16. **g**ide _____

Challenge Yourself

Write the Challenge Word for each clue. Check the Spelling Dictionary to see if you are right. Then use separate paper to write sentences showing that you understand the meaning of each Challenge Word.

Challenge Words

Blvd.   North Pole
Jupiter   Memorial Day

17. This is the day when people remember those who died for their country. _____

18. This abbreviation names a kind of road. _____

19. This planet was named after the ruler of the ancient Roman gods.

    _____

20. You'll need your warmest clothes if you travel here. _____

Unit 1 Review
Lessons 1–5

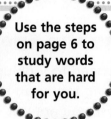 Use the steps on page 6 to study words that are hard for you.

1

sandwich
factory
half
laughter

Words with /ă/

Write the spelling word for each clue.

1. Two fourths of something equals this.

_____

2. This is where workers and machines make things.

_____

3. This has meat between two slices of bread.

_____

4. When people respond to a funny joke, you hear this.

_____

2

escape
parade
bakery
holiday
container
neighbor
break

Words with /ā/

Write the spelling word for each definition.

5. a public event for a special occasion _____

6. a place where bread is sold _____

7. a person who lives nearby _____

8. a day such as Thanksgiving _____

9. to break loose or get away _____

10. a gap or opening _____

11. a box, jar, or can used to hold something

_____

3

depth
wealth
breath
treasure
friendly

Words with /ĕ/

Write the spelling word that completes each analogy.

12. *Sociable* is to _____ as *bashful* is to *shy.*

13. *Brain* is to *thought* as *lung* is to

_____.

14. *Cookie* is to *jar* as _____ is to *chest*.

15. *Riches* is to _____ as *story* is to *tale*.

16. *Mountain* is to *ocean* as *height* is to _____.

4

length
special
exercise
excellent
vegetable

More Words with /ĕ/

Write the spelling word that belongs in each group.

17. fruit, grain, _____

18. outstanding, wonderful, _____

19. width, height, _____

20. different, unique, _____

21. diet, rest, _____

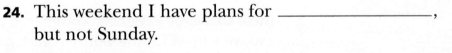

5

Tuesday
Saturday
January
February

Capitalized Words

Write the spelling word that completes each sentence.

22. The month of _____ is the shortest month of all.

23. Ling went to bed late Monday night and overslept _____ morning.

24. This weekend I have plans for _____, but not Sunday.

25. The new year for many people begins in the month of _____.

26. /ă/ Words

_____

_____

27. /ā/ Words

_____

_____

_____

_____

_____

_____

28. /ĕ/ Words

_____

_____

_____

_____

_____

_____

_____

_____

_____

_____

_____

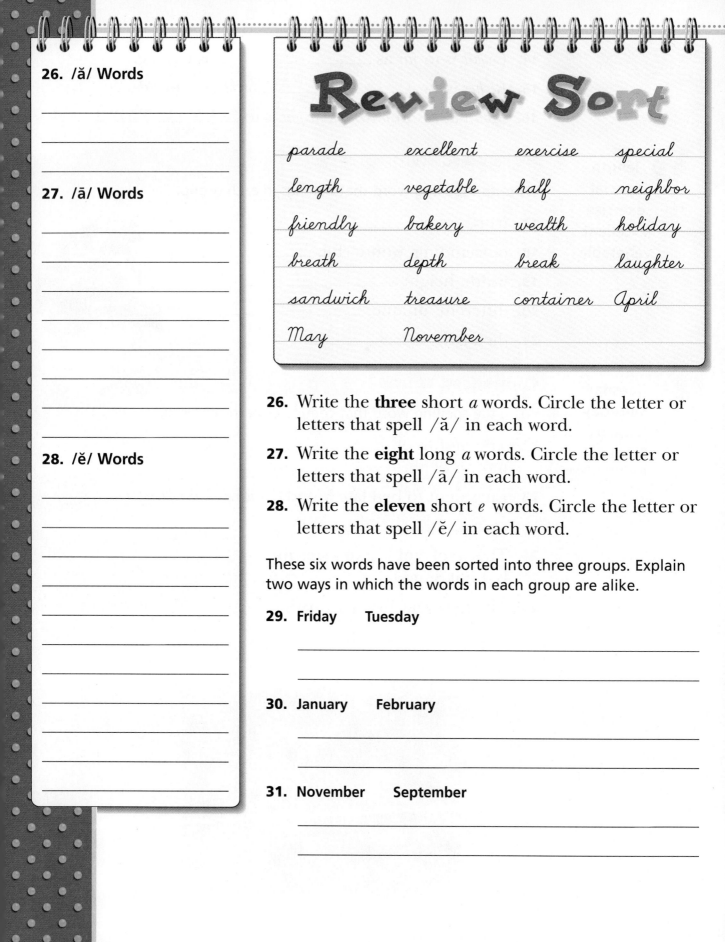

Review Sort

parade	excellent	exercise	special
length	vegetable	half	neighbor
friendly	bakery	wealth	holiday
breath	depth	break	laughter
sandwich	treasure	container	April
May	November		

26. Write the **three** short *a* words. Circle the letter or letters that spell /ă/ in each word.

27. Write the **eight** long *a* words. Circle the letter or letters that spell /ā/ in each word.

28. Write the **eleven** short *e* words. Circle the letter or letters that spell /ĕ/ in each word.

These six words have been sorted into three groups. Explain two ways in which the words in each group are alike.

29. Friday   Tuesday

_____

_____

30. January   February

_____

_____

31. November   September

_____

_____

Writer's Workshop

A Personal Narrative

In a personal narrative, a writer tells a true story about his or her own life. The writer chooses a special memory that might be good, bad, or funny, or an event that changed his or her life. Because he or she is the person telling the story, the writer uses first person words such as *I* and *me*. Here is part of Midori's personal narrative about the time her cat disappeared.

Prewriting   To write her personal narrative, Midori followed the steps in the writing process. She used a chain of events chart to plan her narrative. The chart helped her to remember events. It also helped her to put the events in the order in which they happened. Part of Midori's chain of events chart is shown here. Study what Midori did.

The Search for Shadow

When my cat, Shadow, didn't show up for dinner on Friday, I wasn't too worried. Shadow likes to wander. But when he didn't show up for breakfast or lunch the next day, I began to worry. I walked all over the neighborhood, calling him. I looked on the playground and behind the corner store where the trash cans are. Since Shadow had gotten stuck in a tree three times, I checked out all the tall trees.

1
Shadow didn't show up for meals.

↓

2
I walked through the neighborhood, calling him.

↓

3
I looked in the tall trees.

It's Your Turn!

Write your own personal narrative. Choose a special memory that you would enjoy sharing. Decide what to write about, then make a chain of events chart. Then you can follow the other steps in the writing process — writing, revising, proofreading, and publishing. Try to use spelling words from this lesson in your narrative.

Words with /ē/

athlete

1. y Words

_____
_____
_____
_____
_____
_____
_____
_____
_____
_____
_____
_____
_____

2. e-consonant-e Words

_____
_____
_____
_____
_____
_____

3. ie Word

_____

hobby

believe

compete

delivery

angry

evening

tardy

fancy

trapeze

athlete

merry

pretty

penalty

ugly

theme

liberty

empty

shady

busy

complete

Say and Listen

Say each spelling word. Listen for the /ē/ sound you hear in _hobby_.

Think and Sort

Look at the letters in each word. Think about how /ē/ is spelled. Spell each word aloud.

How many spelling patterns for /ē/ do you see?

1. Write the **thirteen** spelling words that have the _y_ pattern.

2. Write the **six** spelling words that have the _e_-consonant-_e_ pattern.

3. Write the **one** spelling word that has the _ie_ pattern.

Use the steps on page 6 to study words that are hard for you.

Spelling Patterns

y	e-consonant-e	ie
hob**b**y	compe**te**	bel**ie**ve

Spelling and Meaning

Classifying Write the spelling word that belongs in each group.

1. swing, acrobat, _____
2. topic, subject, _____
3. displeasing, bad-looking, _____
4. vacant, hollow, _____
5. activity, interest, _____
6. think, suppose, _____
7. shadowy, dark, _____
8. morning, afternoon, _____
9. punishment, fine, _____
10. shipment, distribution, _____

Trading Places Complete each sentence by writing the spelling word that can take the place of the underlined word or words.

11. Our country has many symbols of _____. <u>freedom</u>
12. We sent some _____ flowers to our aunt. <u>lovely</u>
13. I was _____ that I fell down and skinned my knee! <u>furious</u>
14. Matthew was _____ this morning. <u>late</u>
15. Mom wore a _____ gown to the party. <u>elaborate</u>
16. The little man had a _____ laugh. <u>happy</u>
17. Tran leads a _____ life. <u>active</u>
18. This Canadian stamp makes my collection _____. <u>whole</u>
19. Ray will _____ in the race this Saturday. <u>take part</u>

Word Story One spelling word comes from the Greek words *athlos* and *athlon,* which meant "contest" and "prize." We use the spelling word to name a participant in a sport. Write the word.

20. _____

Family Tree: *compete* Compare the spellings, meanings, and pronunciations of the *compete* words. Then add another *compete* word to the tree.

competition   competing

competed   21.

compete   competitor

The Ambassadors

Samantha waited for the ambassadors from the planet Flod to arrive. It was a hot day, so she stood on the _____ side of the landing pad. She
1
checked her watch to make sure she was not _____.
2

When the Flodians stepped off their ship, Samantha stared in amazement. Tall and rainbow-colored, each Flodian wore a uniform _____
3
with an unusual red helmet. Samantha thought that the helmets were very

_____. "Welcome to Earth," she said to them. "I thought you
4
might like to rest while you wait for the _____ of your things to
5
your hotel. What would you like to do this _____?"
6

Flio, the Flodian leader, said, "Samantha, please feel at _____
7
to show us what you think we will like."

Samantha decided to take the Flodians to a magic show. They didn't seem surprised by the magic.

Samantha chose the circus as a _____ for the next day's
8
entertainment. She took her special guests to a store that sold clown puppets.

There were puppets with sad faces and puppets with mean,

_____ faces. There were clown dolls with colorful,
　　　9

_____ costumes. The Flodians seemed to have seen
　　　10

the puppets before. Later at the circus, the ambassadors didn't bat

an eyelash at the man on the flying _____. That
　　　　　　　　　　　　　　　　　11

night Samantha wondered whether the Flodians were upset or

_____. She decided to pay Flio a visit. She found
　　　12

him watching TV.

"I have always been an _____," he told her, "and
　　　　　　　　　　　　　13

football is my _____. I love it so much that I don't
　　　　　　　　14

wear my future-predicting helmet while I watch a game."

Samantha could not _____ her ears. "Flio,
　　　　　　　　　　　　15

knowing everything before it happens can make life dull and

_____," she told him. "Now I know how to make
　　16

your people enjoy their visit more."

Flio listened. The next morning, he and Samantha gathered the

Flodians together. "Today," Samantha said, "you are going to learn

to play football. But first, please remove your red helmets and put

on these football helmets instead." Soon all of the Flodians were

_____ learning how to score a touchdown and how
　　17

to avoid getting a _____. None of the Flodians knew
　　　　　　　　　18

what was going to happen next. They grew very excited.

When it was time for the Flodians to leave, Flio said to Samantha,

"Never have we had such a _____ time. Someday
　　　　　　　　　　　　　19

Flod may _____ against Earth in an intergalactic
　　　　　　20

football game. For now, you have taught us that life is much more

interesting when you don't know what lies ahead."

hobby

believe

compete

delivery

angry

evening

tardy

fancy

trapeze

athlete

merry

pretty

penalty

ugly

theme

liberty

empty

shady

busy

complete

Spelling and Writing

hobby
believe
compete
delivery
angry
evening
tardy
fancy
trapeze
athlete
merry
pretty
penalty
ugly
theme
liberty
empty
shady
busy
complete

Write to the Point

Imagine that you are creating a movie about visitors from outer space. Write a paragraph describing the visitors. What do they look like? How do they move? How do they communicate? Try to use spelling words from this lesson.

Use the strategies on page 7 when you are not sure how to spell a word.

Proofreading

Proofread this paragraph from a book jacket. Use proofreading marks to correct five spelling mistakes, three capitalization mistakes, and two missing words.

Proofreading Marks
◯ spell correctly
≡ capitalize
∧ add

A Martian in the library

It is friday evning. Daniel and Jasmine sit at a table in the library. They are buzy doing a report about life other planets. to their surprise, Martian sits down in the emty seat next to them. The Martian is not only uggly but very angry. Readers won't beleive what happens next in this intergalactic tale of loyalty, liberty, and friendship written by the award-winning author of fiction for young adults, Lisa Lowry.

Dictionary Skills

Multiple Meanings   When you look up the meaning of a word in a sentence, you will often find that the word has several meanings. To know which one the writer intends, you must know the word's part of speech in the sentence. Then you can use other words in the sentence to decide on the correct meaning of the word.

com·plete (kəm plēt′) *adj.* **1.** Whole: *a complete set of the encyclopedia.* **2.** Finished; ended: *My report is complete.* **3.** Fully equipped: *a new car complete with power steering.* —*v.* **com·plet·ed, com·plet·ing.** To finish.

emp·ty (ĕmp′ tē) *adj.* **1.** Containing nothing. **2.** Without meaning: *empty promises.* —*v.* **emp·tied, emp·ty·ing, emp·ties.** To remove the contents of.

Use the dictionary entries above to write the part of speech and definition for *empty* or *complete* in each of the following sentences.

	Part of Speech	Definition
1. Dad bought a sailboat **complete** with sails and motor.	_____	_____
2. My Saturday chore is to **empty** the trash cans.	_____	_____
3. I must **complete** my homework by six o'clock.	_____	_____
4. I wanted some juice, but the pitcher was **empty**.	_____	_____
5. Ashley has a **complete** set of the books you want.	_____	_____
6. The man's **empty** welcome made us feel uneasy.	_____	_____

Challenge Yourself

What do you think each Challenge Word means? Check the Spelling Dictionary to see if you are right. Then use separate paper to write sentences showing that you understand each Challenge Word.

Challenge Words	
canopy	recede
utility	siege

7. Marta's bed has a white lace **canopy** over it.

8. If we have a drought, the water in the lake will **recede**.

9. We get **utility** bills for water, telephone, and electricity.

10. The enemy held the town under **siege**, so no one was allowed to leave.

More Words with /ē/

ski

1. *ea* Words

_____
_____
_____
_____
_____
_____
_____
_____

2. *ee* Words

_____
_____
_____
_____
_____
_____
_____
_____
_____

3. *i* Words

_____
_____
_____

greet
pizza
weak
breathe
freeze
piano
speech
asleep
increase
peace
ski
defeat
reason
needle
steep
sheet
wheat
agree
degree
beneath

Say and Listen

Say each spelling word. Listen for the /ē/ sound.

Think and Sort

Look at the letters in each word. Think about how /ē/ is spelled. Spell each word aloud.

How many spelling patterns for /ē/ do you see?

1. Write the **eight** spelling words that have the *ea* pattern.

2. Write the **nine** spelling words that have the *ee* pattern.

3. Write the **three** spelling words that have the *i* pattern.

Use the steps on page 6 to study words that are hard for you.

Spelling Patterns

ea	ee	i
weak	greet	pizza

Spelling and Meaning

Classifying Write the spelling word that belongs in each group.

1. thread, pins, _____
2. sled, skate, _____
3. inhale, exhale, _____
4. enlarge, grow, _____
5. beat, win, _____
6. under, below, _____
7. corn, oats, _____
8. spaghetti, ravioli, _____
9. ounce, watt, _____
10. guitar, violin, _____
11. pillow, blanket, _____
12. quiet, silence, _____

Rhymes Write the spelling word that completes each sentence and rhymes with the underlined word.

13. Each student had to give a _____.
14. After the race, the winner was too _____ to speak.
15. The raccoons creep up the _____ hill to our house.
16. Snow is the _____ I like the winter season.
17. When you meet them, _____ them with a smile.
18. Please give me my gloves before my hands _____.
19. The tired sheep were _____ in the meadow.

Word Story One spelling word comes from the Old French word *agreer*, which meant "to please." We use the word today to refer to what people do when they have the same opinion or idea. Write the spelling word that comes from *agreer*.

20. _____

Family Tree: *weak* Compare the spellings, meanings, and pronunciations of the *weak* words. Then add another *weak* word to the tree.

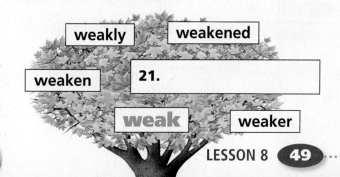

weakly   weakened

weaken   21.

weak   weaker

The Homework Assignment

Claudia sat on her bed, lost in thought. Mr. Costa had given the class a writing assignment for the next day. He asked everyone to write an idea for a story telling what they wanted to be doing in twenty years. Claudia put her pen to the paper.

I am on a _____ **1** *ski slope in Austria. The hill must be at least a 45-*_____ **2** *angle. The snow on the hill is covered with a thin sheet of ice because there was a hard* _____ **3** *last night. I know the slope is dangerous, but I'm not afraid. I can* _____ **4** *better than anyone I know. I take a deep breath, forcing myself to* _____ **5** *slowly and evenly. I concentrate on the* _____ **6** *and quiet here on the mountain. I count down very slowly and push off. The ice* _____ **7** *my skis feels slippery. I push off and fly down the hill faster, faster, faster.*

Claudia's stomach growled. She thought about the _____ **8** she would eat with Mattie this evening. She knew she had to finish her homework before she went to Mattie's house. She wrinkled her brow and kept writing.

As I enter the crowded auditorium, the Prime Minister smiles and stands up to _____ **9** *me. I begin to give my* _____ **10**. *Several people in the back of the hall begin to boo because they disagree with my opinions. I see that I will have to give them a good* _____ **11** *to vote for me, or else my opponent will* _____ **12** *me in this important election.*

"Maybe I'll just sneak into the kitchen for a slice of Mom's whole-_____ bread," Claudia said to herself.
13
"All this homework sure makes me hungry!" Then she thought of something else she would like to be doing in twenty years.

I am sitting at a concert grand _____. I have just
14
finished playing Beethoven's "Moonlight Sonata." The crowd is going wild. I take one bow, two bows, three bows. They are still clapping wildly. Finally I _____ to play one more piece. The crowd is silent as
15
I raise my hands to begin.

Just then, Claudia remembered the dream she had the night before while she was _____. She got out another
16
sheet of paper.

I am in the operating room. The patient is covered with a heavy cotton _____. He was very _____ when they
17 **18**
brought him in, and he is getting weaker every minute. The nurse put a bandage on his arm so that his wound wouldn't bleed. There is only one way to _____ his chances of getting well. I ask the
19
nurse for the _____ and give him a shot. I am the best
20
doctor in the country. If anyone can save him, I can.

When the doorbell rang, Claudia looked at the clock. "Wow! It's been an hour, and I don't have one idea for a story—I have four!" She smiled and ran downstairs to meet Mattie.

greet
pizza
weak
breathe
freeze
piano
speech
asleep
increase
peace
ski
defeat
reason
needle
steep
sheet
wheat
agree
degree
beneath

greet
pizza
weak
breathe
freeze
piano
speech
asleep
increase
peace
ski
defeat
reason
needle
steep
sheet
wheat
agree
degree
beneath

Write to the Point

Write a paragraph that tells what you would like to be doing twenty years from now. What kind of work will you do? What kind of hobbies will you have? Try to use spelling words from this lesson in your paragraph.

Use the strategies on page 7 when you are not sure how to spell a word.

Proofreading

Proofread the paragraph below. Use proofreading marks to correct five spelling mistakes, three capitalization mistakes, and two unnecessary words.

Proofreading Marks
◯ spell correctly
≡ capitalize
⌿ take out

A Baker's Life

Uncle Al gets up early and is open for business when I go to school. Sometimes I stop in, and we eat hot doughnuts together. When i enter to his bakery and breeth in, lovely aromas greet me. that is one reazon why I am want to be a baker. I also like to help Uncle Al toss the wheet dough for pitza or roll it into balls for rolls. I enjoy taking baked cookies off the big cookie sheat, too. a baker's life is the life for me!

Language Connection

Predicates   Every sentence has two main parts, the complete subject and the complete predicate. The complete subject includes all the words that tell whom or what the sentence is about. The complete predicate includes all the words that tell what the subject does or is.

Complete Subject	Complete Predicate
The little gray kitten	followed me all the way to the fair.

Use the words in the boxes to complete each sentence below. Then circle the complete predicate.

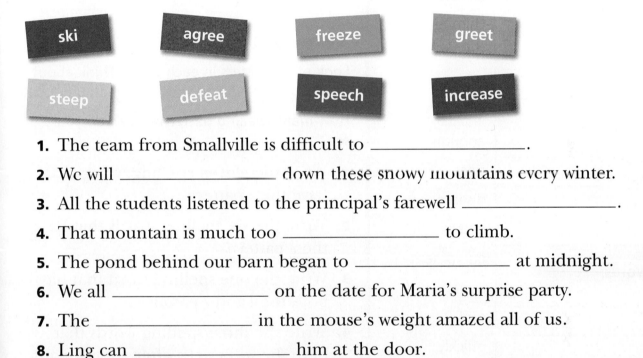

ski   agree   freeze   greet
steep   defeat   speech   increase

1. The team from Smallville is difficult to _____.

2. We will _____ down these snowy mountains every winter.

3. All the students listened to the principal's farewell _____.

4. That mountain is much too _____ to climb.

5. The pond behind our barn began to _____ at midnight.

6. We all _____ on the date for Maria's surprise party.

7. The _____ in the mouse's weight amazed all of us.

8. Ling can _____ him at the door.

Challenge Yourself

Write the Challenge Word for each clue. Check the Spelling Dictionary to see if you are right. Then use separate paper to write sentences showing that you understand the meaning of each Challenge Word.

Challenge Words	
easel	tweed
meager	safari

9. Clothing made of this helps keep people warm in winter. _____

10. This is part of an artist's equipment. _____

11. If you like wild animals but don't like zoos, you can go on this with a camera. _____

12. This serving of food leaves you hungry. _____

Lesson 9

Words with /ĭ/

guitar

Say and Listen

Say each spelling word. Listen for the /ĭ/ sound you hear in *wrist*.

Think and Sort

Look at the letters in each word. Think about how /ĭ/ is spelled. Spell each word aloud.

How many spelling patterns for /ĭ/ do you see?

1. Write the **eleven** spelling words that have the *i* pattern.

2. Write the **six** spelling words that have the *e* pattern.

3. Write the **one** spelling word that has both the *i* and *e* patterns.

4. Write the **three** spelling words that have the *ui* pattern after a consonant other than *q*.

Use the steps on page 6 to study words that are hard for you.

1. *i* Words

_____
_____
_____
_____
_____
_____
_____
_____
_____
_____
_____

2. *e* Words

_____
_____
_____
_____
_____
_____

3. *i* and *e* Word

_____

4. *ui* Words

_____
_____
_____

wrist
guitar
expect
chimney
riddle
bridge
guilty
enough
since
disease
except
equipment
built
quit
quickly
relax
review
different
discuss
divide

Spelling Patterns

i	e	ui
wrist	**expect**	**built**

Spelling and Meaning

Analogies   Write the spelling word that completes each analogy.

1. *Under* is to *tunnel* as *over* is to _____.

2. *Ankle* is to *leg* as _____ is to *arm*.

3. *Add* is to *subtract* as *multiply* is to _____.

4. *Wrong* is to *right* as _____ is to *innocent*.

5. *Water* is to *faucet* as *smoke* is to _____.

6. *Stop* is to _____ as *start* is to *begin*.

7. *Walk* is to *slowly* as *run* is to _____.

8. *Same* is to *like* as _____ is to *unlike*.

9. *Jog* is to *exercise* as *nap* is to _____.

10. *Before* is to *preview* as *after* is to _____.

Clues   Write the spelling word for each clue.

11. You have this if you have as much as you need.   _____

12. You did this if you made a house.   _____

13. Baseball bats, balls, and gloves are this.   _____

14. You play this by strumming its strings.   _____

15. This kind of joke asks a question.   _____

16. This is another word for *because*.   _____

17. You do this when you think a thing will happen.   _____

18. People do this when they talk about something.   _____

19. You might use this word instead of *but*.   _____

Word Story   One spelling word comes from the Old French word *desaise,* which meant "without ease." Over time the word came to mean "a sickness." Write the spelling word that comes from *desaise.*

20. _____

Family Tree: *divide*   Compare the spellings, meanings, and pronunciations of the *divide* words. Then add another *divide* word to the tree.

divider

division

undivided

dividing

21.

divide

Use each spelling word once to complete the selection.

Picking and Strumming

Imagine a day in the woods. You and your friends are hiking back to the cabin where your family is gathering. You cross a covered _____
1
over a bubbling brook and notice the smoke curling from the _____ of the cabin. As you go nearer,
2
you hear the strumming of a _____. "What beautiful music!"
3
you exclaim. That's when the idea hits—you want to learn to play the guitar.

Playing the guitar is a great hobby, _____ a guitar is easy to
4
take with you wherever you go. You don't need a lot of _____
5
to play one. You need only a guitar and a pick. Learning to play the guitar takes time and patience, though. You cannot _____ to play well at
6
first. The good news is that you can play a lot of songs after learning only a few chords.

First, choose your guitar. There are many types, including folk, classical, and electric. Look for a guitar that is _____ for a person your size.
7
Then have someone show you how to tune it.

Second, plan a way to _____ your time between school,
8
family, and the guitar. Then _____ with your family the best
9
times to practice. You don't want to bother anyone with your picking and strumming, _____, of course, for those times when you'd *like*
10
someone to listen.

Third, find a teacher. Remember that _____ people teach in
11
different ways. Talk to other guitar players to help you choose the right instructor.

Fourth, go to your guitar lessons. You might learn the history of the guitar or how plucking a string makes sounds. You will definitely learn chords and scales.

You need nimble fingers to change chords or play scales _____. Some chords and scales may strain your

fingers or even your _____. A _____

12   13   14

or injury that interferes with the movement of your fingers may slow you down. Talk to your doctor if you notice such a problem.

Do not let playing a few scales each day discourage you. Think of

each one as a kind of musical puzzle or _____ to

15

solve. Play the notes, _____ your lessons, and then

16

practice, practice, practice. Remember that you can never practice

_____. With time, you will play better and better.

17

The most important thing is to never _____ trying.

18

If you give up too soon you may feel _____ later.

19

Instead, _____, play your guitar, and enjoy making

20

beautiful music for your family and friends!

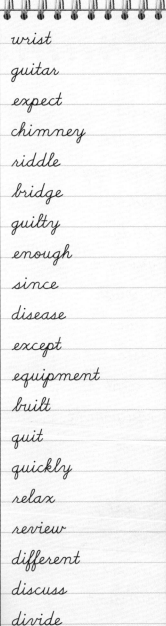

wrist
guitar
expect
chimney
riddle
bridge
guilty
enough
since
disease
except
equipment
built
quit
quickly
relax
review
different
discuss
divide

Spelling and Writing

wrist
guitar
expect
chimney
riddle
bridge
guilty
enough
since
disease
except
equipment
built
quit
quickly
relax
review
different
discuss
divide

Write to the Point

What instrument would you like to play? Write a letter to a friend, telling about the instrument, why you want to learn to play it, and what you might have to do to learn how to play it. Try to use spelling words from this lesson.

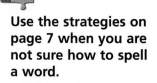

Use the strategies on page 7 when you are not sure how to spell a word.

Proofreading

Proofread the letter below. Use proofreading marks to correct five spelling mistakes, three capitalization mistakes, and two punctuation mistakes.

Proofreading Marks
◯ spell correctly
≡ capitalize
⊙ add period

14th Street SW

Calgary, AB

Canada T2T 3Y9

May 7, 2003

Dear Marty,

you asked how I learned to play the keyboard

It's been a year sinse I started lessons There are so

many diferent things to learn, and i wanted to learn

everything quikly. The best thing I learned is to relaax.

I just remember to take it slowly and never qwit.

Your friend,

ted

Language Connection

Capitalization   Capitalize the names of days and months.

> Sally was born on a **Friday** in **December**.

The following scrambled sentences contain errors in capitalization and spelling. Unscramble each sentence and write it correctly.

1. my april broke last I rist.

_____

2. our sinse february had We've trampoline.

_____

3. field discus june Let's go where our on trip in we'll.

_____

4. chimley september built Dad our a house new last on.

_____

5. and july expeck can really august weather We hot in.

_____

6. before to I tuesday our test riview need my notes on.

_____

7. theater saturday go diffrent We'll to move a next.

_____

Challenge Yourself

Use the Spelling Dictionary to answer these questions. Then use separate paper to write sentences showing that you understand the meaning of each Challenge Word.

Challenge Words	
quizzical	bliss
commit	pinnacle

8. When people are puzzled, do their faces sometimes have a **quizzical** look? _____

9. Do most people feel **bliss** if they do badly on a test? _____

10. Is a detective's job to catch people who **commit** crimes? _____

11. If you were climbing a steep mountain, would you start at the **pinnacle**?

_____

More Words with /ĭ/

cottage

Spelling list

business
system
package
skill
chicken
mystery
arithmetic
film
message
picnic
kitchen
damage
village
sixth
garbage
pitch
insect
cottage
insist
timid

1. *i* Words

_____
_____
_____
_____
_____
_____
_____
_____
_____
_____
_____

2. *y* Words

_____
_____

3. *a* Words

_____
_____
_____
_____
_____

4. *i* and *a* Word

_____

5. *u* Word

_____

Say and Listen

Say each spelling word. Listen for the /ĭ/ sound.

Think and Sort

Look at the letters in each word. Think about how /ĭ/ is spelled. Spell each word aloud.

How many spelling patterns for /ĭ/ do you see?

1. Write the **eleven** spelling words that have the *i* pattern.

2. Write the **two** spelling words that have the *y* pattern.

3. Write the **five** spelling words that have the *a* pattern.

4. Write the **one** spelling word that has the *i* and *a* patterns.

5. Write the **one** spelling word that has the *u* pattern.

Use the steps on page 6 to study words that are hard for you.

Spelling Patterns

i	y	a	u
film	**mystery**	**cottage**	**business**

Spelling and Meaning

Making Connections   Write the spelling word that relates to each person listed below.

1. a farmer _____
2. a baseball player _____
3. a movie director _____
4. a math teacher _____
5. a chef _____
6. a mail carrier _____

Definitions   Write the spelling word for each definition. Use the Spelling Dictionary if you need to.

7. a group of related things that make up a whole _____
8. a meal eaten outside _____
9. a small group of houses and businesses _____
10. trash _____
11. a small house _____
12. one of six equal parts _____
13. shy or lacking in self-confidence _____
14. news sent from one person to another _____
15. injury or harm _____
16. the ability to do something well _____
17. to take a stand or demand strongly _____
18. a small animal with wings and six legs _____
19. what a person does to earn a living _____

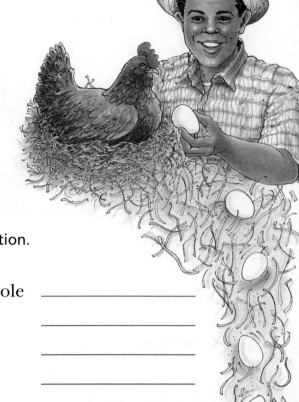

Word Story   One spelling word comes from the Greek word *myein,* which meant "to shut the eyes." The spelling word means "something people don't know." Write the word.

20. _____

Family Tree: *insist*   Compare the spellings, meanings, and pronunciations of the *insist* words. Then add another *insist* word to the tree.

insistent

insisted

insisting

21.

insists

insist

Use each spelling word once to complete the selection.

CRAZY ABOUT ANTS!

Ants can be found in almost every city, town, and

_____ in the world. Whether you live in
1

a huge house or a tiny _____, you can
2

find these small creatures nearby. You don't need radar or a _____
3

sense to locate them, either. Just put out some food crumbs and wait. When it comes

to food crumbs, ants are not _____. Sooner or later, you will see
4

these busy little animals.

Ants are social insects that depend on each other to stay alive. They live in a

colony, or group, with other ants. A colony has one or more queens, a few males,

and many workers. The workers must find food for the other ants. When a worker

finds food, it signals other workers with its antennae. When the others receive the

_____, they hurry to find the food.
5

Ants will eat anything from a candy bar to another _____, and it
6

does not matter where the food is. In your home, ants will eat bread crumbs you

drop on your _____ floor. At a _____, they will
7 8

eat a sandwich or a _____ leg. They will crawl inside an open box
9

of crackers or a _____ of cookies. Ants are very willing to take
10

people's leftovers. Who needs a _____ disposal when you
11

have ants? At a crowded baseball stadium, ants will drink from soda cups. They go

merrily about their _____, paying no attention to a powerful hit or
12

a great _____ of a ball.
13

Once ants find food, they usually carry it back to their nest. Using great

strength and _____, they often carry loads that weigh more
14

than 50 times their body weight. If you want to know what that is like for a human, do the _____.

15

It's like a 150-pound person lifting more than 6,000 pounds!

Some people _____

16

that all ants are pests. They argue that ants sting people and ruin picnics. Ants' usefulness, however, is no big secret or _____. Scientists have studied ant behavior

17

and even captured it on _____ with special cameras.

18

What scientists have learned is that ants are helpful. They eat insects that _____ crops. Ants also help keep soil in good

19

shape. They dig an elaborate _____ of underground

20

tunnels. The tunnels allow air to flow through the soil. Ants are also useful in another important way. What would spiders, frogs, and birds do without ants for food?

Although ants bother almost everyone at one time or another, they are useful animals. The next time you see a group of them, spend some time watching these amazing little creatures.

business
system
package
skill
chicken
mystery
arithmetic
film
message
picnic
kitchen
damage
village
sixth
garbage
pitch
insect
cottage
insist
timid

Spelling and Writing

business
system
package
skill
chicken
mystery
arithmetic
film
message
picnic
kitchen
damage
village
sixth
garbage
pitch
insect
cottage
insist
timid

Write to the Point

Ants are fascinating insects. Write a paragraph about an insect that you see often. Tell what it looks like and interesting facts about it. Try to use spelling words from this lesson.

Proofreading

Proofread this paragraph. Use proofreading marks to correct five spelling mistakes, three capitalization mistakes, and two punctuation mistakes.

Use the strategies on page 7 when you are not sure how to spell a word.

Proofreading Marks
◯ spell correctly
≡ capitalize
⊙ add period

Bees in our House!

We had bees in our kytchen, but not for long. My dad is good at catching them. he showed me how he does it. First, he lowers a glass carefully over the bee. Next, he slips a postcard under the glass Then, he takes the whole thing outside and lets the bee go. i tried to catch one of the bees in our kitchen, but I couldn't get the glass over it because the bee scared me A bee is not a timud insec. Last year I was stung near a garbige can at a picnec. Since then I've never cared much for picnics—or bees.

Language Connection

Commas A series is a list of three or more items. The items can be single words or groups of words. A comma is used to separate the items in a series.

> Bill had a sandwich, a piece of pie, and a glass of milk.
> Then he gathered up his baseball glove, bat, and ball.

Write the following sentences correctly, adding commas where they are needed and correcting the misspelled words.

1. I need a pencil an eraser and some paper to do my arithmatick.

   _____

2. Chikcen can be fried broiled or baked.

   _____

3. We saw tulips roses and daisies outside the cottige.

   _____

4. The villaje had a bakery a post office and a town hall.

   _____

5. Lynn wanted to study history bizness and medicine.

   _____

6. The timmid elephant was afraid of mice snakes and his own shadow!

   _____

⭐ Challenge Yourself

Write the Challenge Word for each clue. Check the Spelling Dictionary to see if you are right. Then use separate paper to write sentences showing that you understand the meaning of each Challenge Word.

Challenge Words	
rummage	symptom
abyss	lyrics

7. You might hum a song because you can't remember these.

   _____

8. When someone is getting a cold, the first one might be a sore throat.

   _____

9. You may have to do this to find a pencil in a messy desk drawer.

   _____

10. Drop something into this, and you may never see it again. _____

Lesson 11

Plural Words

sandwiches

1. -s Plurals

_____
_____
_____
_____
_____
_____

2. -es Plurals with No Base Word Changes

_____
_____
_____
_____
_____
_____
_____

3. -es Plurals with Base Word Changes

_____
_____
_____
_____
_____
_____
_____

stories

wives

benches

skis

calves

sandwiches

branches

athletes

parties

companies

neighbors

hobbies

exercises

penalties

degrees

vegetables

speeches

crashes

wishes

businesses

Say and Listen

Say the spelling words. Notice the ending sounds and letters.

Think and Sort

A **plural** is a word that names more than one thing. A **base word** is a word to which suffixes, prefixes, and endings can be added. All of the spelling words are plurals. Most plurals are formed by adding -s to a base word. Other plurals are formed by adding -es.

The spelling of some base words changes when -es is added. A final y is often changed to i. An f is often changed to v.

Look at the spelling words. Think about how each plural is formed. Spell each word aloud.

1. Write the **six** spelling words formed by adding -s to the base word.

2. Write the **seven** -es spelling words that have no changes in the base word.

3. Write the **seven** -es spelling words that have changes in the spelling of the base word.

> Use the steps on page 6 to study words that are hard for you.

Spelling Patterns

-s	-es
skis	benches stories wives

Spelling and Meaning

Clues   Write the spelling word for each clue.

1. Corn and spinach are kinds of these. _____

2. You can use these to slide over snow. _____

3. You make these with bread and a filling. _____

4. These are very young cows. _____

5. These people live next door to you. _____

6. These women have husbands. _____

7. These reach out from tree trunks. _____

8. You sit on these in a park. _____

9. These happen when cars hit other cars. _____

10. Collecting stamps is an example of these. _____

11. Doing these can make you stronger. _____

12. Runners and gymnasts are these. _____

13. These can be about real or made-up events. _____

14. Referees give these to rule-breakers. _____

15. These places make things to sell. _____

Rhymes   Write the spelling word that completes each sentence and rhymes with the underlined word.

16. James _____ that he hadn't broken the dishes.

17. When it was twenty _____, my nose began to freeze!

18. Ms. Lowe teaches us how to give _____.

19. Everyone loves to go to Artie's birthday _____.

Word Story   One spelling word comes from the word *bisiness*. Long ago, *bisiness* meant "the state of being busy, eager, or anxious." The meaning and spelling of *bisiness* changed over time. Write the spelling that we use today.

20. _____

Family Tree: *athletes*   *Athletes* is a form of the word *athlete*. Compare the spellings, meanings, and pronunciations of the *athlete* words. Then add another *athlete* word to the tree.

athletically

athletes

21.

athleticism

athletics

athlete

Use each spelling word once to complete the selection.

In the Sky, on the Water, and in the Backyard

goldfinches

Birds fascinate us. We write _____ 1 and poems about them. Some of us give heartfelt _____ 2 asking others to help save them. Many of us spend hours watching them. Bird watching is one of the most popular _____ 3 for people of all ages.

Sometimes it takes years for bird watchers to spot a rare bird such as a whooping crane or a sandhill crane. Some people travel many miles to make their _____ 4 come true. To see a whooping crane, they might go to Ontario or Texas. They even throw bird-watching _____ 5 while waiting for sandhill cranes to gather each spring at the Platte River in Nebraska.

sandhill crane

Some birds can be found in many different places. Sit with friends on some park _____ 6 at lunch time. Toss out little pieces of bread from your _____ 7. Then watch the pigeons flock! Birds don't often gather for carrots or other _____ 8, however. Stick with bread or seeds.

Other birds, such as seagulls, can be found only in certain areas. Seagulls are so plentiful in coastal areas that people on water _____ 9 must keep a lookout for them to avoid any collisions or _____ 10! The cowbird can be found on ranch land. Cowbirds follow cows and their _____ 11 and wait for the cattle to stir up tasty insects. Falcons are not as easy to spot but are worth the effort. Similar to well-trained _____ 12,

seagull

they are strong and swift. Falcons can be trained

to hunt for certain animals. The training

_____ involve searching for
         13

small animals and diving at high speeds. At one

time peregrine falcons were few in number. Then

the government set strict _____
                                    14

for harming them. Now people sometimes see

falcons perched on telephone poles and bare tree _____.
                                                              15

A hawk or a falcon is usually spotted sitting by itself. However,

scientists believe that both hawks and falcons live in pairs like husbands

and _____. They work together to raise their young.
           16

Don't try to get close to a nest, though. They are very protective parents!

Birds' sweet songs and colorful feathers make them interesting

friends and _____. Many _____
                      17   **18**

and factories manufacture binoculars, birdhouses, and bird feeders for

bird watchers. This equipment, as well as seed, is sold in local stores and

_____.
         19

Do not expect to see many birds in snowy, icy weather. If the

thermometer drops by many _____, birds tend to
                                        20

migrate to warmer climates. Wait until spring. They'll be back!

prairie falcon

stories
wives
benches
skis
calves
sandwiches
branches
athletes
parties
companies
neighbors
hobbies
exercises
penalties
degrees
vegetables
speeches
crashes
wishes
businesses

migrating geese

stories
wives
benches
skis
calves
sandwiches
branches
athletes
parties
companies
neighbors
hobbies
exercises
penalties
degrees
vegetables
speeches
crashes
wishes
businesses

Write to the Point

Do you have a hobby, or is there one you'd like to have? Write a paragraph telling about the hobby. Try to use spelling words from this lesson.

Proofreading

Proofread the paragraph below. Use proofreading marks to correct five spelling mistakes, three capitalization mistakes, and two punctuation mistakes.

Use the strategies on page 7 when you are not sure how to spell a word.

Proofreading Marks
◯ spell correctly
≡ capitalize
⊙ add period

Up and Away

I learned about model airplanes from my neighbors,

Victor and melinda Last Saturday we sat on the

benchs in their yard, ate sandwitches, and talked about

planes. They showed me their models and told storyes

about each one Victor's favorite model is one that his

great-grandfather gave him. It's a Spitfire, an

airplane used by the Royal Air Force in World War II.

Victor's great-grandfather flew a Spitfire in that

war. i decided to build my own models. Victor said

that of all the hobies, building model airplanes is his

favorite. now it's mine, too. My father is helping me

build a Spitfire and a Hornet.

Language Connection

Subject-Verb Agreement The subject and the verb of a sentence must "agree" in number. A plural subject must have a plural verb. A singular subject must have a singular verb.

Singular Subject	Plural Subject
This **story** is about a zookeeper.	**All** of the stories are interesting.

The subject of each of the following sentences appears in dark type. Choose the correct verb for the subject. Then write the sentence correctly.

1. My **neighbor** (was, were) upset about losing her parrot.

_____

2. The **vegetables** in our garden (is, are) ready to be picked.

_____

3. The mayor's **speech** (seem, seems) too long and too serious.

_____

4. These cucumber **sandwiches** really (does, do) taste good.

_____

5. Our **calves** (spends, spend) most of the day playing.

_____

6. The **benches** at the city park (need, needs) to be replaced.

_____

7. His father's **company** (build, builds) parts for computers.

_____

Challenge Yourself

Write the Challenge Word for each clue. Check the Spelling Dictionary to see if you are right. Then use separate paper to write sentences showing that you understand the meaning of each Challenge Word.

Challenge Words	
cosmetics	scarves
apologies	actresses

8. They can be skinny or wide, plain or fancy, woolly or silky. _____

9. Some of these are well-known stars. _____

10. People use these to look more attractive. _____

11. When you make serious mistakes, you need to make these. _____

Lesson 12

Unit 2 Review
Lessons 7–11

Use the steps on page 6 to study words that are hard for you.

7 delivery
empty
athlete
evening
believe

Words with /ē/

Write the spelling word that completes each sentence.

1. The _____ trained every day.

2. Every _____ after dinner, we play a word game.

3. Tell the truth so that people will always _____ you.

4. Joe's Pizza Place has free _____ service.

5. I spent all my money, so my wallet is _____.

8 weak
reason
breathe
speech
piano

More Words with /ē/

Write the spelling word for each clue.

6. This is a musical instrument with keys.

_____

7. If something is not strong, then it's this.

_____

8. Humans do this to get air. _____

9. This tells why something is the way it is.

_____

10. You give one of these when you give a talk.

_____

9 different
chimney
except
enough
guilty

Words with /ĭ/

Write the spelling word for each definition.

11. a tall structure through which smoke can flow _____

12. feeling that one has done something wrong _____

13. outside of or apart from _____

14. not the same as _____

15. as much as is needed _____

10

kitchen
mystery
garbage
message
business

More Words with /ĭ/

Write the spelling word that completes each analogy.

16. *Trash* is to _____ as *bag* is to *sack*.

17. *Store* is to _____ as *cottage* is to *house*.

18. *Passage* is to *hall* as *letter* is to _____.

19. *Piece* is to *puzzle* as *clue* is to _____.

20. *Bedroom* is to *sleep* as _____ is to *cook*.

11

skis
businesses
companies
calves
wives

Plural Words

Write the spelling word that answers each question.

21. What are baby cows called? _____

22. What is another word for *businesses*? _____

23. What do people use to go down a snowy mountain?

_____

24. What do husbands have? _____

25. What can you see on the main streets of small towns?

_____

26. /ē/ Words

_____
_____
_____
_____
_____
_____
_____
_____
_____

27. /ĭ/ Words

_____
_____
_____
_____
_____
_____
_____

28. /ē/ and /ĭ/ Words

_____
_____
_____
_____

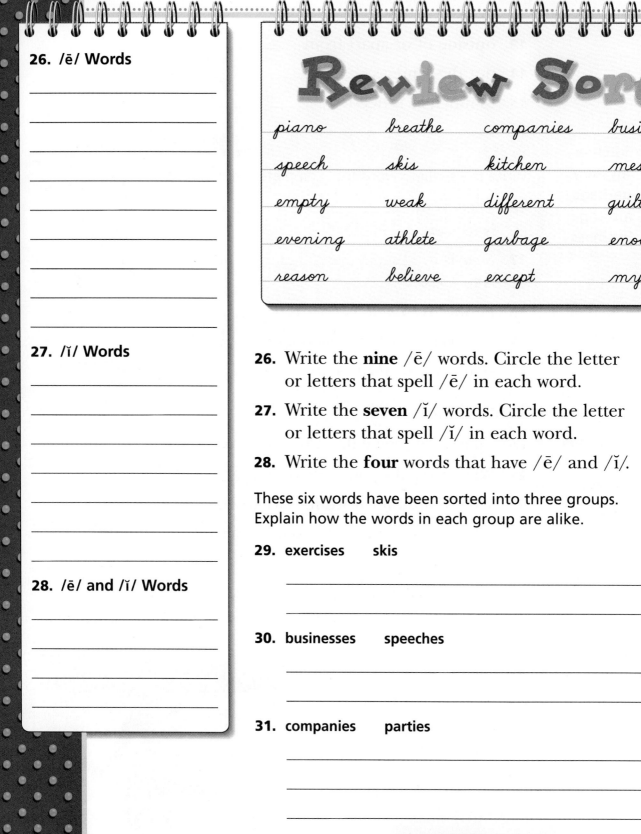

Review Sort

piano	breathe	companies	business
speech	skis	kitchen	message
empty	weak	different	guilty
evening	athlete	garbage	enough
reason	believe	except	mystery

26. Write the **nine** /ē/ words. Circle the letter or letters that spell /ē/ in each word.

27. Write the **seven** /ĭ/ words. Circle the letter or letters that spell /ĭ/ in each word.

28. Write the **four** words that have /ē/ and /ĭ/.

These six words have been sorted into three groups. Explain how the words in each group are alike.

29. exercises   skis

_____
_____

30. businesses   speeches

_____
_____

31. companies   parties

_____
_____
_____

Writer's Workshop

A Narrative

A narrative is a story. Every good story has a beginning, a middle, and an end. In the beginning, the author usually introduces the main character and the problem that the main character must solve. In the middle of the story, the main character tries to solve the problem. The end of the story tells how the problem is solved. Notice how Diego introduces the main character and the problem in the beginning of his story "The Hardest Race."

Prewriting   To write his story, Diego followed the steps in the writing process. First he chose the kind of story he wanted to write and who the main character would be. Then he used a story map to plan the the beginning, the middle, and the end of the story. Look at Diego's story map. Study what he did.

The Hardest Race
Luke knew he should be training for the big race next week, but he didn't feel like it. Usually he loved to race. He spent all his free time getting into shape. This time it was different, though, because Luke would be racing against his best friend, Carlos. Winning against Carlos wouldn't be any fun, and losing might feel even worse.

Beginning
Luke must race against his best friend, Carlos.

Middle
Luke wins the race.

End
Carlos is a good sport.

It's Your Turn!

Write your own narrative. You can create a realistic story like Diego's, a mystery, a fairy tale, a science fiction story, or any kind you wish. After you have decided what to write about, make a story map. Then follow the other steps in the writing process—writing, revising, proofreading, and publishing. Try to use spelling words from this lesson in your story.

Lesson 13
Words with /ī/

island

1. i-consonant-e Words

_____
_____
_____
_____
_____
_____
_____

2. i Words

_____
_____
_____
_____
_____
_____
_____
_____
_____
_____
_____

3. ie Word

_____

4. ui Word

_____

mild	
library	
science	
guide	
idea	
quite	
awhile	
ninth	
pirate	
polite	
tried	
decide	
remind	
revise	
island	
grind	
knife	
climb	
invite	
blind	

Say and Listen

Say each spelling word. Listen for the /ī/ sound you hear in *mild*.

Think and Sort

Look at the letters in each word. Think about how /ī/ is spelled. Spell each word aloud.

How many spelling patterns for /ī/ do you see?

1. Write the **seven** spelling words that have the *i*-consonant-*e* pattern.

2. Write the **eleven** spelling words that have the *i* pattern.

3. Write the **one** spelling word that has the *ie* pattern.

4. Write the **one** spelling word that has the *ui* pattern after a consonant other than *q*.

Use the steps on page 6 to study words that are hard for you.

Spelling Patterns

i-consonant-e	i	ie	ui
quite	mild	tried	guide

Spelling and Meaning

Classifying   Write the spelling word that belongs in each group.

1. mathematics, reading, _____
2. lead, direct, _____
3. robber, thief, _____
4. chop, crush, _____
5. change, edit, _____
6. spear, dagger, _____
7. tested, attempted, _____
8. thought, opinion, _____
9. calm, gentle, _____
10. seventh, eighth, _____

Definitions   Write the spelling word for each definition.
Use the Spelling Dictionary if you need to.

11. to go or move up   _____
12. to come to a conclusion   _____
13. unable to see   _____
14. completely or very   _____
15. to ask someone to go somewhere   _____
16. for a brief period of time   _____
17. a place with books and reference materials   _____
18. to make a person remember   _____
19. a piece of land completely surrounded by water   _____

Word Story   One spelling word comes from the Latin word *politus,* which meant "polished." It was used to refer to someone who had good manners. Today the word is used in the same way. Write the spelling word that comes from *politus.*

20. _____

Family Tree: *decide*   Compare the spellings, meanings, and pronunciations of the *decide* words. Then add another *decide* word to the tree.

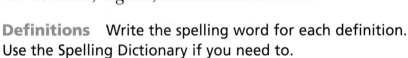

indecisive

undecided

indecision

decision

21.

decide

decisive

LOST AT SEA

June 6, 1843

    We have been at sea for eight months, and all that time the weather has been pleasant and _____. Once, we were almost attacked by a
                              1
_____ ship, but we got away.
        2

    I like my life as a sailor on board the <u>Fairweather</u>. Each day after I finish my work, I _____ to the top of the main mast and watch the
                          3
sea. I am _____ happy.
            4

July 1, 1843

    This is the first day of the _____ month of our voyage,
                          5
and the weather has changed. The sky is very dark and a great wind is blowing.

July 3, 1843

    The storm grew much worse. A huge wave crashed over the deck and threw me into the sea. I watched in horror as the ship sailed on without me. This morning I found myself on the shore of a small _____.
                          6
All I have are the clothes I am wearing and this diary, which I had wrapped in oilcloth and put in a pocket. I _____ to discover where I
                          7
was. But without a compass or a map, I had no _____. I could
                          8
not _____ what to do. Then I saw a boy about my own age
      9
walking toward me. I wanted to be _____, so I bowed to him.
                        10
He bowed back and offered to _____ me through the forest
                    11
to his family's hut. Although we didn't speak the same language, we were able to understand each other by using sign language.

When we got to the hut, he introduced me to his family. They pointed to a cooking pot, and I understood that they wanted to

_____ me to eat with them. They used a stone to
12

_____ some spices into a fine powder. Then they
13

sliced some vegetables with a _____. They fried
14

them and added the spices and some rice. It was the most

delicious meal I have ever eaten. Whenever I eat vegetables and

rice in the future, they will _____ me of this meal.
15

May 10, 1844

Today a ship sailed into the bay. I can't believe

I'm going home. My island friends asked me to

stay _____ longer. But I have
16

to return to my family.

I have had plenty of time to _____
17

my opinion of a sailor's life. How could I have been

so _____ to the dangers of a life
18

at sea? I could have drowned when the huge wave

threw me into the ocean. When I reach home, I

will study _____ and spend my
19

life in a laboratory. Or perhaps I'll just

read about the sea in a _____.
20

I will definitely not be a sailor.

mild
library
science
guide
idea
quite
awhile
ninth
pirate
polite
tried
decide
remind
revise
island
grind
knife
climb
invite
blind

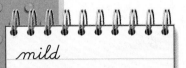

mild
library
science
guide
idea
quite
awhile
ninth
pirate
polite
tried
decide
remind
revise
island
grind
knife
climb
invite
blind

Write to the Point

Pretend that you are having an adventure. Write three diary entries telling about your adventure. Begin each entry with a date so that the reader will know how much time has passed. Try to use spelling words from this lesson.

> **Use the strategies on page 7 when you are not sure how to spell a word.**

Proofreading

Proofread this paragraph from a short story. Use proofreading marks to correct five spelling mistakes, two punctuation mistakes, and three unnecessary words.

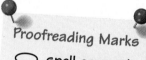

Proofreading Marks
⬭ spell correctly
? add question mark
✎ take out

The Decision

The sailor depended on the stars that twinkled in the black night sky to giude him along his course. Tonight, however, a thick fog had stolen in and a covered everything in a thick, wet blanket. The sailor had no iddea where he was, and he couldn't deside what to do. Should he drop it the ship's anchor and wait for awile Would the that just invite a pyrate attack The choice that he made in this moment could change the rest of his life.

Do you have sick friends in the _____ **?**
11

Finding the right gift for patients is not an unusual problem. In fact, it's very _____. Give our
12

Intergalactic Environmental Unit.

By setting the buttons, your friends can feel as if they have _____ earth under their
13

feet. It also can make your friends feel like they are at the

_____ of the ocean. No more dusty feelers!
14

No more sticky bimnuls! The IEU is small enough to store in

a _____ and comes in your choice of a silver or
15

_____ case.   **7000 Bloteems**
16

Tired of bumping around while flying

through space? Try our sturdy Querk

_____ absorbers. They will
17

get rid of that awful _____.
18

Set of 4 only 150 Bloteems

To order a gift from this book, log onto our Web address.

Be sure to use a _____, not a period, after
19

Querk. Have your space card number handy. Remember, three

Bloteems equal one _____ ($1.00).
20

www.Querk,com

dollar
honor
collar
closet
common
lobster
quantity
hospital
solid
copper
wander
problem
object
comma
watch
bother
bottom
shock
honest
promise

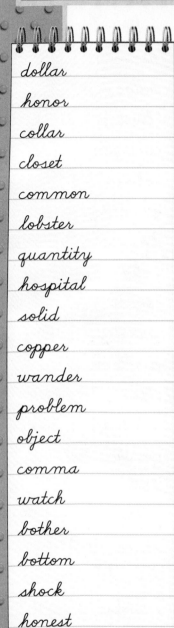

dollar
honor
collar
closet
common
lobster
quantity
hospital
solid
copper
wander
problem
object
comma
watch
bother
bottom
shock
honest
promise

Write to the Point

Think of an idea for a fantastic and useful new product. Then write an ad for the product. Explain what it does and why it makes an excellent gift. Give the price, too. Try to use spelling words from this lesson in your ad.

Use the strategies on page 7 when you are not sure how to spell a word.

Proofreading

Proofread the e-mail below. Use proofreading marks to correct five spelling mistakes, three capitalization mistakes, and two unnecessary words.

Proofreading Marks
◯ spell correctly
≡ capitalize
ꝰ take out

e-mail

| Address Book | Attachment | Check Spelling | Send | Save Draft | Cancel |

Dear Customer Service:

Help! do you promis to return my money if I can't use

an objikt that I bought? I don't want my dog to wandur

when I walk him on Mars, so i ordered a coller and

leash from the spring issue of your a catalog. Here is

my problum. the items that I ordered only work with

Rover space suits, and and my dog has a Fido suit.

Will you refund my money if I return these items?

Please respond soon!

Loraina Burton

Language Connection

Simple Subjects   The simple subject of a sentence tells who or what is doing the action of the verb or is being talked about. The simple subject is the main word of the complete subject. In the following sentence, the complete subject is underlined. The simple subject appears in dark type.

> The **boy** in the blue shirt won the race.

Write the simple subject of each sentence below.

1. The local hospital was a busy place on Saturday. _____

2. Fresh lobster is a tasty meat. _____

3. A comma is a punctuation mark. _____

4. The closet in your room is a mess. _____

5. A dollar is worth ten dimes. _____

6. My new gold watch is broken. _____

7. A promise should not be broken. _____

8. The bottom of the page is empty. _____

9. The soldier's honor was at stake. _____

10. Copper is a reddish-brown metal. _____

11. The object of the game is simple. _____

12. Dina saw the deer through the trees. _____

13. The dog's collar was lying in the mud. _____

14. The engine problem can easily be solved. _____

Challenge Yourself

What do you think each Challenge Word means? Check the Spelling Dictionary to see if you are right. Then use separate paper to write sentences showing the meaning of each Challenge Word.

Challenge Words	
solitude	jot
jostled	dislodge

15. The author needed **solitude** to write her book, so she worked alone in her room for hours.

16. You had better **jot** down this address in case you forget it.

17. The people **jostled** one another as they tried to get off the crowded bus.

18. I shook the piggy bank to **dislodge** the coin that was stuck in the slot.

Words with /ō/

telephone

1. o-consonant-e Words

_____
_____
_____
_____
_____
_____
_____
_____
_____

2. ow Words

_____
_____
_____
_____
_____
_____
_____
_____
_____
_____

3. ew Word

_____

vote

zone

known

follow

alone

microscope

arrow

grown

borrow

swallow

tomorrow

telephone

code

suppose

chose

sew

throw

bowl

owe

elbow

Say and Listen

Say each spelling word. Listen for the /ō/ sound you hear in *vote*.

Think and Sort

Look at the letters in each word. Think about how /ō/ is spelled. Spell each word aloud.

How many spelling patterns for /ō/ do you see?

1. Write the **nine** spelling words that have the *o-consonant-e* pattern.

2. Write the **ten** spelling words that have the *ow* pattern.

3. Write the **one** word that has the *ew* pattern.

Use the steps on page 6 to study words that are hard for you.

Spelling Patterns

o-consonant-e	ow	ew
vote	arrow	sew

Spelling and Meaning

Classifying Write the spelling word that belongs in each group.

1. pitch, hurl, _____

2. plate, cup, _____

3. yesterday, today, _____

4. grow, grew, _____

5. mend, stitch, _____

6. imagine, expect, _____

7. know, knew, _____

8. area, district, _____

9. dart, spear, _____

10. telescope, kaleidoscope, _____

11. picked, selected, _____

12. puzzle, signal, _____

What's Missing? Write the missing spelling word.

13. Leave me _____!

14. Answer the _____, please.

15. _____ the leader.

16. The pill was hard to _____.

17. You _____ me a favor.

18. May I _____ your pencil?

19. Let's _____ on it.

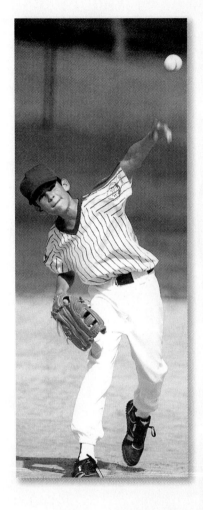

Word Story One spelling word developed from the Old English word *elnboga*. *Eln* meant "length of arm" and *boga* meant "arch." Today the word names a part of the body. Write the spelling word that comes from *elnboga*.

20. _____

Family Tree: *known* *Known* is a form of *know.* Compare the spellings, meanings, and pronunciations of the *know* words. Then add another *know* word to the tree.

known

knowing

knowledge

21. _____

unknown

know

Use each spelling word once to complete the story.

Letter from the Science Fair

Dear Hannah,

Every year at our school, the science teachers choose one student to go to the state science fair in South Bend. This year they _____ [1] me! The teachers took a _____ [2], and I won!

You know I've always wanted to be a scientist. I _____ [3] it all started when I found out that a caterpillar turns into a butterfly. Ever since then, I've wanted to learn everything about nature.

I'm going to look really nice at the science fair. Mom worked all last weekend to _____ [4] a new skirt for me. My friend Taylor let me _____ [5] her new blue sweater. It matches the skirt perfectly.

Today was the first time I've ever traveled _____ [6]. I felt really _____ [7] up. I also felt a little bit lonely. I wish now that I had _____ [8] someone else on the train because I didn't have anyone to talk to. I propped an _____ [9] on the armrest by the window and watched the miles go by.

When we got to the train station in South Bend, the conductor told me to _____ [10] him to a taxi. Then he folded my chair and put it in the taxi for me. The taxi took me to a dorm at the university where I'll spend the night. Then I went over to the main building of the university. Just inside the front door I saw an _____ [11] pointing to a large room. A sign read "INDIANA SCIENCE FAIR." I really began to get excited then.

A woman met me at the door and explained that the room was divided into several zones. My table is in the _____ 12 reserved for fifth graders. I began to unpack my project immediately. I was a little worried about the _____ 13 and slides, so I checked them first. They were fine. I put one of the slides on the microscope and then set up the rest of my exhibit.

When I finished setting up, I found a _____ and 14 called home. I had never called long distance before, so I forgot to dial our area _____. I finally got it right, though. 15 Mom and Dad were glad to hear I had arrived safely.

I bought some toast on the train, but I was so excited that I could hardly _____ a bite. Now I'm hungry. When I 16 finish this letter, I think I'll _____ on my coat and 17 go to the cafeteria for a _____ of chili. 18

Well, _____ is the big day, so wish me luck! It 19 feels great to be at the science fair. I _____ it all 20 to that caterpillar!

Your friend,

Gabby

vote

zone

known

follow

alone

microscope

arrow

grown

borrow

swallow

tomorrow

telephone

code

suppose

chose

sew

throw

bowl

owe

elbow

vote
zone
known
follow
alone
microscope
arrow
grown
borrow
swallow
tomorrow
telephone
code
suppose
chose
sew
throw
bowl
owe
elbow

Write to the Point

Write a letter to a friend or relative, telling that person some of the news in your life. Try to use spelling words from this lesson.

Use the strategies on page 7 when you are not sure how to spell a word.

Proofreading

Proofread the journal entry below. Use proofreading marks to correct five spelling mistakes, three capitalization mistakes, and two mistakes in word order.

Proofreading Marks

◯ spell correctly
≡ capitalize
∿ trade places

april 8

Tommorrow I give will my science report. It's called "The Amazing microscope." I choze the microscope as a topic because have I grone very interested in tiny living things. The only way to see them is to view them through a microscope. without this important invention, we would never have knoan why people get typhoid fever and food poisoning. I suppows that we wouldn't be able to see what a flea or a mite really looks like, either. I hope everyone likes my report. I've tried to make it fun and interesting.

Language Connection

Verbs   The complete predicate is the part of a sentence that tells what the subject does or is. The verb is the main word or words in the predicate. In the sentences below, *Chelsey* is the subject, and the words in dark type are the verbs.

| Chelsey | **will jog** to school today. |
| Chelsey | **is** a very good athlete. |

Write each of the following sentences, correcting the spelling errors and underlining the verbs.

1. I oew Jo Anne a dollar.

_____

2. Noah can borow my bike.

_____

3. I soe my own clothes.

_____

4. Tyler and Cody folloe directions well.

_____

5. Zoey answered the telefone.

_____

6. Rosie put the slide under the microskope.

_____

Challenge Yourself

Write the Challenge Word for each clue. Check the Spelling Dictionary to see if you are right. Then use separate paper to write sentences showing that you understand the meaning of each Challenge Word.

Challenge Words	
disclose	wallow
stowaway	brooch

7. This person gets a free ride by hiding on a ship. _____

8. You do this to a secret when you tell it to someone. _____

9. This pin is a piece of jewelry. _____

10. Pigs do this in mud to cool themselves off. _____

More Words with /ō/

tornado

oak
hotel
coach
notice
dough
yolk
boast
poem
groan
echo
float
control
tornado
hero
coast
though
throat
clothing
scold
roast

Say and Listen

Say each spelling word. Listen for the /ō/ sound.

Think and Sort

Look at the letters in each word. Think about how /ō/ is spelled. Spell each word aloud.

How many spelling patterns for /ō/ do you see?

1. Write the **ten** spelling words that have the *o* pattern.

2. Write the **eight** spelling words that have the *oa* pattern.

3. Write the **two** spelling words that have the *ough* pattern.

1. *o* Words
_____
_____
_____
_____
_____
_____
_____
_____
_____
_____

2. *oa* Words
_____
_____
_____
_____
_____
_____
_____
_____

3. *ough* Words
_____
_____

Use the steps on page 6 to study words that are hard for you.

Spelling Patterns

o	oa	ough
y**o**lk	**oa**k	th**ough**

Classifying   Write the spelling word that belongs in each group.

1. hats, shoes, _____

2. egg white, eggshell, egg _____

3. resound, repeat, _____

4. elm, birch, _____

5. ear, nose, _____

6. since, however, _____

7. direct, operate, _____

8. lecture, yell, _____

9. crust, batter, _____

10. manager, trainer, _____

11. motel, inn, _____

12. see, observe, _____

13. drift, bob, _____

Synonyms   Complete each sentence by writing the spelling word that is a synonym for the underlined word.

14. The champion of the chess match was our _____.

15. This _____ is verse that doesn't rhyme.

16. Sail along the _____ and stop near the shore.

17. A stomachache can make you moan and _____.

18. Some people brag and _____ when they win a game.

19. Should I bake the chicken and _____ the corn?

Word Story   One spelling word names a violent wind that can spin at 300 miles per hour. It takes its name from the Spanish word *tronada*. Write the spelling word.

20. _____

Family Tree: *control*   Compare the spellings, meanings, and pronunciations of the *control* words. Then add another *control* word to the tree.

controls

controllable

uncontrollable

21.

controlled

control

uncontrolled

Use each spelling word once to complete the story.

Hurricane!

Maria's father was the head chef at Casa Grande, the most famous seaside _____ on the western
1

_____ of the island. Maria often helped in the kitchen. Today
2

was no different. While her father kneaded _____ for bread and
3

put a _____ in the oven, Maria cracked four eggs and stirred each
4

_____ into cake batter.
5

When she was finished, she changed from her work _____ to her
6

swimsuit. The kitchen had been hot. Now she was ready to _____ on
7

the gentle waves of the sea. On her way down to the beach, she saw Hector, the hotel

manager, looking out at the choppy waves and dark storm clouds. "Looks like a

hurricane is moving our way," he said.

One guest, a softball trainer and _____, didn't seem afraid. In
8

fact, she began to _____ about all the storms she had seen. "No
9

_____ or hurricane can scare me," she bragged.
10

A second guest began to moan and _____ when he heard the news.
11

"I'm no _____," he said. "I've never been so scared in all my life!"
12

Just then, Hector announced over a loudspeaker that everyone should take shelter

in the hotel. The guests listened to his voice _____ up and down the
13

beach for a long moment. Then Maria took them to the hotel's kitchen, which was in

the basement. They would be safe there.

Even in the basement, they could hear the wind roaring and the huge waves

crashing over the beach. The guests tried hard to _____ their rising
14

fears. Even the brave coach felt her _____ become so tight that she
15

couldn't swallow. Then she began to _____ herself for
16
being so afraid.

Maria decided she had to do something to take the guests' minds off
the storm. She grabbed some paper and pencils. "May I please have
your attention?" she shouted above the noise of the storm. "Even
_____ we're stuck in the kitchen until the storm blows
17
over, there's no reason we can't have a good time. Let's all sit around
this big _____ table and write poems. There will be a
18
prize for the best _____ about the storm." Everyone
19
scrambled for seats and began to write.

After a while, no one seemed to _____ the storm.
20
Maria breathed a deep sigh as she heard the storm die down. Everyone
was safe. Hector announced that the prize for the writing contest would
be a free dinner. Then he thanked Maria for entertaining the guests and
keeping them busy during the storm.

Maria often helped in the kitchen, but today her kitchen work
included helping people as well as preparing food.

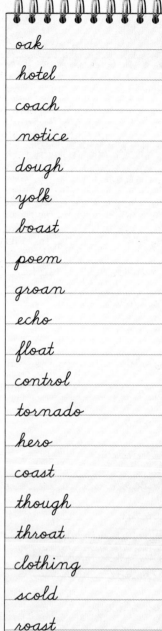

oak
hotel
coach
notice
dough
yolk
boast
poem
groan
echo
float
control
tornado
hero
coast
though
throat
clothing
scold
roast

oak
hotel
coach
notice
dough
yolk
boast
poem
groan
echo
float
control
tornado
hero
coast
though
throat
clothing
scold
roast

Write to the Point

Write a list of rules telling what to do in a certain kind of emergency or how to prevent an emergency from happening. Try to use spelling words from this lesson.

Use the strategies on page 7 when you are not sure how to spell a word.

Proofreading

Proofread the diary entry below. Use proofreading marks to correct five spelling mistakes, three capitalization mistakes, and two punctuation mistakes.

Proofreading Marks
◯ spell correctly
/ make lowercase
⊙ add period

Dear Diary,

Last night a tornadoe hit our Town. I've never been so scared in all my life. I woke up around Midnight when our house began to grone. I looked outside and saw lawn chairs and branches flying through the air. Dad said we had to get somewhere in the middle of the house, so we gathered in the hall Soon we heard nothing but the roaring wind spinning out of controle. This morning we saw that the roof of the hotell next door was gone. The oke tree in our yard had been pulled up by the roots. I'm grateful that We are all unharmed

Dictionary Skills

Parts of Speech The parts of speech include noun (*n.*), verb (*v.*), adverb (*adv.*), and preposition (*prep.*). Some words can be used as more than one part of speech. The parts of speech for those words are usually listed within one dictionary entry.

coast (kōst) *n.* The edge of land along the sea. —*v.* **coast·ed, coast·ing.** To move without power or effort: *coast down a hill.*

con·trol (kən trōl′) *v.* **con·trolled, con·trol·ling.** To have power over: *control a country; control a car.* —*n.* **1.** Authority or power: *the athlete's control over his body.* **2. controls.** Instruments for operating a machine.

Both *coast* and *control* can be used as a noun and a verb. Use the words to complete the sentences below. Then write *noun* or *verb* after each to tell how it is used in each sentence.

1. Joan couldn't _____ the frisky pony. _____

2. I like to _____ down the hill on my skateboard.

   _____

3. We rented a house on the _____ of Florida. _____

4. Gymnasts have remarkable _____ over their body.

   _____

5. The hotel guests' fear seemed out of _____.

   _____

6. We drove along the _____ today. _____

⭐ Challenge Yourself

Use the Spelling Dictionary to answer these questions. Then use separate paper to write sentences showing that you understand the meaning of each Challenge Word.

Challenge Words	
loathe	nomad
token	smolder

7. Would the coals from a fire **smolder** if you didn't

   put the fire out completely? _____

8. Would someone who is a **nomad** stay in one place all her life?

   _____

9. Could a photograph be a **token** of a special day? _____

10. If you care for someone very much, do you **loathe** that person?

    _____

Lesson 17

Media Words

newspaper

1. Words with Two Syllables

_____

_____

_____

_____

_____

_____

_____

2. Words with Three Syllables

_____

_____

_____

_____

_____

_____

_____

_____

_____

_____

3. Words with More Than Three Syllables

_____

_____

_____

graphics

animation

columnist

byline

studio

earphones

producer

commercial

recorder

video

network

camera

newspaper

director

television

editorial

headline

musician

masthead

broadcast

Say and Listen

Say each spelling word. Listen for the number of syllables in each word.

Think and Sort

Look at the letters in each word. Spell each word aloud.

1. Write the **seven** spelling words that have two syllables.

2. Write the **ten** spelling words that have three syllables.

3. Write the **three** spelling words that have more than three syllables.

4. Look up the spelling words in the Spelling Dictionary and draw lines between the syllables of each word.

Use the steps on page 6 to study words that are hard for you.

Spelling Patterns

Two Syllables	Three Syllables	More Than Three Syllables
graph·ics	di·rec·tor	an·i·ma·tion

Compound Words   Write the spelling word that is made from the two underlined words in each sentence.

1. The phones were close to my right ear.   _____

2. The horse's head has a white line on it.   _____

3. We walked by the line for the movie.   _____

4. Lee cast a glance over the broad meadow.   _____

5. I bumped my head on the sailboat's mast.   _____

6. Will this net work in the river?   _____

7. The reporter read the news from a sheet of paper.   _____

Clues   Write the spelling word for each clue.

8. an ad on TV   _____

9. someone who plays a musical instrument   _____

10. a person who writes a daily or weekly feature   _____

11. a newspaper column that tells the writer's opinion   _____

12. a movie put on tape for viewing on television   _____

13. a device for taking pictures   _____

14. a way to bring drawings to life   _____

15. a person who instructs movie actors and crew   _____

16. a place where TV shows and movies are filmed   _____

17. the person who manages the making of a TV show   _____

18. a device that saves sounds on magnetic tape   _____

19. artwork in a video game   _____

Word Story   One spelling word comes from two words, *telos* and *video*. *Telos* is Greek. It means "far away." *Video* comes from Latin and means "I see." Write the spelling word.

20. _____

Family Tree: *recorder*   *Recorder* is a form of *record*. Compare the spellings, meanings, and pronunciations of the *record* words. Then add another *record* word to the tree.

recording

recorder

prerecorded

21.

unrecorded

record

Use each spelling word once to complete the story.

Multimedia

Both of my parents work for media companies. My mom works for a television _____, and my dad works for a newspaper.

1

I went to visit both of them at their jobs to see what they do each day.

My mom is a _____ of a television show. Her job is to plan

2

each show. The show is _____ at 9:00 every Wednesday evening.

3

Mom's job also includes choosing other people who work on the show. One of

the most important people she chooses is the program's _____.

4

He directs people in the show.

Two days ago I went with Mom to the _____ where

5

the show is filmed. First she met with the director. He introduced us to

the _____, who was wearing _____. He was

6 **7**

listening to the music for the show on a multitrack _____.

8

Mom and the director went over the script for the show. They decided which

_____ would be used

9

to film each live action scene.

They also decided to include some cartoon _____.

10

Then they reviewed a tape of the show to see where to break for a

_____. I was surprised to find out how much work

11

it takes to put together one half-hour _____ show.

12

My dad also does a lot of work to put together his column. My

dad works at the *Daily Times*. He writes a daily column about

television shows. He is a _____. His name appears

13

in the _____ that follows his column.

14

Yesterday I visited my dad at his office. He showed me a copy of

the _____ from the day he started work there. He

15

pointed to the _____, which listed the name of the

16

paper and the date. Then we watched a _____ of

17

the program he was reviewing for his column. After Dad wrote his

column, I helped him write the _____ for it. We

18

decided on "A Show Worth Seaing: Ocean Watch." Then he chose

_____ to illustrate his review. Dad's column appears

19

on the page across from the _____ page, where all

20

of the editorials and letters to the editor appear.

I really enjoyed visiting my mom and dad at their work. I think

I will work in media when I grow up!

graphics
animation
columnist
byline
studio
earphones
producer
commercial
recorder
video
network
camera
newspaper
director
television
editorial
headline
musician
masthead
broadcast

Write to the Point

Write a paragraph giving your opinion of television. What is good about it? What could be better? Support your opinions with reasons and examples. Try to use spelling words from this lesson.

> Use the strategies on page 7 when you are not sure how to spell a word.

Proofreading

Proofread the help-wanted ad below. Use proofreading marks to correct five spelling mistakes, three capitalization mistakes, and two mistakes in word order.

Proofreading Marks
- ◯ spell correctly
- ≡ capitalize
- ∼ trade places

Spelling word list:
- graphics
- animation
- columnist
- byline
- studio
- earphones
- producer
- commercial
- recorder
- video
- network
- camera
- newspaper
- director
- television
- editorial
- headline
- musician
- masthead
- broadcast

Help Wanted!

KNBE, the most popular network in North America, is seeking a praducer and a director for its new telavision show. the show about is a newspaper columist and a musician who are roommates. job requirements include a bachelor's degree in theater arts or radio/TV, three years' experience working on similar small-screen projects, camara knowledge, and a stable work history. if are you interested, contact the KNBE stewdio at 305-4444 for an application. KNBE is an equal opportunity employer.

Language Connection

Capitalization   Names of cities, states, countries, bodies of water, mountains, and streets are capitalized.

> Larry visited **S**an **F**rancisco, **C**alifornia, last summer. He saw the **P**acific **O**cean.

The following scrambled sentences contain errors in capitalization. Unscramble each sentence and write it correctly.

1. broadcast came The new york from.

_____

2. the was commercial rocky mountains The filmed in.

_____

3. mentioned The washington, d.c., headline virginia and.

_____

4. was arctic ocean The about newspaper the article.

_____

5. a hollywood We studio visited.

_____

6. lives director paris in The of that film.

_____

7. The show atlantic ocean television was about the.

_____

Challenge Yourself

Challenge Words

journalism
periodical
audio
microphone

Use the Spelling Dictionary to answer these questions. Then use separate paper to write sentences showing that you understand the meaning of each Challenge Word.

8. Would a person who likes writing about people and

events enjoy a job in **journalism**? _____

9. Is a novel an example of a **periodical**? _____

10. Can you call the sounds heard on a TV show the **audio**? _____

11. Do you listen to sound through a **microphone**? _____

Lesson 18

Unit 3 Review
Lessons 13–17

Use the steps on page 6 to study words that are hard for you.

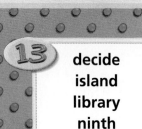

13
decide
island
library
ninth
science
guide

Words with /ī/

Write the spelling word that completes each analogy.

1. *Cloud* is to *sky* as _____ is to *sea*.

2. *Reside* is to *residence* as _____ is to *decision*.

3. *Eight* is to *eighth* as *nine* is to _____.

4. *Scientist* is to _____ as *historian* is to *history*.

5. *Leader* is to _____ as *path* is to *trail*.

6. *Teacher* is to *classroom* as *librarian* is to _____.

14
collar
common
hospital
promise
wander

Words with /ŏ/

Write the spelling word that belongs in each group.

7. waistband, cuff, _____

8. doctor's office, clinic, _____

9. usual, ordinary, _____

10. guarantee, oath, _____

11. roam, drift, _____

15
telephone
owe
borrow
sew

Words with /ō/

Write the spelling word that answers each question.

12. What can you use to call a friend? _____

13. What can you do if you forget your pencil? _____

14. How do you attach a missing button to a coat? _____

15. What word has the meaning "to be in debt"? _____

16

echo
notice
yolk
groan
throat
though

More Words with /ō/

Write the spelling word for each definition.

16. a repeating or bouncing sound _____

17. a narrow passage or entryway _____

18. even if; in spite of the fact that _____

19. a printed announcement _____

20. to moan deeply or sadly _____

21. the yellow part of an egg _____

17

musician
camera
commercial
graphics

Media Words

Write the spelling word that completes each sentence.

22. The girl was a brilliant _____.

23. Kayla liked the _____ on her computer screen.

24. My new _____ has a zoom lens.

25. The new pizza _____ features a singing parrot.

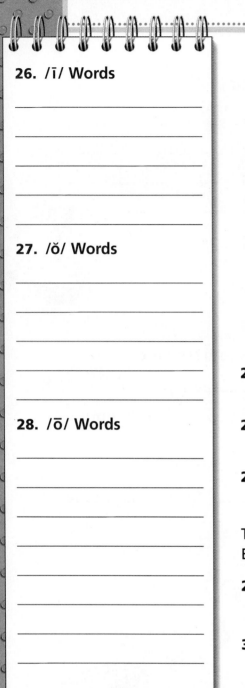

26. /ī/ Words

_____

_____

_____

_____

_____

27. /ŏ/ Words

_____

_____

_____

_____

_____

28. /ō/ Words

_____

_____

_____

_____

_____

_____

_____

_____

_____

Review Sort

ninth	though	promise	echo
common	library	owe	collar
notice	throat	island	telephone
yolk	wander	sew	guide
decide	groan	hospital	

26. Write the **five** long *i* words. Circle the letter or letters that spell /ī/ in each word.

27. Write the **five** short *o* words. Circle the letter that spells /ŏ/ in each word.

28. Write the **nine** long *o* words. Circle the letter or letters that spell /ō/ in each word.

These seven words have been sorted into three groups. Explain how the words in each group are alike.

29. commercial   musician

_____

30. graphics   network

_____

31. earphones   newspaper   headline

_____

Writer's Workshop

A Business Letter

Suppose that you read a great book and wanted to write a letter to the author to tell him or her how much you liked the book. You would need the author's address. One way to get the address is to write a business letter to the book publisher. Here is a business letter that Lena wrote to a publisher.

27 Palm Road
Jacksonville, FL 32216
May 3, 2003

Hall Publishing Company
157 Madison Avenue
New York, NY 10023

Dear Hall Publishing Company:
    I really enjoyed the book South Pacific Adventure by Kate Rossini. Please send me Ms. Rossini's address so that I can tell her how much I liked the book. Thank you.

    Sincerely,
    Lena Yu

Prewriting To write her business letter, Lena followed the steps in the writing process. As a prewriting activity, she made a list of the parts of a business letter. Lena's list is shown under her letter. Study what Lena did. Use the list to identify each part of Lena's letter.

Heading
Inside address
Greeting
Body
Closing
Signature

It's Your Turn!

Choose a company that sells books or games through a catalog. Write a letter to the company, asking for a copy of the catalog. When you have decided what company to write to, make a list of the parts of a business letter. Then follow the other steps in the writing process—writing, revising, proofreading, and publishing. Try to use spelling words from this lesson in your letter.

Lesson 19

Words with /ŭ/

compass

1. u Words

_____
_____
_____
_____
_____
_____
_____
_____

2. o Words

_____
_____
_____
_____
_____
_____
_____

3. ou Words

_____
_____
_____

4. oo Words

_____
_____

crush
judge
rough
husband
tongue
pumpkin
monkey
onion
touch
hundred
jungle
compass
blood
among
knuckle
flood
instruct
country
dozen
wonderful

Say and Listen

Say each spelling word. Listen for the /ŭ/ sound you hear in _crush._

Think and Sort

Look at the letters in each word. Think about how /ŭ/ is spelled. Spell each word aloud.

How many spelling patterns for /ŭ/ do you see?

1. Write the **eight** spelling words that have the _u_ pattern.

2. Write the **seven** spelling words that have the _o_ pattern.

3. Write the **three** spelling words that have the _ou_ pattern.

4. Write the **two** spelling words that have the _oo_ pattern.

Use the steps on page 6 to study words that are hard for you.

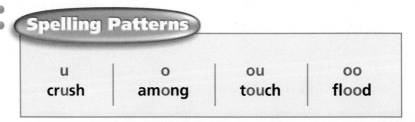

Spelling Patterns

u	o	ou	oo
crush	among	touch	flood

Spelling and Meaning

Classifying Write the spelling word that belongs in each group.

1. courtroom, lawyer, _____
2. pepper, garlic, _____
3. desert, plains, _____
4. teeth, gums, _____
5. map, backpack, _____
6. hand, finger, _____

Clues Write the spelling word for each clue.

7. If you pound ice into pieces, you do this. _____
8. This red liquid is pumped through the body. _____
9. This is a married man. _____
10. This is a group of twelve. _____
11. This word means "excellent." _____
12. A wagon bounces over this kind of road. _____
13. If you teach, you do this. _____
14. This is ten times ten. _____
15. This is another word for *nation*. _____
16. When you have a lot of rain, you might get this. _____
17. This word means "in the company of." _____
18. This is what you don't do to a hot stove. _____
19. This animal has hands with thumbs. _____

Word Story One of the spelling words comes from the Greek word *pessein,* meaning "to cook." The word names a fruit that is "cooked by the sun." Write the spelling word that comes from *pessein.*

20. _____

Family Tree: *instruct* Compare the spellings, meanings, and pronunciations of the *instruct* words. Then add another *instruct* word to the tree.

instructive

instructor

instructions

21.

instructed

instruct

Use each spelling word once to complete the selection.

Advertising World

Insta-Boat

Do you live near a river?

Do you worry when heavy

rains come? Here's a great way to

prepare for a _____.
1

Buy an Insta-Boat. It inflates with a _____ of a finger. For
2

easy storage just _____ it into a ball. Comes in one size
3

large enough for the whole family: wife, _____, children,
4

and grandparents.

Compass Ring

Going for a sail, a trip to another _____,
5

a hike through _____ and rocky terrain?
6

The _____ ring is a must! Don't just take our word for it.
7

_____ for yourself. Just program in your address, and the
8

compass ring will always point home. You may not be able to get there, but

you will always know where it is! Adjustable band slips easily over the largest

_____. Makes a _____ gift.
9   10

Coward's Bandages

Can't stand the sight of _____? Try Coward's Bandages.
11

As soon as you cut yourself, simply place a bandage over your eyes and stop

worrying. When the bleeding stops, remove bandages from the eyes and place

them on the wound. Order a _____ now so you'll have plenty!
12

Be a Monkey's Uncle

You can be a monkey's uncle. That's right! The Amazon

_____ is fast disappearing. You can change
　　　13

that. For just one _____ dollars, you can help
　　　　　　　　　　　14

save a _____ and its habitat. Choose from
　　　　15

_____ the thousands of monkeys available.
　　16

Every month you'll receive a photograph and a handwritten

letter from your monkey.

Pumpions

Try this exciting taste treat and give your _____ a
　　　　　　　　　　　　　　　　　　　　17

surprise. As its name implies, the pumpion is a cross between a

_____ and an _____. It's sweet
　　18　　　　　　　　　　　　19

enough for dessert but snappy enough to add zest to any casserole.

We'll also send our full-color idea book at no cost to you. It will

_____ you in the fine art of preparing french-fried
　　20

pumpion rings and homemade pumpion pie.

crush
judge
rough
husband
tongue
pumpkin
monkey
onion
touch
hundred
jungle
compass
blood
among
knuckle
flood
instruct
country
dozen
wonderful

Spelling and Writing

crush
judge
rough
husband
tongue
pumpkin
monkey
onion
touch
hundred
jungle
compass
blood
among
knuckle
flood
instruct
country
dozen
wonderful

Write to the Point

Satisfied customers often appear in television commercials. They tell why they are pleased with a product. Imagine that you tried one of the "Advertising World" products and are a satisfied customer. Write what you would say in a commercial for the product. Try to use spelling words from this lesson.

Use the strategies on page 7 when you are not sure how to spell a word.

Proofreading

Proofread the advertisement below. Use proofreading marks to correct five spelling mistakes, two punctuation mistakes, and three missing words.

Proofreading Marks

◯ spell correctly

? add question mark

∧ add

Try No-Cry!

Do you cry when peel an uniun Have you tried chilling it, peeling it underwater, or shutting your eyes As you know, these old-fashioned remedies don't work, but we have a new one does. Now is the time to try No-Cry!

Just place two No-Cry pills on your tung. No tears will stream down your face. Your eyes will not sting.

No store in the countre sells these pills, so order a bottle now. In fact, order two. Each bottle contains a dozan pills.

They wonderfull!

Dictionary Skills

Homographs Some words are spelled exactly like other words but have different meanings and different origins. Some are also pronounced differently. These words are called homographs. *Homo* means "same," and *graph* means "write." Homographs appear as separate entry words in dictionaries, and they are numbered.

bowl¹ (bōl) *n.* **1.** A round dish used to hold things. **2.** Something shaped like a bowl.

bowl² (bōl) *v.* **bowled, bowl·ing. 1.** To play the game of bowling: *Rita likes to bowl after school.* **2.** To roll a ball in the game of bowling: *Who bowls first?*

des·ert¹ (dĕz′ ərt) *n.* A dry, sandy region.

de·sert² (dĭ zûrt′) *v.* **de·sert·ed, de·sert·ing.** To forsake; abandon: *She did not desert her friends when they needed her.*

Complete each sentence with one of the homographs above. Then write the entry number for the homograph.

1. May I have a _____ of soup? _____

2. I like to _____ with my team on Saturdays. _____

3. I hope I _____ a few strikes. _____

4. The _____ had not seen rain in two years. _____

5. The students walked down into the rocky _____ left by the meteorite. _____

6. Don't _____ a person in need. _____

Challenge Yourself

What do you think each Challenge Word means? Check the Spelling Dictionary to see if you are right. Then use separate paper to write sentences showing that you understand the meaning of each Challenge Word.

Challenge Words

blunt
budget
doubly
stomachache

7. A pencil lead starts out sharp but grows **blunt** as you write with it.

8. We made a **budget** for the party to avoid spending too much money.

9. To finish an hour's work in half an hour, you must work **doubly** fast.

10. Eating too much food can give you a **stomachache**.

autumn

1. a Words

_____

_____

2. o Words

_____

_____

3. au Words

_____

_____

_____

4. aw Words

_____

_____

_____

_____

_____

_____

5. augh, ough Words

_____

_____

_____

_____

_____

_____

_____

dawn

raw

autumn

crawl

thought

fault

lawn

automobile

fought

straw

daughter

all right

caught

already

bought

brought

wrong

taught

often

awful

Say and Listen

Say each spelling word. Listen for the /ô/ sound you hear in _dawn._

Think and Sort

Look at the letters in each word. Think about how /ô/ is spelled. Spell each word aloud.

How many spelling patterns for /ô/ do you see?

1. Write the **two** spelling words that have the _a_ pattern.

2. Write the **two** spelling words that have the _o_ pattern.

3. Write the **three** spelling words that have the _au_ pattern.

4. Write the **six** spelling words that have the _aw_ pattern.

5. Write the **seven** spelling words that have the _augh_ or _ough_ pattern.

> Use the steps on page 6 to study words that are hard for you.

Spelling Patterns

a	o	au	aw	augh	ough
already	wr**o**ng	f**au**lt	d**aw**n	t**augh**t	f**ough**t

Spelling and Meaning

Antonyms   Antonyms are words that have opposite meanings. Write the spelling word that is an antonym of each word below.

1. dusk   _____

2. sold   _____

3. right   _____

4. seldom   _____

5. wonderful   _____

6. cooked   _____

7. unsatisfactory _____

8. learned   _____

Analogies   Write the spelling word that completes each analogy.

9. *Spring* is to *warm* as _____ is to *cool.*

10. *Tell* is to *told* as *catch* is to _____.

11. *Grass* is to _____ as *leaves* are to *tree.*

12. *Fast* is to *run* as *slow* is to _____.

13. Fight is to _____ as *sing* is to *sang.*

14. _____ is to *past* as *right away* is to *soon.*

15. *Eat* is to *ate* as *think* is to _____.

16. *Mother* is to _____ as *father* is to *son.*

17. *Pillow* is to *feather* as *scarecrow* is to _____.

18. *Asked* is to *ask* as _____ is to *bring.*

19. *Find* is to *locate* as *mistake* is to _____.

Word Story   One spelling word comes from the Greek word *auto,* which meant "self," and the Latin word *mobilis,* which meant "moving." The word used today names a means of transportation. Write the word.

20. _____

Family Tree: *thought*   Compare the spellings, meanings, and pronunciations of the *thought* words. Then add another *thought* word to the tree.

thoughtless

thoughtfulness   thoughtfully

thoughtlessly   21.

thoughtful   thought

Use each spelling word once to complete the selection.

Camp Mail

Dear Mom and Dad,

I know it isn't your _____. Next time, though, I'll read
                                    1

between the lines in any camp ad that says "GET READY TO LAUNCH

INTO AN EXCITING SUMMER!" The only thing we've launched is a canoe.

Our counselors woke us up at _____ this morning and
                                          2

drove us twenty miles upriver in their ancient _____. When
                                                          3

we stopped, I _____ that the counselors would help us.
                      4

Guess who got to carry the canoe to the water.

When the canoe was in the river, we all _____ for the
                                                   5

best seats. It took awhile, because you can't stand up in a canoe. You

must hold the sides and _____ to your seat.
                                 6

We pulled up to the bank at noon for lunch. We cooked stew while the

counselors made fruit salad. Our stew wasn't very good. In fact, it was

_____. Some of the meat was still _____,
        7   8

and the beans were as dry as _____. Luckily the fruit
                                       9

salad was _____.
                 10

We finally got back to camp late this afternoon. The counselors

_____ some fish for supper. Then they _____
        11   12

us how to clean them. I hope that the fish tastes better than our stew.

Your homesick _____,
                          13

Alison

July 7, 2003

Dear Alison,

Your letter was by far the nicest thing the mail carrier _____ 14 us today. We know you think the camp ad gave you the _____ 15 impression. Just remember that you won't be there forever. Later on when you look back on this summer, you'll probably think that it was exciting. When _____ 16 comes, you'll probably miss your summer friends and the counselors more than you can imagine.

Our _____ 17 doesn't look the same since you left. Your long-lost friend, the lawnmower, is always asking for you. I am sure, though, that it is one friend you are happy to be away from.

Uncle Todd passed his exams to become a lawyer. To celebrate, we _____ 18 him a book by his favorite writer.

It's noon _____ 19 and just about time for the mail carrier to pick up the mail. I promise to write again soon. We think of you _____ 20.

Love,
Mom

dawn
raw
autumn
crawl
thought
fault
lawn
automobile
fought
straw
daughter
all right
caught
already
bought
brought
wrong
taught
often
awful

Spelling and Writing

Write to the Point

Is there a summer that you remember especially well because something unusual, funny, or exciting took place? Write the true story of what happened. Try to use spelling words from this lesson in your story.

Use the strategies on page 7 when you are not sure how to spell a word.

Proofreading

Proofread the e-mail below. Use proofreading marks to correct five spelling mistakes, three capitalization mistakes, and two punctuation mistakes.

Proofreading Marks
◯ spell correctly
≡ capitalize
⊙ add period

| e-mail |
| Address Book | Attachment | Check Spelling | Send | Save Draft | Cancel |

Hi, Aunt sylvia!

Did you have a good summer? I did, except for one problem. I was supposed to mow mrs. Hu's laun each week until she returned in the awtumn. She taght me how to start her mower, and I thought I had caught on. I was rong

After ten days, her yard looked auful. I finally asked a neighbor what to do. he showed me how to start the mower, and everything was fine I hope I can do it again next summer.

Raymond

Language Connection

Apostrophes   A contraction is a shortened form of two or more words in which one or more letters are left out. An apostrophe shows where the letters have been left out.

> had + n**o**t hadn't

A possessive noun is a noun form that shows ownership. An apostrophe and -*s* are used to form the possessive of a singular noun. An apostrophe and -*s* are also used to form the possessive of a plural noun that does not end in -*s*. If a plural noun ends in -*s,* only an apostrophe is used.

Singular Possessives	Plural Possessives
the dog**'s** house	the mice**'s** cage
	the girls**'** dresses

The following sentences contain spelling errors and apostrophe errors. Write each sentence correctly.

1. Mom: Ive brawt you a surprise.

_____

2. Stuart: I thawt youd forgotten my birthday.

_____

3. Mom: Its all boys favorite means of transportation.

_____

4. Stuart: You bougt me a car like Dads!

_____

5. Mom: Youre rong, silly boy. Its a bicycle.

_____

Challenge Yourself

Write the Challenge Word for each clue. Check the Spelling Dictionary to see if you are right. Then use separate paper to write sentences showing that you understand the meaning of each Challenge Word.

Challenge Words	
authentic	nautical
fraud	awning

6. This word describes an anchor, a sail, and a sailor's cap. _____

7. To put your name on a painting by someone else is this. _____

8. This is the opposite of *fake.* _____

9. This is good to stand under if you're caught in the rain. _____

Lesson 21

Words with /oo/

kangaroo

1. oo Words

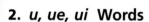
_____
_____
_____
_____
_____
_____
_____

2. u, ue, ui Words

_____
_____
_____
_____
_____

3. o-consonant-e, oe, o Words

_____
_____
_____
_____
_____
_____

choose
loose
lose
rooster
balloon
shampoo
improve
clue
kangaroo
fruit
proof
prove
truth
foolish
shoe
whom
juice
whose
raccoon
glue

Say and Listen

Say each spelling word. Listen for the /oo/ sound you hear in *choose*.

Think and Sort

Look at the letters in each word. Think about how /oo/ is spelled. Spell each word aloud.

How many spelling patterns for /oo/ do you see?

1. Write the **nine** spelling words that have the *oo* pattern.

2. Write the **five** spelling words that have the *u, ue,* or *ui* pattern.

3. Write the **six** spelling words that have the *o*-consonant-*e, oe,* or *o* pattern.

> Use the steps on page 6 to study words that are hard for you.

Spelling Patterns

oo	u	ue	ui
choose	truth	glue	fruit

o-consonant-e	oe	o
whose	shoe	whom

Spelling and Meaning

Hink Pinks   Write the spelling word that completes each hink pink.

1. colored paste   blue _____

2. song sung by a masked animal   _____ tune

2. drink for large animal with antlers   moose _____

4. an unattached train car   _____ caboose

5. honesty from a ten-year-old   youth _____

6. what puppies make from footwear   _____ chew

Clues   Write the spelling word for each clue.

7. This is a form of *who*.   _____

8. An apple is this kind of food.   _____

9. You do this when you show a thing is true. _____

10. This word is a homophone for *who's*.   _____

11. People use this to wash their hair.   _____

12. A lawyer presents this to a jury.   _____

13. This is the opposite of *wise*.   _____

14. This animal crows in the morning.   _____

15. People fill this with air.   _____

16. This is the opposite of *find*.   _____

17. You do this when you pick something.   _____

18. You practice so that you will do this.   _____

19. A detective looks for this.   _____

Word Story   When Captain James Cook sailed to Australia in the 1700s, he met the people who had lived there for 12,000 years. He wrote the names of plants and animals as the people pronounced them. He wrote one spelling word as *kanguru*. Write the spelling we use today.

20. _____

Family Tree: *prove*   Compare the spellings, meanings, and pronunciations of the *prove* words. Then add another *prove* word to the tree.

proves

proving

disprove

proven

21.

unproven

prove

Use each spelling word once to complete the story.

The Case of the Missing Shoe

One day last week, I was sitting in my office, drinking a glass of orange _____ 1 , when a call came from the head of the city zoo, Mrs. Annie Mall. I'm Pry Vitigh, private eye. I solve mysteries.

I went to Mrs. Mall's zoo and rang the bell. She answered it herself. Right away, I knew something was wrong. She was wearing two socks but only one _____ 2 .

"That's the mystery," she told me. "I took a little nap after lunch, and I took off my shoes. When I woke up, one shoe was gone. I know I didn't _____ 3 one shoe. Somebody must have taken it."

I asked Mrs. Mall who she thought might be guilty. This is _____ 4 she suspected:

• the baboon, a really strong character who could easily walk off with a shoe,

• the _____ 5 , whose mask looked very odd,

• the _____ 6 , whose pocket could hide more than you think,

• the _____ 7 , a loud, sneaky character not to be trusted.

Mrs. Mall said, "Those are the ones that could have done it. But I can't _____ 8 anything."

"Don't worry," I told her. "We'll learn the _____ 9 , and I'll show you _____ 10 ."

First I searched the house from the basement to the roof.

I couldn't find a single _____. I had to admit that it
                                11

was a tough case. But I did notice some _____ tiles
                                              12

on the roof.

Then I went to see the baboon. He was in the kitchen eating

some _____. When I tried to question him, I
         13

couldn't understand him because his mouth was so full of food.

I decided to go on to the next suspect.

The raccoon was a smart animal, even though she looked kind

of _____ in that strange mask. When I tried to
       14

question her, she stared at me and bit into a crab with some very

sharp teeth. I didn't _____ to stick around.
                             15

I needed to _____ my method of questioning
                   16

suspects. I decided to go and get Mrs. Mall. After all, she was the

one _____ shoe was missing. Let her face the other
        17

two suspects with me.

When I got back to the living room, a boy came in the front door.

In one hand he held a long string with a _____ tied
                                                 18

to it. In the other hand he held a paper bag.

"Hi, Mom," the boy said. "I took your

shoe over to the repair shop. They'll

_____ on a new sole
        19

this afternoon. I also bought some

_____ so you can wash
        20

your hair, just like you asked me.

Another case was solved.

Word list (notepad):
- choose
- loose
- lose
- rooster
- balloon
- shampoo
- improve
- clue
- kangaroo
- fruit
- proof
- prove
- truth
- foolish
- shoe
- whom
- juice
- whose
- raccoon
- glue

choose
loose
lose
rooster
balloon
shampoo
improve
clue
kangaroo
fruit
proof
prove
truth
foolish
shoe
whom
juice
whose
raccoon
glue

Write to the Point

Suppose Mrs. Mall's son had not taken the missing shoe. How else might the shoe have disappeared? Write a new ending for the story. Tell what happened to the shoe and how Pry Vitigh solved the mystery. Try to use spelling words from this lesson.

Use the strategies on page 7 when you are not sure how to spell a word.

Proofreading

Proofread the paragraph below from a book report. Use proofreading marks to correct five spelling mistakes, three capitalization mistakes, and two punctuation mistakes.

Proofreading Marks

◯ spell correctly

／ make lower case

⊙ add period

Jeremy Garza   Benton Middle School

Fourth Period   January 5, 2003

"The Grape Mystery"

"The Grape Mystery" is a short Story by Anna Heglin

The main character is a detective named Reba Barberra.

Reba needs to solve a mystery about a Missing diamond

necklace. Reba suspects the next door neighbor, whooz wife

is going on a long voyage. Reba's clew is a spot on the floor

Someone has stepped on a grape and smashed it. Now she

has to find a shoo with Smashed fruite on the bottom of

it. Will that be enough for Reba to proove this person is

the thief?

Dictionary Skills

Pronunciation A dictionary lists the pronunciation for each entry word. The pronunciation is written in special symbols. To know what sound each of the symbols stands for, you must refer to the pronunciation key. It lists the symbols and gives examples of words that have the sounds of the symbols.

Write the word for each pronunciation below. Check your answers in the Spelling Dictionary.

Pronunciation Key

ă	pat	ŏ	pot	ŭ	cut
ā	pay	ō	toe	ûr	urge
âr	care	ô	paw, for	ə	about,
ä	father	oi	noise		item,
ĕ	pet	ŏŏ	took		edible,
ē	bee	ōō	boot		gallop,
ĭ	pit	ou	out		circus
ī	pie	th	thin	ər	butter
îr	deer	*th*	this		

1. (ră koon′) _____
2. (joos) _____
3. (bə loon′) _____
4. (trooth) _____
5. (ĭm proov′) _____
6. (proof) _____
7. (loos) _____
8. (roo′ stər) _____
9. (shăm poo′) _____
10. (foo′ lĭsh) _____
11. (looz) _____
12. (gloo) _____

Challenge Yourself

Use the Spelling Dictionary to answer these questions. Then use separate paper to write sentences showing that you understand the meaning of each Challenge Word.

Challenge Words

feud	mutual
presume	maroon

13. If two friends always agree on everything, are they having a **feud**? _____

14. If you and a friend both like to skate, is skating your **mutual** interest? _____

15. Can you **presume** that people who smile are happy? _____

16. Would you call the color of a lemon **maroon**? _____

Words with /oi/

voyage

1. oy Words

_____
_____
_____
_____
_____
_____
_____
_____
_____
_____

2. oi Words

_____
_____
_____
_____
_____
_____
_____
_____
_____
_____

noise

destroy

annoy

enjoy

choice

appoint

moisture

employment

boiler

oyster

coin

loyal

avoid

loyalty

voice

voyage

royal

broil

employ

appointment

Say and Listen

Say each spelling word. Listen for the /oi/ sound you hear in *noise*.

Think and Sort

Look at the letters in each word. Think about how /oi/ is spelled. Spell each word aloud.

How many spelling patterns for /oi/ do you see?

1. Write the **ten** spelling words that have the *oy* pattern.

2. Write the **ten** spelling words that have the *oi* pattern.

Use the steps on page 6 to study words that are hard for you.

Spelling Patterns

oy	oi
l**oy**al	n**oi**se

What's the Answer? Write the spelling word that answers each question.

1. An opera singer uses what to make music? _____

2. A diver might find a pearl in what? _____

3. What do you need in order to see the doctor? _____

4. What do you want if you're looking for a job? _____

5. What do you feel when you walk barefoot on damp grass? _____

6. What is a trip on a ship called? _____

7. Where does the steam to power a steamboat come from? _____

8. You do what when you name someone to do something? _____

9. What word describes the palace of a king? _____

Synonyms Complete each sentence by writing the spelling word that is a synonym for the underlined word.

10. Pele knew the rain would <u>wreck</u> his sand castle. _____

11. The coat with the hood is my <u>selection</u>. _____

12. Mr. Bander will <u>grill</u> hamburgers and chicken. _____

13. A dog can be a <u>faithful</u> friend. _____

14. Students who talk out of turn <u>bother</u> Mrs. Reyna. _____

15. The department store will <u>hire</u> ten new clerks. _____

16. Sam showed his <u>faithfulness</u> by keeping Ann's secret. _____

17. Jordan will do anything to <u>escape</u> yardwork. _____

18. A loud, frightening <u>sound</u> blared from the foghorn. _____

19. Ping and Sara really <u>like</u> opera music. _____

Word Story One spelling word comes from the Latin word *cuneus,* which meant "wedge." It described the wedge-shaped tool that was used to stamp pieces of money. Later the word became *coinen,* which meant "to mint." Write the word we use today.

20. _____

Family Tree: *appoint* Compare the spellings, meanings, and pronunciations of the *appoint* words. Then add another *appoint* word to the tree.

appointed

appoints

reappoint

appointing

21.

appoint

Use each spelling word once to complete the selection.

Do What You Like

What kind of job would you like to get when you finish school? It's hard to

make a _____ about a career. Sometimes people make an

          1

_____ to see a career counselor. A career counselor can help

          2

you decide what kind of job you would like to do.

You'll be happiest if you pick something you _____ doing. If

                                              3

you have a _____ collection, you might buy and sell coins for a

          4

living. If you like to sing and you have a good _____, you might

                                                5

want to become a professional singer. Do you like to cook? Do you know how to

_____ foods and how to use a double _____?

          6   7

Can you grill a steak or whip up a tasty _____ stew? Look for

                                          8

_____ as a chef in a restaurant.

          9

Would you like to see other parts of the world? You can take a free ocean

_____ if you get someone to _____ you to a

          10   11

ship's crew. Do you like to _____ things? Get a job with a

                             12

wrecking company. Then you can knock down some old buildings.
If you like the idea of keeping a palace neat and clean, try getting
a job as a housekeeper for a _____ family.
13
If you'd like to report the _____ in the air as well as
14
the temperature, weather forecasting might be the job for you.

It's best to stay away from things you don't like. If animals
_____ you, _____ a job in a pet
15   16
store. If you don't like lots of _____, don't ask a
17
music store to _____ you. You won't feel any
18
_____ to a job you hate. But you'll find that it's
19
easy to be _____ to a job you like. It's more likely
20
that you'll be good at it, too.

Spelling and Writing

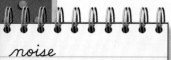

noise
destroy
annoy
enjoy
choice
appoint
moisture
employment
boiler
oyster
coin
loyal
avoid
loyalty
voice
voyage
royal
broil
employ
appointment

Write to the Point

Think of all the jobs in your community. Think of the people who teach, build things, own shops, and fight fires. Choose one job and write a paragraph about it. Tell what you would like and not like about the job. Try to use spelling words from this lesson.

Use the strategies on page 7 when you are not sure how to spell a word.

Proofreading

Proofread the journal entry below. Use proofreading marks to correct five spelling mistakes, two capitalization mistakes, and three unnecessary words.

Proofreading Marks
◯ spell correctly
≡ capitalize
ℰ take out

April 5

   maria wants to be a doctor, and Rita hopes

to be a a ballet dancer. But I enjoye so many

things that it's hard to decide on just one

career. Each day i have a new idea and make a

new choyce.

   I'd like to to avoid being a singer, because my

voyce sounds more like noyze than music! I love

horses, so maybe I could work with with them.

Maybe someone would employe me to train and

ride their horses.

13. *Dark* is to *light* as *lie* is to _____.

14. *It's* is to *its* as *who's* is to _____.

15. *Flour* is to *wheat* as _____ is to *orange*.

16. *Scarlet* is to *red* as *hint* is to _____.

17. *Pencil* is to *what* as *person* is to _____.

22

annoy
destroy
appointment
avoid
choice

Words with /oi/

Write the spelling word for each definition. Use the Spelling Dictionary if you need to.

18. something that is chosen _____

19. to bother _____

20. to make useless _____

21. to stay away from _____

22. an arrangement to meet at a specific time and place _____

23

cycling
amateur
champion

Sports Words

Write the spelling word that answers each question.

23. What do you call someone who plays a sport for fun?

_____

24. What sport involves riding a bike? _____

25. What do you call someone who wins first prize in a contest? _____

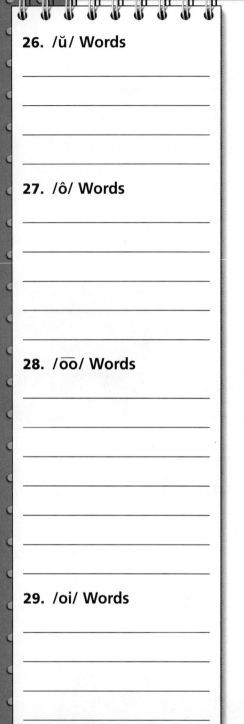

26. /ŭ/ Words

_____

_____

_____

27. /ô/ Words

_____

_____

_____

_____

28. /ōo/ Words

_____

_____

_____

_____

_____

_____

_____

29. /oi/ Words

_____

_____

_____

_____

Review Sort

tongue	all right	shoe	avoid
flood	fought	choice	juice
awful	whom	fault	rough
often	raccoon	clue	annoy
whose	destroy	truth	judge

26. Write the **four** /ŭ/ words. Circle the letter or letters that spell /ŭ/ in each word.

27. Write the **five** /ô/ words. Circle the letter or letters that spell /ô/ in each word.

28. Write the **seven** /ōo/ words. Circle the letter or letters that spell /ōo/ in each word.

29. Write the **four** /oi/ words. Circle the letters that spell /oi/ in each word.

These five words have been sorted into two groups. Explain how the words in each group are alike.

30. amateur   basketball   champion

_____

_____

31. soccer   hockey

_____

_____

Writer's Workshop

A Description

When you write a description, you picture something in your mind and then use words to help your reader see or imagine the same thing. A description can tell what something looks like as well as how it sounds, feels, smells, or tastes. To engage their readers' senses, writers choose the most vivid details possible. Here is part of Mark's description of the ocean.

Prewriting   To write his description, Mark followed the steps in the writing process. Once he had chosen a topic, he created a senses web. The web helped Mark think of words and phrases to describe the ocean. Part of Mark's senses web is shown here. Study what Mark did.

The Ocean

The ocean stretched as far as I could see. White gulls soared above it in the blue sky. The waves rolled and sparkled in the sun. They rumbled and roared where they met rocks. They slapped and splashed where they met sand, bursting into white foam. Walking into the water, I felt the slippery seaweed and the rough pebbles under my feet.

Ocean

Hearing
waves
rumbled
roared
slapped
splashed

It's Your Turn!

Write your own description. Choose a favorite object or a place that you can picture in your mind. Once you have decided on a subject, make a senses web. Then follow the other steps in the writing process—writing, revising, proofreading, and publishing. Try to use spelling words from this lesson in your description.

More Words with /ô/

orchard

1. o-consonant-e Words

_____
_____
_____
_____
_____
_____

2. o Words

_____
_____
_____
_____
_____
_____

3. a Words

_____
_____
_____
_____

4. ou Words

_____
_____

5. oa Words

_____
_____

score
quarrel
court
adore
roar
shore
before
reward
course
board
wore
warn
tore
export
toward
perform
fortunate
orchard
import
important

Say and Listen

Say each spelling word. Listen for the /ô/ sound you hear in *score*.

Think and Sort

Look at the letters in each word. Think about how /ô/ is spelled. Spell each word aloud.

How many spelling patterns for /ô/ do you see?

1. Write the **six** spelling words that have the *o*-consonant-*e* pattern.

2. Write the **six** spelling words that have the *o* pattern.

3. Write the **four** spelling words that have the *a* pattern.

4. Write the **two** spelling words that have the *ou* pattern.

5. Write the **two** spelling words that have the *oa* pattern.

Use the steps on page 6 to study words that are hard for you.

Spelling Patterns

o-consonant-e	o	a	ou	oa
score	perform	warn	court	roar

Spelling and Meaning

Synonyms   Write the spelling word that is a synonym for each word below.

1. act _____

2. love _____

3. plank _____

4. caution _____

5. direction _____

6. ripped _____

7. argue _____

8. earlier _____

9. to _____

Clues   Write the spelling word for each clue.

10. the past tense of *wear* _____

11. where people play tennis _____

12. what is often offered for finding a lost pet _____

13. the number of points in a game _____

14. where sandcastles are found _____

15. what a lucky person is _____

16. the place to find apples _____

17. worth noticing _____

18. what lions and tigers do _____

19. what people do in selling goods to another country _____

Word Story   One spelling word comes from the Latin word *importare*, which meant "bring in." Today the word means "to bring in from another country." Write the spelling word that comes from *importare*.

20. _____

Family Tree: *adore*   Compare the spellings, meanings, and pronunciations of the *adore* words. Then add another *adore* word to the tree.

adoration

adored

21.

adoringly

adore

adores

Use each spelling word once to complete the story.

The Daily

Scientist's New Discovery

Mr. Ifor Gott, who works for Sigh Ents Company, has discovered a formula that improves the memory. "With this pill," explained Mr. Gott, "you can remember just about anything."

Mr. Gott says he got the idea for his formula while looking at the ocean. "I was walking along the _____. I just

1

_____ the sea. I forget exactly when it was, and I forget how I

2

worked the formula out, but it's written in my notes somewhere. Or maybe I

_____ that page out. I'm not sure."

3

Ms. Selma Gradey, President of the Sigh Ents Company, said, "We couldn't be more pleased with Mr. Gott's idea. For years our major business has been to _____ pieces of pottery from other countries. Then we

4

_____ them to other places. But now we'll be famous."

5

Can the formula do any harm? Mr. Gott told us, "We did lots of tests, but I forget what the results were."

Fleas Flee Flue's Flea Circus

Ten performing fleas escaped from Flue's Fabulous Flea Circus early last night. "The fleas were just about ready to _____ the most

6

_____ part of their act. That's the part where they jump off a

7

tiny diving _____," Mr. Flue said. "Just _____

8   9

they began, a dog came into the hall. Before I knew it, my fleas were rushing

Herald

_____ the dog. That was the last time I saw them.
10

The dog made a noise between a howl and a _____
11

and raced out of the room."

"Those fleas are very unusual," Flue went on to comment.

"I was extremely _____ to get them. I'll organize a
12

search party, of _____, but I fear the worst. I may
13

have to find a new source of income."

The dog was last seen near the apple _____ on
14

the Edgeware farm. It _____ a black collar. Mr. Flue
15

is offering a _____
16

of $25 for the return of his fleas.

Sports

Lowe High Wins Title

Lowe High School won the city pinky wrestling championship,

but it was a rough match. The match was held on Lowe High's

basketball _____. It was attended by several noisy
17

fans who began to argue about the game rules. The referee had to

_____ the fans not to _____. The
18   19

final _____ was tied 1–1, but Lowe's rivals decided
20

to let Lowe have the title so that they could go home.

Word list (spiral notepad):

score
quarrel
court
adore
roar
shore
before
reward
course
board
wore
warn
tore
export
toward
perform
fortunate
orchard
import
important

score
quarrel
court
adore
roar
shore
before
reward
course
board
wore
warn
tore
export
toward
perform
fortunate
orchard
import
important

Write to the Point

Imagine that you are a reporter. Write another funny news article like the ones in *The Daily Herald.* Choose a subject that you might find in a real newspaper. Then have some fun with it. Try to use spelling words from this lesson.

Use the strategies on page 7 when you are not sure how to spell a word.

Proofreading

Proofread the part of a newspaper article below. Use proofreading marks to correct five spelling mistakes, three capitalization mistakes, and two punctuation mistakes.

Proofreading Marks

◯ spell correctly
≡ capitalize
⊙ add period

A Heady Discovery

In a press conference on thursday, Dr. G.Y. Nott announced an importent discovery Standing befour reporters in a derby hat with a large feather, he read the findings of a four-year study. according to Dr. Nott, the people in his study who woar funny hats usually didn't kwarrel with one another Dr. Nott added that these findings made him feel very fortunat. he himself adores funny hats.

Dictionary Skills

Multiple Pronunciations   Some words may be pronounced in more than one way. A dictionary gives all the acceptable pronunciations for these words, but the one listed first is usually the most common or the preferred.

Look at the pronunciations for *quarrel* given in the entry below. Notice that the /ə/ in the first pronunciation is not in the second. If a word has more than one syllable, only the syllable that is pronounced in different ways is repeated in the Spelling Dictionary. Say *quarrel* to yourself and see which pronunciation you use.

> **quar·rel** (**kwôr′** əl) *or* (**kwŏr′-**) *n.* A fight with
> words; an argument. —*v.* **quar·reled,**
> **quar·rel·ing.** To have a fight with words.

Each of the following words has more than one pronunciation. Look up each word in the Spelling Dictionary. Write the complete pronunciation that you use.

1. course _____
2. score _____
3. export _____
4. import _____
5. toward _____
6. aunt _____
7. aurora _____
8. chorus _____
9. closet _____
10. compass _____
11. perfume _____
12. program _____
13. absurd _____
14. meteor _____
15. pumpkin _____
16. story _____

Challenge Yourself

What do you think each Challenge Word means? Check the Spelling Dictionary to see if you are right. Then use separate paper to write sentences showing that you understand the meaning of each Challenge Word.

Challenge Words	
pores	furor
resourceful	distort

17. You sweat through the **pores** in your skin.

18. The crowd was in a **furor** because the band never showed up for the concert.

19. A **resourceful** student uses library books to find and check facts.

20. A mirror that is bent or cracked can **distort** your image.

Words with /ûr/

pearl

1. er Words

_____
_____
_____
_____
_____
_____

2. ir Words

_____
_____
_____
_____
_____

3. ur words

_____
_____
_____
_____

4. ear Words

_____
_____
_____
_____
_____

skirt

purpose

earn

certain

dirty

service

furnish

early

thirteen

perfect

permit

firm

hurt

furniture

learning

heard

perfume

third

pearl

personal

Say and Listen

Say each spelling word. Listen for the /ûr/ sound you hear in _skirt_.

Think and Sort

Look at the letters in each word. Think about how /ûr/ is spelled. Spell each word aloud.

How many spelling patterns for /ûr/ do you see?

1. Write the **six** spelling words that have the _er_ pattern.

2. Write the **five** spelling words that have the _ir_ pattern.

3. Write the **four** spelling words that have the _ur_ pattern.

4. Write the **five** spelling words that have the _ear_ pattern.

Use the steps on page 6 to study words that are hard for you.

Spelling Patterns

er	ir	ur	ear
p**er**mit	sk**ir**t	h**ur**t	p**ear**l

Spelling and Meaning

Classifying   Write the spelling word that belongs in each group.

1. fragrance, scent, _____

2. sure, positive, _____

3. spotless, flawless, _____

4. eleven, twelve, _____

5. private, inner, _____

6. late, on time, _____

7. researching, studying, _____

8. curtains, rugs, _____

9. supply, provide, _____

10. allow, let, _____

11. assistance, help, _____

12. aim, goal, _____

13. solid, hard, _____

Rhymes   Write the spelling word that completes each sentence and rhymes with the underlined word.

14. There are <u>thirty</u> _____ shirts in the laundry.

15. I need to <u>learn</u> some ways to _____ money.

16. We _____ a <u>bird</u> singing in a tree.

17. Carmen wore a yellow <u>shirt</u> that matched her _____.

18. The <u>girl</u> found a huge white _____ in the oyster.

19. Mr. <u>Byrd</u> lives in the _____ house on the left.

Word Story   One spelling word comes from the Old German word *hurten,* which meant "to run at." In Old English it meant "to harm." Now the word means not only "to harm" but also "an injury; pain." Write the spelling word that comes from *hurten.*

20. _____

Family Tree: *perfect*   Compare the spellings, meanings, and pronunciations of the *perfect* words. Then add another *perfect* word to the tree.

perfection   perfectly

imperfect   21.

perfectionist

perfect

A Pearl of a Problem

Every time our family tells "remember when" stories, the story of Mom's

missing ring is _____ to come up. Here's what happened. One
                              1

afternoon Mom was getting ready to roast a chicken and bake a cherry pie. She

put an apron on over her new _____, took off her beautiful
                                        2

_____ ring, and laid it on the kitchen table. Just then the
            3

doorbell rang, and our neighbor came in. She likes to _____
                                                                4

extra money by selling _____ and soap to her friends.
                                  5

When the neighbor left, Mom started supper. I _____
                                                            6

someone at the front door. It was the delivery man with a new piece of

_____ that Mom and Dad had bought. I showed him where to
        7

put it and went upstairs to write in my _____ diary. I have a
                                                    8

_____ rule: I don't _____ anyone to come in
            9   10

the room when I'm writing in my diary!

A little while later, my brother, Jake, came home with some friends who

are in the school band. They began practicing. They weren't very good.

One boy made _____ mistakes in one song. My ears began
                        11

to _____. I complained to Mom, but she said, "They're
            12

_____, dear. And if you're finished with your diary, you can
        13

help in the kitchen."

It was after I started washing the _____ dishes that Mom
                                              14

noticed her ring was gone. We looked on the table, on the floor, and in the

sink. Mom was really upset. Dad had given her the ring for their anniversary.

She kept saying, "I'm sure no one took it on _____. Someone
                                                        15

must be playing a joke."

We had dinner _____ that night. I dished out
16
the chicken and dressing. Jake laughed and said, "Now that's what

I call _____."
17

Then we all tried to solve the mystery. But no one could

_____ any clues. We couldn't believe that one of
18

the people there that day took the ring.

We finished dinner, and Mom brought in dessert. The cherry

pie was _____. I had eaten all my lima beans to
19

make sure that I'd be allowed a big slice. Mom gave the first piece

to me and the second to Jake. She gave the _____
20

piece to Dad. We all started eating. Then Dad yelled, "Ouch!" He

put his hand to his mouth and out came the pearl ring. We all

cheered. Dad got another piece of pie.

skirt
purpose
earn
certain
dirty
service
furnish
early
thirteen
perfect
permit
firm
hurt
furniture
learning
heard
perfume
third
pearl
personal

skirt
purpose
earn
certain
dirty
service
furnish
early
thirteen
perfect
permit
firm
hurt
furniture
learning
heard
perfume
third
pearl
personal

Write to the Point

Write a "remember when" story about something interesting that happened in your family. Use colorful, specific words to show readers why the story is worth remembering. Try to use spelling words from this lesson.

Use the strategies on page 7 when you are not sure how to spell a word.

Proofreading

Proofread the letter below. Use proofreading marks to correct five spelling mistakes, two punctuation mistakes, and three unnecessary words.

Proofreading Marks

◯ spell correctly

⊙ add period

ℰ take out

295 Hill Drive

Billings, MT 59102

September 9, 2003

Dear Aunt Libby,

Mom told me that when you were thurteen, you did extra chores for money She said your perpose was to to buy Grandma Dora a sertain kind of pirfume. The day you you bought it, Uncle Benny spilled the whole bottle on Grandma's skurt What a smell it must have made!

I'm trying to earn money to buy a gift for Mom. Do you you have any ideas for me?

Love,

Madison

Language Connection

Adjectives   An adjective describes a noun or pronoun by telling which one, what kind, or how many.

> A **colorful** bird was singing in the **old** tree.
>
> A **big fat** cat scared it away.

The following sentences contain adjectives and misspelled words. Write the sentences, spelling the misspelled words correctly and underlining the adjectives.

1. We made new ferniture for the treehouse.

_____

2. I herd there is a fantastic movie downtown.

_____

3. The urly bird catches the worm.

_____

4. I'd like to fernish my room with large green plants.

_____

5. I hert my foot when I dropped the heavy suitcase.

_____

6. Jennifer wants a perl necklace for her birthday.

_____

Challenge Yourself

Use the Spelling Dictionary to answer these questions. Then use separate paper to write sentences showing that you understand the meaning of each Challenge Word.

Challenge Words	
conserve	absurd
earthenware	virtual

7. Does turning off the water while brushing your teeth help to **conserve** our water?   _____

8. Would it be **absurd** to ride a bicycle while wearing ice skates?

_____

9. Are cars and airplanes made out of **earthenware**?   _____

10. Is a **virtual** fact a completely true fact?   _____

harvest

1. /âr/ Words

_____
_____
_____
_____
_____
_____
_____
_____

2. /är/ Words

_____
_____
_____
_____
_____
_____
_____
_____
_____

share

charge

discharge

aware

harvest

prepare

fare

alarm

farther

stare

carefully

starve

margin

depart

declare

compare

square

marbles

apartment

bare

Say and Listen

Say each spelling word. Listen for the /âr/ sounds you hear in *share* and the /är/ sounds you hear in *charge*.

Think and Sort

Look at the letters in each word. Think about how /âr/ or /är/ is spelled. Spell each word aloud.

How many spelling patterns for /âr/ and /är/ do you see?

1. Write the **ten** spelling words that have /âr/. Circle the letters that spell /âr/.

2. Write the **ten** spelling words that have /är/. Circle the letters that spell /är/.

Use the steps on page 6 to study words that are hard for you.

Spelling Patterns

are	ar
sh**are**	ch**ar**ge

Making Connections   Complete each sentence with the spelling word that goes with the underlined group of people.

1. <u>Firefighters</u> respond to a fire _____.

2. <u>Children</u> often play the game of _____.

3. <u>Doctors</u> _____ well hospital patients.

4. <u>Bus drivers</u> collect a _____ from each passenger.

5. <u>Math teachers</u> teach about the triangle and the _____.

Clues   Write the spelling word for each clue.

6. This word describes feet without shoes or socks.   _____

7. People do this with their eyes.   _____

8. Without food, people and animals do this.   _____

9. It's good to do this for a test.   _____

10. This is how you should handle sharp things.   _____

11. People do this to see how things are alike.   _____

12. This is the outer edge of paper.   _____

13. People do this when they take part of something.   _____

14. This word is the opposite of *nearer*.   _____

15. If you know there is danger ahead, you are this.   _____

16. This is a type of home.   _____

17. A bull does this when it sees a waving cape.   _____

18. Trains do this when they leave the station.   _____

19. If you announce, you do this.   _____

Word Story   One of the spelling words comes from the Old English word *hærfest,* which meant "autumn." Autumn was the time for reaping and gathering in crops. Write the spelling word that comes from *hærfest.*

20. _____

Family Tree: *prepare*   Compare the spellings, meanings, and pronunciations of the *prepare* words. Then add another *prepare* word to the tree.

preparation

prepared

unprepared

21.

preparing

preparer

prepare

The Broadway Limited

Would you like to travel in style while taking in the beautiful scenery of the Northeast? Take the Broadway Limited from New York to Chicago. Pay your _____ at New York's Penn Station, check your baggage
1

_____ to make sure you packed all you need, and board the
2

train! Then _____ yourself for the 18-hour trip as the conductor
3

comes by and punches holes in the _____ of your ticket.
4

As you _____ from New York, you travel
5

through the tunnel under the Hudson River. When you come

out in New Jersey, you can see New York's tall office and

_____ buildings in the distance. As the train
6

rolls _____ away from New York, factories
7

give way to hills and woods. You can _____
8

in wonder at the scenery and _____ the
9

different areas of New Jersey and Pennsylvania. You then become

_____ of flatlands and farms. Along the way, the train stops to
10

take on and _____ passengers and freight.
11

Traveling through Pennsylvania into Ohio, you see Lake

Erie. As the sun begins to set, the lake takes on the color of

blue toy _____. As you go farther west into
12

Ohio, you see farms and fields. Each field looks like a

_____ in a giant patchwork quilt. If it's
13

_____ time, you can watch as big machines
14

cut the crops.

If you get hungry, you won't _____ 15 _____ on the
Broadway Limited! Experience fine dining in the dining car. There is
an additional _____ 16 _____ for eating there. Then move
from the dining car to your bunk in the sleeping car. You can rest
as the train speeds west through Ohio and Indiana. Set your

_____ 17 _____ for an early wake-up to hear the conductor

_____ 18 _____ that the next stop is Gary, Indiana. Soon

you see the big steel-manufacturing town.

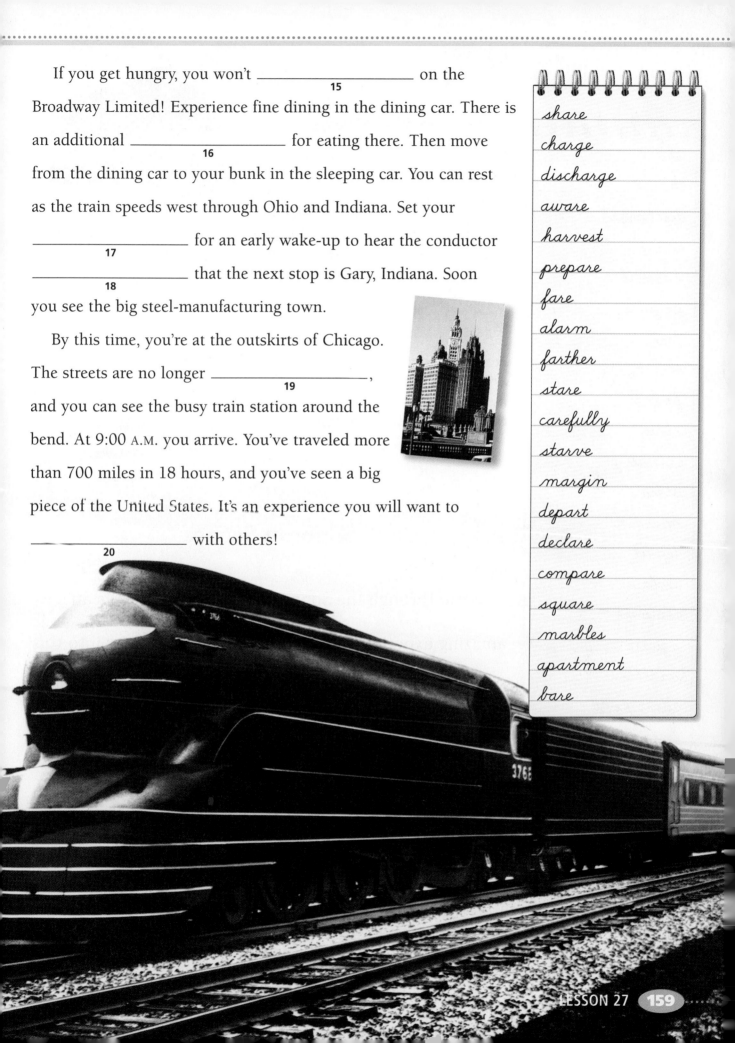

By this time, you're at the outskirts of Chicago.
The streets are no longer _____ 19 _____,
and you can see the busy train station around the
bend. At 9:00 A.M. you arrive. You've traveled more
than 700 miles in 18 hours, and you've seen a big
piece of the United States. It's an experience you will want to

_____ 20 _____ with others!

share
charge
discharge
aware
harvest
prepare
fare
alarm
farther
stare
carefully
starve
margin
depart
declare
compare
square
marbles
apartment
bare

share
charge
discharge
aware
harvest
prepare
fare
alarm
farther
stare
carefully
starve
margin
depart
declare
compare
square
marbles
apartment
bare

Write to the Point

Think about a trip you have taken and write a paragraph about something you saw on your trip. You might write about a nature park near your home or about a beautiful lake farther away. Try to use spelling words from this lesson in your paragraph.

Use the strategies on page 7 when you are not sure how to spell a word.

Proofreading

Proofread this paragraph from a travel article. Use proofreading marks to correct five spelling mistakes, three capitalization mistakes, and two unnecessary words.

Proofreading Marks
◯ spell correctly
≡ capitalize
◞ take out

Sonoran Scenes

a trip through the Sonoran Desert in arizona is an amazing experience. You don't have to travel far into this national treasure to become awair of its beauty. Nothing can compair to to the rich colors and gorgeous sunsets. The the flat landscape spreads farthur than the eye can see. although land appears baer, it does have a variety of plant and animal life. But it is hot. You must prepaar for the dry and scorching heat. Tour guides constantly remind visitors to bring lots of water.

Dictionary Skills

Multiple Meanings Some words can be used as different parts of speech and may have more than one meaning. The dictionary entries for these words list the parts of speech and different definitions. Study the dictionary entry below.

> **a·larm** (ə lärm′) *n.* **1.** Sudden fear caused by a feeling of danger: *The animals ran away in alarm.* **2.** A warning that danger is near. **3.** A warning signal, such as a bell: *The alarm woke me up too early.* —*v.* **a·larmed, a·larm·ing.** To frighten.

Use the Spelling Dictionary to identify the part of speech for the underlined word in each sentence. Then write the number of the definition.

1. The fire <u>alarm</u> rang out in the night. _____ _____

2. The club asked Maria to be in <u>charge</u> of fundraising. _____ _____

3. The town <u>square</u> is filled with beautiful green trees. _____ _____

4. Please <u>share</u> the cookies with all the children. _____ _____

5. The farmers had an early <u>harvest</u> last year. _____ _____

6. The train will <u>depart</u> at noon. _____ _____

⭐ Challenge Yourself

What do you think each Challenge Word means? Check the Spelling Dictionary to see if you are right. Then use separate paper to write sentences showing that you understand the meaning of each Challenge Word.

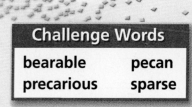

Challenge Words	
bearable	pecan
precarious	sparse

7. The aspirin didn't stop the pain, but it made it **bearable**.

8. Mr. Ono looked down from his **precarious** position at the top of the wobbly ladder.

9. A **pecan** looks like a skinny walnut with a smooth shell.

10. The grass that once was thick now grows in **sparse** patches.

Compound Words

grasshopper

1. Two-Syllable Words

_____
_____
_____
_____
_____
_____
_____
_____
_____
_____
_____
_____
_____
_____
_____

2. Three-Syllable Words

_____
_____
_____
_____
_____

thunderstorm

strawberry

birthday

sailboat

cheeseburger

hallway

nightmare

notebook

upset

cartwheel

flashlight

chalkboard

grasshopper

suitcase

sawdust

uproar

weekend

homework

blueberry

breakfast

Say and Listen

Remember that a syllable is a word part or word with one vowel sound. Say each spelling word. Listen for the number of syllables.

Think and Sort

Each of the spelling words is a compound word. Because a compound word is made from two words, it has at least two syllables.

Look at the syllables in each word. Think about how each syllable is spelled. Spell each word aloud.

1. Write the **fifteen** spelling words that have two syllables.

2. Write the **five** spelling words that have three syllables.

Use the steps on page 6 to study words that are hard for you.

Spelling Patterns

Two Syllables	Three Syllables
up·set	grass·hop·per

Spelling and Meaning

Definitions   Write the spelling word for each definition.

1. the first meal of the day _____
2. a surface to write on with chalk _____
3. a hamburger with cheese _____
4. loud noise _____
5. bits of wood left over after sawing _____
6. a passageway, walkway, or corridor _____
7. a small red fruit with many seeds _____
8. a storm that includes lightning and thunder _____
9. a boat powered by wind _____
10. to cause someone to be worried or disturbed _____
11. schoolwork done at home or away from school _____
12. a very small blue fruit that grows on bushes _____

Compound Words   Write the spelling word that is made from the two underlined words in each sentence.

13. Sam's <u>book</u> has a <u>note</u> in it. _____
14. Dad's black <u>case</u> holds a <u>suit</u> and six pairs of jeans. _____
15. The insect in the <u>grass</u> was a <u>hopper</u>, not a crawler. _____
16. What is the <u>day</u> of your <u>birth</u>? _____
17. At the <u>end</u> of next <u>week</u>, we are going on a camping trip. _____
18. The <u>mare</u> whinnied loudly all <u>night</u>. _____
19. The clown hopped over the <u>wheel</u> of the popcorn <u>cart</u>. _____

Word Story   Sometimes Americans and the British use different words for the same thing. The British word for *car hood* is *bonnet*. One spelling word is called a *torch* in England and means "a small light." Write the spelling word.

20. _____

Family Tree: *breakfast*   *Breakfast* comes from the word *break*. Compare the spellings, meanings, and pronunciations of the *break* words. Then add another *break* word to the tree.

breaking

breakfast

21. _____

breakable

break   rebreak

LESSON 28   **163**

Use each spelling word once to complete the story.

Stormy Weather

My sister Lisa is a singer. She sings in small restaurants and hopes someone will discover her. Last _____ she almost became a star.

Lisa was singing at the Dew Drop Inn. The Dew Drop is a lakeside restaurant. It has a small dock where you can leave your _____. Lots of boaters stop at the Dew Drop Inn for a bite to eat. You can get _____, lunch, or dinner. They have great pancakes and tasty _____ shortcake. Their specialty is a _____ made with three different kinds of cheese. Everything they serve is written on a dusty _____. At night they have live musical entertainment.

The owner had just introduced Lisa to the audience when I saw a well-dressed man walk in the front door. I watched him walk all the way down the _____ into the room. He stood in the back and listened to Lisa for a few minutes. Then he took a small spiral _____ out of his _____ and began to take notes. I realized he was a talent scout! Lisa must have sensed something special was happening. She sang her heart out. It was clear that my sister had done her _____. All that practicing was really

<u>10</u>

starting to pay off.

Lisa had just begun to sing "You Are My Sunshine" when

lighting flashed, and a terrible, loud _____

<u>11</u>

began. Within a few seconds the lights went out. Lisa just

kept singing, "You are my sunshine, my only sunshine. . . ."

Everyone started laughing loudly. There was quite an

_____. The talent scout tried to move

<u>12</u>

closer to the stage to hear Lisa. In the dark he bumped into

a chair and slipped in the _____ covering

<u>13</u>

the floor. Someone turned on a _____ just

<u>14</u>

as the man's long legs went out from under him. He looked

like a _____ doing a _____.

<u>15</u>   <u>16</u>

The man was still on the floor when the lights went on. The

audience couldn't stop laughing.

I went over to Lisa to tell her about the scout. (She had wisely

stopped singing by this time.) She ran to help the scout and try to talk

to him. The man said, "This has been a total _____.

<u>17</u>

I want to forget this place, forget you, and forget every song with the

word *sunshine.*" He was out the door before Lisa could reply.

As you can imagine, Lisa was very _____.

<u>18</u>

We made her favorite _____ muffins

<u>19</u>

to cheer her up. We usually only make them for her on her

_____. Lisa instantly perked up.

<u>20</u>

My sister's a trooper. The next night she was back on

stage—but with a new act. Now her best number is

"Stormy Weather"!

thunderstorm
strawberry
birthday
sailboat
cheeseburger
hallway
nightmare
notebook
upset
cartwheel
flashlight
chalkboard
grasshopper
suitcase
sawdust
uproar
weekend
homework
blueberry
breakfast

Spelling and Writing

Write to the Point

A restaurant review is an article that tells what the writer likes and dislikes about a restaurant. Write your own review of a real or imaginary restaurant. Tell what food you ate, what you liked and disliked about the food, and what the service at the restaurant was like. Try to use spelling words from this lesson in your review.

Use the strategies on page 7 when you are not sure how to spell a word.

Proofreading

Proofread this excerpt from a restaurant review. Use proofreading marks to correct five spelling mistakes, three capitalization mistakes, and two punctuation mistakes.

Proofreading Marks
- ◯ spell correctly
- ≡ capitalize
- ⊙ add period

RESTAURANT REVIEW

The Dew drop Inn is a wonderful place to eat Several friends suggested that I eat there and try the bluberry pancakes. Last wekend was my birthday, so my mother and I ate brekkfast there. The pancakes were melt-in-your-mouth moist, and the strawbury jam was delicious. just as I was jotting my thoughts in my noetbook, the waiters came out and sang "Happy birthday" to me This restaurant is a good place to go for both food and fun!

Language Connection

Possessive Nouns   A possessive noun is a noun that shows possession, or ownership. To form the possessive of a singular noun, add -'s. To form the possessive of a plural noun that ends in s, add only an apostrophe. If a plural noun does not end in s, add -'s to form the possessive.

Singular Possesive Nouns	Plural Possesive Nouns
Sam**'s** notebook	the boys**'** homework
the mouse**'s** fur	the women**'s** sailboat

The sentences below contain apostrophe errors and spelling errors. Write each sentence correctly.

1. Lings flashlite was lying by the door.

_____

2. The mens' chessburgers came quickly.

_____

3. The childrens pet grasshoper was in a cage.

_____

4. Mrs. Sperrys' chalkbored was clean.

_____

5. The six performers cartwheals were magnificent.

_____

Challenge Yourself

Use the Spelling Dictionary to answer these questions. Then use separate paper to write sentences showing that you understand the meaning of each Challenge Word.

Challenge Words

sweatshirt
tablespoon
roommate
handmade

6. What is one kind of measuring tool that can be found in most kitchens? _____

7. What piece of clothing might keep you warm on a chilly day? _____

8. What word might describe a sweater knitted by a person at home?

_____

9. What is a person that shares a room with another person? _____

Lesson 29 · Space Words

telescope

Notepad Word List

1. Two-Syllable Words

_____
_____
_____
_____
_____
_____
_____
_____
_____

2. Three-Syllable Words

_____
_____
_____
_____
_____
_____
_____
_____

3. Four-Syllable Words

_____
_____
_____

shuttle
celestial
astronomy
revolution
comet
galaxy
axis
orbit
meteors
motion
universe
light-year
solar
rotation
telescope
asteroids
eclipse
satellite
constellation
lunar

Say and Listen

Say each spelling word. Listen for the number of syllables.

Think and Sort

Look at the syllables in each word. Think about how each syllable is spelled. Spell each word aloud.

How many syllables does each word have?

1. Write the **nine** spelling words that have two syllables.

2. Write the **eight** spelling words that have three syllables.

3. Write the **three** spelling words that have four syllables.

Use the steps on page 6 to study words that are hard for you.

Spelling Patterns

Two Syllables	Three Syllables	Four Syllables
so·lar	u·ni·verse	as·tron·o·my

Spelling and Meaning

Classifying   Write the spelling word that belongs in each group.

1. meteor, asteroid, _____
2. mathematics, geology, _____
3. rotation, single turn, _____
4. rocket, spaceship, _____
5. microscope, gyroscope, _____

Clues   Write the spelling word for each clue.

6. the turning of Earth _____
7. a measure of distance in space _____
8. a straight line around which Earth turns _____
9. having to do with the sun _____
10. having to do with the moon _____
11. a kind of star formation _____
12. the path a planet travels around the sun _____
13. a man-made object that orbits Earth _____
14. shooting stars _____
15. relating to the heavens or skies _____
16. the Milky Way _____
17. Earth, space, and all things in it _____
18. occurs when light from the sun is cut off _____
19. a synonym for *movement* _____

Word Story   One spelling word comes from two Greek words. *Aster* meant "star," and *eidos* meant "form." The two words put together made the word *asteroeides*. *Asteroeides* meant "starlike." Today the word names any of the many small objects between Mars and Jupiter. Write the spelling word.

20. _____

Family Tree: *revolution*   *Revolution* is a form of the word *revolve*. Compare the spellings, meanings, and pronunciations of the *revolve* words. Then add another *revolve* word to the tree.

revolving   revolves

revolution   21.

revolve

LESSON 29   **169**

Use each spelling word once to complete the selection.

Star Light, Star Bright: The Story of Astronomy

a comet

The stars and planets are called heavenly, or _____ ,
1
bodies. Even very long ago, they interested people. What did early
people think when a _____ blazed across the sky?
2
What did they think when an _____ made day
3
become night? We know that they tried to predict eclipses of the sun
and moon. The _____ and _____
4   5
eclipses were wondrous and frightening to them. It's no wonder that the study
of celestial bodies, _____ , is one of the oldest sciences.
6

Early people didn't understand that Earth rotates on its _____
7
or that the _____ of Earth on its axis causes day and night.
8
People had their own explanations for what happened in space. They made up
stories to explain a group of stars, or _____ . Shooting stars, or
9
_____ , were thought to be messages from gods.
10

Early Greeks, however, had some surprisingly correct ideas about the heavens.
Two men stand out. Thales is known as the father of astronomy. He observed
that the moon moved in an _____ around Earth. He also
11
thought that the whole universe was always in _____ .
12
Pythagoras believed that Earth was not the center of the _____ .
13
We know now that Earth revolves around the sun. But thousands of years ago,
the idea of the _____ of Earth around the sun was an idea that
14
caused many arguments!

the moon Earth

Most people continued to believe that the sun and stars moved around Earth until the _____ proved the idea
15
wrong. With the telescope, people such as Copernicus were able to prove that Pythagoras was right! The telescope revealed that the moon was the only _____ of Earth.
16

Technology improved our knowledge of astronomy. New tools enabled scientists to watch the many _____
17
between Mars and Jupiter. When astronomers realized the huge distances between stars, the _____ became the
18
way to measure space.

a solar eclipse

Today we are accustomed to having people travel to the moon. The day when we can hop on an intergalactic space _____ and visit
19
another _____ may not
20
be far away, thanks to astronomy.

shuttle
celestial
astronomy
revolution
comet
galaxy
axis
orbit
meteors
motion
universe
light-year
solar
rotation
telescope
asteroids
eclipse
satellite
constellation
lunar

Galileo at work

shuttle

celestial

astronomy

revolution

comet

galaxy

axis

orbit

meteors

motion

universe

light-year

solar

rotation

telescope

asteroids

eclipse

satellite

constellation

lunar

Write to the Point

Write an explanation like the ancient Greeks did for an event or thing in nature, such as the sunset or the stars in the sky. Try to use spelling words from this lesson.

Use the strategies on page 7 when you are not sure how to spell a word.

Proofreading

Proofread this paragraph from an essay. Use proofreading marks to correct five spelling mistakes, three capitalization mistakes, and two punctuation mistakes.

Proofreading Marks

◯ spell correctly

≡ capitalize

? add question mark

Space travel Far from Earth

Did you ever wonder if we could really reach other solur systems Other stars are at least a liteyear away. a space shuttel traveling to another star would face many problems. it could crash into astoroids. It might not be able to carry enough fuel for the trip. But perhaps it could reach another galixy. What kinds of great discoveries might we make Perhaps we would find new planets with different types of animals and plants.

Language Connection

Greek and Latin Word Parts   Many English words come from Greek and Latin word parts. For example, *telescope* comes from the Greek word *tele.* Complete the chart below by writing the missing words.

Word Part	Meaning	Word	Meaning
tele	distant; far away	telescope	an instrument for viewing faraway things
uni	one	_____	everything in existence; Earth, the heavens, and all of space
		_____	an imaginary animal that looks like a white horse with a single horn on its forehead
		_____	a vehicle with one wheel
		_____	a special set of clothes that identifies the wearer as a member of one group
		_____	to make one; combine
ast	star	_____	the many small rocky bodies revolving around the sun, mainly between Mars and Jupiter
		_____	the science that deals with the sun, moon, stars, planets, and other heavenly bodies
		_____	a person who travels in a spacecraft to outer space
		_____	a star-shaped garden flower

Challenge Yourself

Write the Challenge Word for each clue. Check the Spelling Dictionary to see if you are right. Then write sentences showing that you understand the meaning of each Challenge Word.

Challenge Words

hemisphere   cosmos
velocity   aurora

1. This light is a beautiful sight to see in the night sky. _____

2. This is an orderly universe. _____

3. This is what each half of Earth is called. _____

4. How long it takes you to get somewhere depends on this and the distance you are traveling. _____

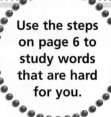
Unit 5 Review
Lessons 25–29

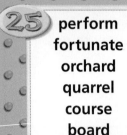

25 perform
fortunate
orchard
quarrel
course
board

More Words with /ô/

Write the spelling word that matches each definition.

1. a flat piece of lumber _____

2. lucky _____

3. a path or direction _____

4. to do something _____

5. to argue _____

6. an area where fruit trees grow _____

26 certain
service
perfect
firm
furniture
pearl

Words with /ûr/

Write the spelling word for each clue.

7. People can sleep or sit on this. _____

8. People are this when they are really sure.

   _____

9. This describes something that is hard or solid.

   _____

10. This can be found inside some oysters.

    _____

11. This is the kind of score students like to get on a test.

    _____

12. When someone does something useful, he or she provides

    this. _____

27

prepare
carefully
declare
compare
marbles
apartment
starve
margin

Words with /âr/ and /är/

Write the spelling word that completes each analogy.

13. *Rehearse* is to *play* as _____ is to *dinner.*

14. *Quickly* is to *slowly* as *carelessly* is to _____.

15. *Ask* is to *question* as _____ is to *statement.*

16. *Shoot* is to _____ as *throw* is to *darts.*

17. *Stuff* is to _____ as *swell* is to *shrink.*

18. *Middle* is to *center* as *edge* is to _____.

19. *Stall* is to *horse* as _____ is to *person.*

20. *Different* is to *similar* as *contrast* is to _____.

28

suitcase
nightmare

Compound Words

Write the spelling word that completes each sentence.

21. Beth's _____ was the worst
dream she'd ever had.

22. Jason forgot his black _____ at
the airport.

29

celestial
meteors
astronomy

Space Words

Write the spelling word that answers each question.

23. What might you see falling toward
Earth from outer space? _____

24. The moon and stars are
what kind of bodies? _____

25. What is the science of the sun,
moon, and planets? _____

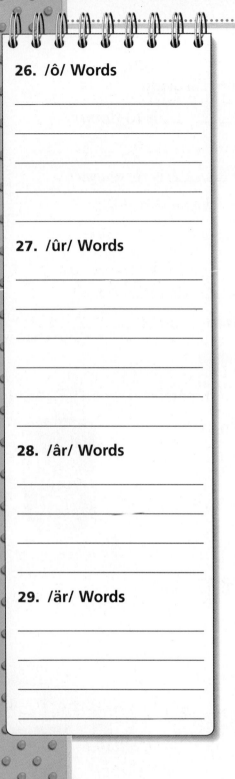

26. /ô/ Words

_____

_____

_____

_____

_____

27. /ûr/ Words

_____

_____

_____

_____

_____

_____

28. /âr/ Words

_____

_____

_____

_____

29. /är/ Words

_____

_____

_____

_____

Review Sort

quarrel	carefully	certain	orchard
board	fortunate	declare	starve
service	compare	marbles	perfect
furniture	firm	apartment	pearl
prepare	margin	course	

26. Write the **five** /ô/ words. Circle the letter or letters that spell /ô/ in each word.

27. Write the **six** /ûr/ words. Circle the letters that spell /ûr/ in each word.

28. Write the **four** /âr/ words. Circle the letters that spell /âr/ in each word.

29. Write the **four** /är/ words. Circle the letters that spell /är/ in each word.

Use the Spelling Table on page 213 to write the sound symbol for each vowel sound in each of the following words.

30. nightmare _____

31. suitcase _____

32. astronomy _____

33. celestial _____

34. meteors _____

Oxcarts lumber along roads and paths. The forests full of wildlife are also full of mosquitoes, so you will need to keep plenty of _____ repellent handy.
_____
10

Costa Rica's _____ tries to protect its forests.
_____
11
Their lawmakers _____ of conserving trees. They
_____
12
are _____ cutting down lots of timber. Because
_____
13
fruit farming is a large _____ in Costa Rica, the
_____
14
country has many pineapple and _____ plantations.
_____
15
Costa Rica does not grow oranges or other _____
_____
16
fruits, however.

All tourists and visitors must _____ to enter
_____
17
Costa Rica. For people from North America, qualifying means having a valid passport. People from other places may need other papers. Even an aunt, uncle, or _____ of a person
_____
18
already living in Costa Rica must have the right documents.

Costa Rica is a magical place that you may want to visit
_____ and again. Each time, you will leave with a
_____
19
wonderful _____ of your trip.
_____
20

season
ocean
qualify
memory
citrus
chorus
government
again
approve
cousin
dangerous
against
industry
perhaps
banana
surprise
beautiful
canoe
mosquito
comfort

season

ocean

qualify

memory

citrus

chorus

government

again

approve

cousin

dangerous

against

industry

perhaps

banana

surprise

beautiful

canoe

mosquito

comfort

Write to the Point

Write a short travel article that will make people want to visit your town or city. Describe the weather and the scenery of a special park or other beautiful place. Try to use spelling words from this lesson in your article.

Use the strategies on page 7 when you are not sure how to spell a word.

Proofreading

Proofread this paragraph from a tourist brochure. Use proofreading marks to correct five spelling mistakes, two words that are out of order, and one unnecessary word.

Proofreading Marks

◯ spell correctly

∿ trade places

ℓ take out

Maine a is beautyful state in any seasen, but fall is a truly spectacular time of year. Although the state has been given the nickname "the Pine Tree State," Maine is home to many trees whose leaves turn color every autumn. Drive along tree-lined streets and gaze in wunder at the brilliant colors the of foliage. Stand along the edge of the ocian and watch the waves crash agenst the shore. Maine will delight and surprise you. Come see why Maine is the the jewel of the Northeast.

Language Connection

Titles Capitalize the first word, the last word, and all other important words in a title. Underline titles of books, movies, magazines, television programs, and newspapers. Put quotation marks around titles of short works such as book chapters, stories, poems, songs, and magazine articles.

> <u>James and the Giant Peach</u>   "How to Get Organized"

The words in parentheses after each title tell what kind of title it is. Write each title correctly.

1. a beautiful memory (book chapter)

_____

2. highlights (magazine)

_____

3. chicago tribune (newspaper)

_____

4. the canoe (book)

_____

5. computer tips for kids (magazine article)

_____

6. industry and the canadian government (book)

_____

7. stopping by woods on a snowy evening (poem)

_____

Challenge Yourself

What do you think each Challenge Word means? Check the Spelling Dictionary to see if you are right. Then use separate paper to write sentences showing that you understand the meaning of each Challenge Word.

Challenge Words	
tyrant	omen
ultimate	random

8. We hoped the king would be just, but he turned out to be a **tyrant**.

9. Some people think finding a four-leaf clover is a good **omen**.

10. I have read ten pages, but my **ultimate** goal is to finish the book.

11. You can plan the colors of your design or choose **random** colors.

Words with /əl/

puzzle

1. /əl/ Words with *al*

_____
_____
_____
_____
_____
_____

2. /əl/ Words with *el*

_____
_____

3. /əl/ Words with *le*

_____
_____
_____
_____
_____
_____
_____
_____
_____
_____
_____
_____

nickel
whistle
general
simple
animal
final
pickles
trouble
double
puzzle
natural
tumble
barrel
tremble
musical
example
sample
wrinkle
couple
signal

Say and Listen

Say each spelling word. Listen for the /əl/ sounds you hear at the end of *nickel.*

Think and Sort

Look at the letters in each word. Think about how /əl/ is spelled. Spell each word aloud. How many spelling patterns for /əl/ do you see?

1. Write the **six** spelling words that have /əl/ spelled *al.*

2. Write the **two** spelling words that have /əl/ spelled *el.*

3. Write the **twelve** spelling words that have /əl/ spelled *le.*

Use the steps on page 6 to study words that are hard for you.

Spelling Patterns

al	el	le
final	**nickel**	**double**

Spelling and Meaning

Clues Write the spelling word for each clue.

1. small cucumbers _____
2. something to copy or imitate _____
3. a sign _____
4. twice as much of something _____
5. a game or riddle to solve _____
6. to try a small piece _____
7. a sound made by blowing air out _____
8. a movie with songs _____
9. not specific _____
10. not fake _____
11. a five-cent coin _____

Synonyms Write the spelling word that is a synonym for the underlined word.

12. We watched the book <u>fall</u> down the stairs. _____
13. One <u>creature</u> at the zoo was very strange. _____
14. Jamal could not answer the <u>last</u> question. _____
15. The pioneer collected rainwater in a large <u>keg</u>. _____
16. Jack and Jill are a well-known <u>pair</u>. _____
17. Most people think playing checkers is <u>easy</u>. _____
18. My dad had a lot of <u>difficulty</u> changing the flat tire. _____
19. The cold weather made the crossing guard <u>shiver</u>. _____

Word Story   One of the spelling words may have come from the Old English word *gewrinclod. Gewrinclod* probably came from the word *wrencan,* which meant "to twist." Write the spelling word.

20. _____

Family Tree: *natural*   *Natural* is a form of *nature.* Compare the spellings, meanings, and pronunciations of the *nature* words. Then add another *nature* word to the tree.

- naturally
- naturalness
- natural
- 21.
- unnatural
- nature
- naturalist

The Case of the Pilfered Pickles

I'm Detective Dill. I work the East Side of Goose Bay. It's a quiet town, and there isn't much for a detective to do. But things turned sour last week, and I made sure I was on the case.

Shifty Louie was causing _____ all over
                                                    1
town by stealing _____. Pickle supplies across
                                    2
the city were dropping sharply. The name of Shifty Louie made
grocery store owners _____.
                                    3

Shifty Louie's latest target was the _____
                                                            4
store here in Goose Bay. Shifty ran into the store and broke
the _____ that contained the pickles. He
                        5
stole a _____ of pickles and ran out of
                        6
the store.

That was the _____ straw for
                                7
me, the detective of Goose Bay. It was only
_____ for me to try to end
                8
this crime wave. I wanted to make an
_____ of Shifty Louie.
                9
But this pickle case wasn't a
_____ one.
                10
That day I called upon an
_____ partner
                11
to help me on the case. His

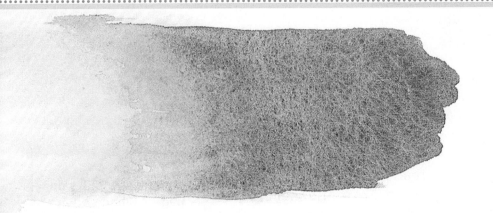

name is Mutt. Mutt is a trained dog that waits patiently and quietly until he is given a _____. When I blow a _____, he corners the thief and waits for help to arrive. I gave Mutt a pickle to _____ so he would be ready to track Shifty's smell.

Together Mutt and I set out to solve the _____ of the missing pickles. We began walking through the streets of Goose Bay. We noticed a light on in a convenience store, even though it was closed. Mutt's nose began to _____ as he caught the scent of Shifty Louie. We went around to the back of the building and waited for Louie to come out the door. When the door opened, Mutt barked, and Louie threw his arms in the air. He dropped several pickles on the ground. I blew my whistle, Mutt jumped, and Louie began to _____ to the ground. I called for backup, and the _____ sound of sirens filled the air.

If I had a _____ for every pickle we found in Louie's coat, I'd _____ my salary. Thanks to Mutt and me, Goose Bay pickle supplies are safe once more.

nickel
whistle
general
simple
animal
final
pickles
trouble
double
puzzle
natural
tumble
barrel
tremble
musical
example
sample
wrinkle
couple
signal

nickel

whistle

general

simple

animal

final

pickles

trouble

double

puzzle

natural

tumble

barrel

tremble

musical

example

sample

wrinkle

couple

signal

Write to the Point

"The Case of the Pilfered Pickles" is a mystery story that involves food. Write your own mystery story about a food. Keep your readers guessing until the mystery is solved. Try to use spelling words from this lesson in your story.

Use the strategies on page 7 when you are not sure how to spell a word.

Proofreading

Proofread the newspaper article below. Use proofreading marks to correct five spelling mistakes, three capitalization errors, and two words that are out of order.

Proofreading Marks

◯ spell correctly

≡ capitalize

∽ trade places

Marbletown Tribune

Friday, october 13, 2003

The Marbletown police responded to a call late Thursday night from the manager the at generel store on bank Street. The manager reported that a couple things of had been stolen—a jar of pickles and a jigsaw puzzel. This was not the first time the manager had reported trubble at the store. Last week a dog collar and a wistle were taken from the pet display. Marbletown Police Chief marvin Cates stated that this was not a simpal case that could be solved quickly.

Language Connection

Adverbs An adverb is a part of speech that tells how, when, where, or in what way. Adverbs tell more about verbs, adjectives, and other adverbs.

> Lauren skates **gracefully**.   Her brother dances **beautifully**.

Write the sentences below, underlining the adverbs.

1. We tremble excitedly.

_____

2. All of the animals wait obediently.

_____

3. A couple of people busily sell souvenirs.

_____

4. Suddenly the signal is given.

_____

5. Each animal steps quickly.

_____

6. The circus parade marches noisily.

_____

7. Two tall clowns dance happily.

_____

Challenge Yourself

Use the Spelling Dictionary to answer these questions. Then use separate paper to write sentences showing that you understand the meaning of each Challenge Word.

Challenge Words	
spaniel	vocal
pedestal	agile

8. Should you keep your **spaniel** on your bookshelf? _____

9. When you give a speech, are you making a **vocal** presentation?

_____

10. Is a **pedestal** something that might be found at the base of a statue?

_____

11. Would it help to be **agile** if you were training to become a gymnast?

_____

Lesson 33 Words with /ər/

toaster

List of Words

teacher
similar
actor
center
toaster
calendar
rather
character
humor
whether
discover
answer
another
silver
cellar
gather
member
polar
master
sugar

Say and Listen

Say each spelling word. Listen for the /ər/ sounds you hear at the end of *teacher*.

Think and Sort

Look at the letters in each word. Think about how /ər/ is spelled. Spell each word aloud. How many spelling patterns for /ər/ do you see?

1. Write the **thirteen** spelling words that have /ər/ spelled *er*.

2. Write the **two** spelling words that have /ər/ spelled *or*.

3. Write the **five** spelling words that have /ər/ spelled *ar*.

1. /ər/ Words with er

_____
_____
_____
_____
_____
_____
_____
_____
_____
_____
_____
_____
_____

2. /ər/ Words with *or*

_____
_____

3. /ər/ Words with *ar*

_____
_____
_____
_____
_____

Use the steps on page 6 to study words that are hard for you.

Spelling Patterns

er	or	ar
teach**er**	hum**or**	sug**ar**

Spelling and Meaning

Classifying   Write the spelling word that belongs in each group.

1. salt, flour, _____

2. alike, same, _____

3. funniness, comedy, _____

4. gold, copper, _____

5. middle, core, _____

6. some other, one more, _____

7. reply, response, _____

8. plot, setting, _____

Analogies   Write the spelling word that completes each analogy.

9. *Basement* is to _____ as *car* is to *automobile*.

10. *Driver* is to *drive* as _____ is to *teach*.

11. *Violinist* is to *orchestra* as _____ is to *play*.

12. *Student* is to *learner* as *expert* is to _____.

13. *If* is to _____ as *comment* is to *remark*.

14. *Hot* is to *tropical* as *cold* is to _____.

15. *Bird* is to *flock* as _____ is to *club*.

16. *Heat* is to _____ as *chill* is to *refrigerator*.

17. *Recover* is to *recovery* as _____ is to *discovery*.

18. *Lake* is to *rake* as *lather* is to _____.

19. *Collect* is to _____ as *scatter* is to *spread*.

Word Story   One of the spelling words comes from the Latin word *calendarium,* which meant "account book." The spelling word is used to name a system for dividing a year into shorter lengths of time. Write the word.

20. _____

Family Tree: *discover*   Compare the spellings, meanings, and pronunciations of the *discover* words. Then add another *discover* word to the tree.

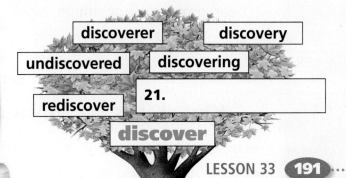

discoverer   discovery

undiscovered   discovering

rediscover   **21.**

discover

An Interview with Roberto Acevito

Many people consider Roberto Acevito to be the greatest movie

_____ alive today. However, not everybody knows that
<u>1</u>

Roberto has held many different jobs. Here, Roberto tells *My Magazine*

(*MM*) about his career.

MM: Roberto, when did you _____ that you wanted to
<u>2</u>

be an actor?

RA: When I saw my first play at the age of eight, I knew right away

that I'd _____ be the _____ of everyone's
<u>3</u>   <u>4</u>

attention than be a _____ of the audience.
<u>5</u>

MM: What was your first acting job?

RA: Well, that's a hard question to _____. When I was
<u>6</u>

nine, my friends and I put on a play in the neighborhood. We held it

downstairs in the _____ of my parent's house. There were
<u>7</u>

lots of acts. I was the _____ of ceremonies.
<u>8</u>

I suppose that my first real acting job was in a TV commercial. I was a

piece of bread popping out of a _____.
<u>9</u>

MM: I _____ that you don't like doing commercials
<u>10</u>

very much.

RA: I found myself doing one after _____ to pay my
<u>11</u>

bills. I played a bowl of _____ and a _____
<u>12</u>   <u>13</u>

bear, among other things. My _____ at acting school taught
<u>14</u>

me to keep a sense of _____. But I often used to wonder
<u>15</u>

_____ I'd ever get a real acting job.
<u>16</u>

MM: What is your favorite _____ to play on stage?
<u>17</u>

■ It's almost _____ time again. Have you signed
                        14
up to vote?

■ Starting your own business? A new book tells how to do it.

Each _____ is clear and easy to follow. Look for
              15
The Business Manager's Guide at your local bookstore. When you

buy the book, just _____ this TV station and get
                            16
a free gift that will aid you in the _____ of office
                                              17
furniture.

■ Don't be fooled by a salesclerk's gift for fast talk. Be careful when

he or she presents you with the latest new _____ to
                                                    18
cut your work to a _____ of its time. All new
                            19
merchandise is tested by the Consumer Watchdog Group. After

_____, the merchandise is rated. Simply call this
        20
station or write Consumer Watchdogs for their free book, *Buying*

the Best for Less.

Spelling and Writing

action
information
education
location
nation
inspection
vacation
pollution
invention
population
section
election
direction
collection
transportation
instruction
fraction
selection
mention
station

Write to the Point

Write an announcement for a real or make-believe event at your school. It could be a meeting, a sporting event, or anything you wish. Give all the information students will need, and tell them why they should attend. Try to use spelling words from this lesson.

Use the strategies on page 7 when you are not sure how to spell a word.

Proofreading

Proofread the announcement below. Use proofreading marks to correct five spelling mistakes, three capitalization mistakes, and two unnecessary words.

Proofreading Marks
◯ spell correctly
≡ capitalize
◞ take out

Pollution Solution Meeting Tonight

Tonight at City Hall, mayor Jim Bond will discuss polution in in our city. Interested citizens are invited to attend. the mayor will mension plans to provide better clean-environment educasion for the entire popullation. School Superintendent Cliff Clayton and several school principals will outline the details. Anyone with ideas for further acttion that will ensure a cleaner, healthier environment is welcome to to speak. the meeting will be held from 7:00 to 8:00 P.M. A panel discussion hosted by the Sierra Club will follow.

road
waist
right
its
hole
whole
write
plain
waste
threw
plane
their
to
it's
there
through
too
rode
they're
two

"I'm pleased to meet you, Jody," said the senator. "I'm going to speak to the Department of Energy. Our country isn't using

_____ natural resources wisely. I want to make
14

people aware of what they can do to help save our resources."

Jody felt proud. He said, "All the kids at school are trying not to

_____ things like paper and electricity. If parents
15

really thought about _____ kids, maybe they wouldn't
16

drive their cars so much. What's going to be left when we grow up?"

"I agree with you, Jody. I'd like to put what you just said in my

speech. Is that all _____ with you?"
17

"Wow! The kids at school are never going _____
18

believe I talked to a real senator! And _____ never
19

going to believe that something I said got into her speech."

"Well, how about some proof?" asked the senator. She took out a

_____ white card and wrote her name on it. On the
20

back she wrote, "Thanks for the help with my speech, Jody."

"Thank you, Senator," said Jody. "Thanks a lot!" He put the card

in his pocket. His trip to Washington, D.C., was off to a great start!

road
waist
right
its
hole
whole
write
plain
waste
threw
plane
their
to
it's
there
through
too
rode
they're
two

Write to the Point

Write a short speech about something that is important to you such as honesty or recycling. Explain why you feel the way you do. Try to use spelling words from this lesson.

Use the strategies on page 7 when you are not sure how to spell a word.

Proofreading

Proofread the book review below. Use proofreading marks to correct five homophone mistakes, three capitalization mistakes, and two words that are out of order.

Proofreading Marks
◯ spell correctly
≡ capitalize
∿ trade places

Wise Words of Warning

In there new book called It's Not Too late, Jarod Marks and emily Davis right that the future the of hole world depends our on stopping the waist of natural resources.

Marks and Davis list hundreds of actions people can take every day to help. for example, turning off the water while we brush our teeth can save millions of gallons of water per day. Marks and Davis say they're is still time to save our planet. Read It's Not Too Late. It can change your life and the world we live in.

Using the Spelling Table

A spelling table can help you find the spelling of a word in a dictionary. Suppose you are not sure how the vowel sound in *prove* is spelled. You can use a spelling table to find the different spellings for the sound. First, find the pronunciation symbol for the sound. Then read the first spelling listed for /o͞o/, and look up *proov* words in the dictionary. Look for each spelling in the dictionary until you find the correct one.

Sound	Spellings	Examples
/o͞o/	oo ew u u_e ue o o_e oe ou ui	loose, grew, truth, presume, clue, whom, prove, shoe, soup, fruit

Write the correct spelling for each word. Use the Spelling Table on page 213 and the Spelling Dictionary.

1. /gŏlf/ _____

2. /klo͞o/ _____

3. /dĭ stroi′/ _____

4. /ûrn/ _____

5. /pə līt′/ _____

6. /sēj/ _____

7. /pĭ kän′/ _____

8. /ē′ zəl/ _____

9. /fyo͞od/ _____

10. /kōd/ _____

Challenge Yourself

Write the Challenge Word for each clue. Check the Spelling Dictionary to see if you are right. Then use separate paper to write sentences showing that you understand the meaning of each Challenge Word.

Challenge Words

alter	altar
chili	chilly

11. You may find this in a church or temple. _____

12. If you like spicy food, you might enjoy this dish. _____

13. This kind of weather makes you want to put on a sweater. _____

14. You do this to pants when you put in a hem to shorten them.

_____

Lesson 36

Unit 6 Review
Lessons 31–35

Use the steps on page 6 to study words that are hard for you.

31 ocean
against
surprise
mosquito
beautiful
dangerous

Words with /ə/

Write the spelling word that completes each sentence.

1. We ended our day at the beach by watching a _____ sunset.
2. My birthday party was a complete _____.
3. Driving in a blizzard can be very _____.
4. A _____ buzzed in my ear all night long.
5. If you want to go deep-sea fishing, you must travel out on the _____.
6. Push firmly _____ the door to open it.

32 general
natural
barrel
couple
example

Words with /əl/

Write the spelling word for each definition.

7. a large, round wooden container _____
8. made by nature _____
9. two of a kind; a pair _____
10. common to most people _____
11. a sample or model _____

33 character
whether
humor
similar
calendar

Words with /ər/

Write the spelling word for each clue.

12. This word means "like something else."

    _____

13. Comedians use this to entertain an audience.

    _____

14. This can help you keep track of the date.

    _____

15. This is a person in a book, movie, or play.

_____

16. _If_ is a synonym for this word. _____

34

invention
direction
collection
education

Words with /shən/

Write the spelling word that completes each analogy.

17. _Collect_ is to _____ as _select_ is to _selection_.

18. _College_ is to _____ as _hospital_ is to _operation_.

19. _Eight_ is to _number_ as _north_ is to _____.

20. _Planet_ is to _discovery_ as _light bulb_ is to _____.

35

its
it's
their
there
they're

Homophones

Write the spelling word that belongs in each group.

21. we're, you're, _____

22. she's, he's, _____

23. our, your, _____

24. his, hers, _____

25. where, here, _____

26. /shən/ Words

_____
_____
_____

27. Words with /ər/

_____
_____
_____
_____
_____

28. Words with /əl/

_____
_____
_____
_____

29. Words with /ə/

_____
_____
_____
_____
_____

Review Sort

example	barrel	calendar	ocean
similar	education	humor	surprise
invention	natural	whether	collection
character	direction	mosquito	couple
against	qualify		

26. Write the **four** spelling words that end in /shən/.

27. Write the **five** spelling words that have /ər/ spelled *er, or,* or *ar.* Circle the letters that spell /ər/.

28. Write the **four** spelling words with /əl/ spelled *le, el,* or *al.* Circle the letters that spell /əl/.

29. Write the **five** spelling words that have /ə/ spelled as *a, o, u,* or *i.* Circle the letter that spells /ə/ in each word.

These five words have been sorted into two groups. Explain how the words in each group are alike and different.

30. its   it's

_____
_____

31. their   there   they're

_____
_____

Writer's Workshop

A Persuasive Letter

If you have a strong opinion that you want someone to share, you can try to convince the person by writing a persuasive letter. When you write the letter, it is important to state your opinion clearly. This helps the reader to know exactly how you feel about the subject. Your letter will be most convincing if you support your opinion with solid reasons and important information. Here is part of Lauretta's persuasive letter.

Prewriting After she chose the opinion she wanted someone to share, Lauretta made a simple outline. First she wrote her opinion and then added reasons to support it. The outline helped Loretta think of and organize ideas. Part of her outline is shown here. Study what Lauretta did.

Dear Dr. Lowenstein,
      The students at Lowe Middle School badly need a covered bench at the corner of Duvall Street and Main Avenue. Right now we students don't have anywhere to sit as we wait for the bus. Some of us have to sit on the curb. This is dangerous! When it rains, we get wet. A covered bench set about ten feet back from the road would keep us safe and dry.

We need a covered bench at Duvall and Main.
      Sitting on curb is dangerous.
      We get wet.

It's Your Turn!

Write your own persuasive letter. You can write to a friend, a teacher, the mayor, or anyone else you wish. After you have decided what to write about, jot down your opinion and reasons in an outline. Then follow the other steps in the writing process—writing, revising, proofreading, and publishing. Try to use spelling words from this lesson in your letter.

Commonly Misspelled Words

again	except	other	through
a lot	exciting	outside	today
always	family	people	together
another	favorite	piece	tomorrow
beautiful	finally	please	too
because	first	pretty	tried
been	friend	probably	until
before	friends	read	upon
beginning	getting	really	usually
believe	goes	right	vacation
birthday	guess	said	very
bought	happened	scared	want
buy	heard	school	weird
children	himself	sent	were
clothes	hospital	should	we're
come	house	since	when
cousin	into	some	where
decided	it's	sometimes	which
different	know	surprise	whole
doesn't	little	their	would
eighth	many	there	write
enough	might	they	writing
especially	morning	they're	wrote
every	myself	though	your
everyone	once	threw	you're

Spelling Table

Sound	Spellings	Examples
/ă/	a ai au	rapid, plaid, aunt
/ā/	a a_e ai ay ea eigh ey	bakery, snake, brain, delay, break, weigh, surveyor
/ä/	a	pecan
/âr/	are air ere eir	aware, fair, there, their
/b/	b bb	bench, hobby
/ch/	ch tch t	orchard, watch, amateur
/d/	d dd	dawn, meddle
/ĕ/	e ea a ai ie ue	bench, health, many, again, friend, guess
/ē/	e e_e ea ee ei eo ey i ie y	female, theme, weak, greet, deceive, people, monkey, ski, believe, tardy
/f/	f ff gh ph	film, different, laugh, elephant
/g/	g gg	golf, jogging
/h/	h wh	here, whole
/ĭ/	i a e ee u ui y	riddle, damage, relax, been, business, build, mystery
/ī/	i i_e ie igh uy y eye	climb, quite, die, right, buy, recycle, eye
/îr/	er ear eer eir ere yr	periodical, hear, cheer, weird, here, lyrics
/j/	j g dg	jot, gentle, pledge
/k/	k c ck ch	kitchen, canoe, chicken, character
/ks/	x	expert
/kw/	qu	quick
/l/	l ll	library, pollution
/m/	m mb mm mn	male, comb, common, condemn
/n/	n kn nn	needle, knife, pinnacle
/ng/	n ng	wrinkle, skating

Sound	Spellings	Examples
/ŏ/	o a	shock, watch
/ō/	o o_e oa oe ou ough ow ew	hero, code, boast, toe, boulder, dough, throw, sew
/oi/	oi oy	coin, enjoy
/ô/	a au aw o ough o_e ou oa	already, autumn, raw, often, thought, score, court, roar
/o͝o/	oo o ou u	rookie, wolf, could, pudding
/o͞o/	oo ew u u_e ue o o_e oe ou ui	loose, grew, truth, presume, clue, whom, prove, shoe, soup, fruit
/ou/	ou ow	ours, towel
/p/	p pp	party, grasshopper
/r/	r rr wr	raw, tomorrow, wrong
/s/	s ss c	solid, message, century
/sh/	sh s ce ci	wishes, sugar, ocean, special
/shən/	tion	competition
/t/	t tt ed	too, bottom, thanked
/th/	th	though
/th/	th	think
/ŭ/	u o o_e oe oo ou	crush, dozen, become, does, blood, touch
/ûr/	ear er ere ir or our ur	earn, certain, were, firm, world, flourish, curve
/v/	v f	vote, of
/w/	w wh o	wish, wheat, once
/y/	y	yolk
/yo͞o/	eau eu u u_e	beautiful, feud, mutual, use
/z/	z zz s	zone, quizzical, busy
/zh/	s	treasure
/ə/	a e i o u	against, elephant, furniture, actor, beautiful

Spelling Dictionary

Major Parts of a Dictionary Entry

The **pronunciation** tells how to pronounce the word.

The **part of speech** is identified by an abbreviation.

The **entry word** is divided into syllables →

Other **major forms** of a verb are given. The plural form of nouns is given.

mas·ter (măs′ tər) *or* (mä′ stər) *n.* **1.** A person who has control of something: *the dog's master; the ship's master.* **2.** A person who has a great skill or ability: *a master of foreign languages.* —*v.* **mas·tered, mas·ter·ing. 1.** To bring under control: *to master your angry feelings.* **2.** To become skilled: *to master your spelling words.*

A **sample phrase or sentence** helps to make the meaning clear.

One or more **definitions** tell you what the word means.

---

absurd | all right

ab·surd (əb sûrd′) *or* (-zûrd′) *adj.* Silly; foolish: *It is absurd to wear a heavy coat when it is very hot outside.*

a·byss (ə bĭs′) *n.* A hole or space so deep that it cannot be measured: *If you looked into an abyss, you probably could not see the bottom.*

act (ăkt) *v.* **act·ed, act·ing. 1.** To do something. **2.** To behave: *act your age.* **3.** To play a part; perform: *Sean acted in the play.* —*n.* **1.** An action: *an act of kindness.* **2.** A part of a play: *Let's rehearse the third act.*

ac·tion (ăk′ shən) *n.* **1.** Something that is done; a deed: *a brave action.* **2.** Motion; activity: *At halftime, the cheerleaders jumped into action.*

ac·tor (ăk′ tər) *n.* A person who acts in a play, in a movie, on television, or on radio.

ac·tress (ăk′ trĭs) *n., pl.* **ac·tress·es.** A girl or woman who acts in a play, in a movie, on television, or on radio.

ad·dress (ə drĕs′) *n.* **1.** (*also* ăd′ rĕs′) The place where someone lives, works, or gets mail. **2.** A formal speech. —*v.* **ad·dressed, ad·dress·ing. 1.** To write the street, city, state, and zip code on an envelope or package: *address an envelope.* **2.** To make a speech to: *address a crowd.*

a·dore (ə dôr′) *v.* **a·dored, a·dor·ing. 1.** To love and admire very greatly. **2.** To like very much.

a·gain (ə gĕn′) *adv.* Once more; another time.

a·gainst (ə gĕnst′) *prep.* **1.** In an opposite direction: *We sailed against the wind.* **2.** In contact with: *The rake is leaning against the fence.* **3.** In opposition to: *Our team will compete against yours and win!*

ag·ile (ăj′ əl) *or* (ăj′ īl′) *adj.* Able to move easily and quickly; nimble: *as agile as a cat.*

a·gree (ə grē′) *v.* **a·greed, a·gree·ing. 1.** To have the same opinion. **2.** To say "yes"; consent: *She agreed to run for president.* **3.** To be the same: *Their stories about the accident do not agree.*

ail·ment (āl′ mənt) *n.* A sickness or disease: *The doctor said that the ailment was not serious.*

a·larm (ə lärm′) *n.* **1.** Sudden fear caused by a feeling of danger: *The animals ran away in alarm.* **2.** A warning that danger is near. **3.** A warning signal, such as a bell: *The alarm woke me up too early.* —*v.* **a·larmed, a·larm·ing.** To frighten.

all right (ôl′ rīt′) *adj.* **1.** Acceptable; satisfactory: *The pizza was all right, but I've tasted better.* **2.** Correct: *His answers are all right.* —*adv.* **1.** Healthy; safe: *I feel all right.* **2.** Yes: *All right, we'll go with you.*

a·lone (ə **lōn′**) *adj.* Not near other people or things: *Sometimes I enjoy being alone.*
    Idiom. **leave well enough alone** *or* **let well enough alone.** To be satisfied with things as they are and not try to change them.

al·read·y (ôl **rĕd′** ē) *adv.* **1.** Before this time: *He had already left when we arrived.* **2.** By this time; even now: *We are already an hour late.*

al·tar (ôl′ tər) *n.* A table or raised place that is used in religious services: *The altar was in the front of the temple. These sound alike:* **altar, alter.**

al·ter (ôl′ tər) *v.* **al·tered, al·ter·ing.** To make or become different; change: *Mother had to alter my dress because I grew two inches taller. These sound alike:* **alter, altar.**

am·a·teur (ăm′ ə tûr′) *or* (-chŏŏr) *or* (-tyŏŏr′) *n.* **1.** A person who does something for pleasure, not for money. **2.** A person who does something in an unskilled way.

a·mong (ə **mŭng′**) *prep.* **1.** In the company of: *a party among friends.* **2.** With a portion for each of: *We divided the clay among the class.* **3.** With or between one another: *Let's not argue among ourselves.*

an·gry (ăng′ grē) *adj.* **an·gri·er, an·gri·est.**
1. Feeling or showing great displeasure or ill will: *an angry look; angry at him.* **2.** Stormy: *angry clouds in the sky.* **3.** Inflamed: *an angry cut on her knee.*

an·i·mal (ăn′ ə məl) *n.* **1.** A living thing that isn't a plant. **2.** Any animal other than a human being.

an·i·ma·tion (ăn′ ə mā′ shən) *n.* **1.** A cartoon motion picture created by photographing a series of drawings: *The movie had both live action and animation.* **2.** Liveliness.

an·noy (ə **noi′**) *v.* **an·noyed, an·noy·ing.** To make angry; bother.

an·oth·er (ə **nŭ**th′ ər) *adj.* **1.** Different: *Let's try another road.* **2.** One more: *May I have another glass of milk?* —*pron.* One of a group: *one problem after another.*

an·swer (ăn′ sər) *n.* **1.** Something said or written in reply: *I received an answer to my letter.* **2.** The solution to a problem: *Did you get the answer to this math problem?* —*v.* **an·swered, an·swer·ing.** To speak or write in reply to something.

a·part·ment (ə pärt′ mənt) *n.* A room or group of rooms to live in, usually found in a large building.

a·pol·o·gy (ə pŏl′ ə jē) *n., pl.* **a·pol·o·gies.** A statement that one is sorry for being rude, doing something wrong, or making a mistake.

ap·point (ə point′) *v.* **ap·point·ed, ap·point·ing. 1.** To select for an office or position: *Jason will appoint a chairman.* **2.** To decide on; set: *We will appoint a time for the meeting.*

Pronunciation Key

ă	pat	ŏ	pot	ŭ	cut
ā	pay	ō	toe	ûr	urge
âr	care	ô	paw, for	ə	about,
ä	father	oi	noise		item,
ĕ	pet	ŏŏ	took		edible,
ē	bee	ōō	boot		gallop,
ĭ	pit	ou	out		circus
ī	pie	th	thin	ər	butter
îr	deer	*th*	**th**is		

ap·point·ment (ə point′ mənt) *n.* **1.** The act of naming someone for an office or position. **2.** An arrangement to meet someone at a certain time and place: *My appointment with the dentist is right after school.*

ap·prove (ə prōōv′) *v.* **ap·proved, ap·prov·ing.**
1. To think or speak well of something: *My parents don't approve of my riding my bike on that busy street.* **2.** To agree or consent to something: *The mayor approved the new city budget.*

A·pril (ā′ prəl) *n.* The fourth month of the year.

a·rith·me·tic (ə rĭth′ mĭ tĭk) *n.* The science of adding, subtracting, multiplying, and dividing numbers.

ar·row (ăr′ ō) *n.* **1.** A thin stick with a point at one end and feathers at the other, made to be shot from a bow. **2.** Anything shaped like an arrow, such as a weather vane.

a·sleep (ə slēp′) *adj.* **1.** Sleeping: *Were you asleep when I called?* **2.** Numb: *My foot was asleep because I crossed my legs.* —*adv.* Into sleep: *She always falls asleep in a car.*

as·ter·oid (ăs′ tə roid′) *n., pl.* **as·ter·oids.** Any of the thousands of small objects that revolve around the sun. Most are between Mars and Jupiter.

as·tron·o·my (ə strŏn′ ə mē) *n.* The science that deals with the sun, moon, stars, planets, and other heavenly bodies.

ath·lete (ăth′ lēt′) *n., pl.* **ath·letes.** A person trained to take an active part in sports.

au·di·o (ô′ dē ō′) *n., pl.* **au·di·os. 1.** Sound reproduction in television and motion pictures: *Most of the audio in the movie was distorted.* **2.** The broadcasting, reproduction, or reception of sound. —*adj.* Involving or used in transmitting, recording, or receiving sound.

au·di·tion (ô dǐsh′ ən) *n.* A short performance that shows the ability of an actor, speaker, singer, or other performer: *The audition for the play is tonight.* —*v.* **au·di·tioned, au·di·tion·ing.** To try out in an audition: *I plan to audition for the main part in the play.*

Au·gust (ô′ gəst) *n.* The eighth month of the year.

aunt (ănt) *or* (änt) *n.* **1.** The sister of one's mother or father. **2.** The wife of one's uncle.

au·ro·ra (ô rôr′ ə) *or* (ə rôr′ ə) *n.* Shining bands of flashing light sometimes seen in the night sky.

au·then·tic (ô thĕn′ tik) *adj.* Real; genuine: *Eduardo has an authentic autograph of a famous baseball player.*

au·to·mo·bile (ô′ tə mō bēl′) *or* (-mō′ bēl′) *n.* A vehicle made to carry passengers; a car.

au·tumn (ô′ təm) *n.* The season of the year between summer and winter; fall.

a·void (ə void′) *v.* **a·void·ed, a·void·ing.** To keep away from: *You should avoid ice cream and cake when you're on a diet.*

a·ware (ə wâr′) *adj.* Having knowledge; realizing: *Be aware of the dangers along the hiking trail.*

aw·ful (ô′ fəl) *adj.* **1.** Causing fear; terrible: *an awful silence in the empty house.* **2.** Very bad: *an awful movie.* **3.** Very large; great: *an awful lot of dishes to wash.*

a·while (ə wīl′) *adv.* For a short time: *We studied awhile before supper.*

awn·ing (ô′ nǐng) *n.* A cover that is like a roof over a window or door: *The awning kept the sun off the porch.*

ax·is (ăk′ sǐs) *n., pl.* **ax·es** (ăk′ sēz′). A straight line around which an object turns or rotates. The axis of the earth runs from the North Pole to the South Pole.

badg·er (băj′ ər) *n.* An animal with thick grayish fur, short legs, and long claws: *Badgers live in holes that they burrow in the ground.*

bak·e·ry (bā′ kə rē) *n., pl.* **bak·e·ries.** A place where bread, pies, cookies, cakes, etc., are baked or sold.

bal·loon (bə loon′) *n.* **1.** A large bag filled with hot air or a gas that is lighter than air, used to lift heavy loads into the air. **2.** A child's toy made of brightly colored rubber that can be blown up by mouth. —*v.* **bal·looned, bal·loon·ing.** To swell out like a balloon: *The sail ballooned in the wind as we raced through the water.*

ba·nan·a (bə năn′ ə) *n.* A slightly curved fruit with yellow or reddish skin that peels easily.

bare (bâr) *adj.* **bar·er, bar·est. 1.** Without covering or clothing: *bare feet.* **2.** Empty: *The room was bare.* **3.** Just enough: *the bare necessities of life.*

bar·rel (băr′ əl) *n.* A large wooden container with round, flat ends of equal size and sides that bulge out slightly.

base·ball (bās′ bôl′) *n.* **1.** A game between two teams of nine players each, played with a ball and bat on a field with four bases that form a diamond pattern. Players score runs by touching all the bases. **2.** The ball used in this game.

bas·ket·ball (băs′ kĭt bôl′) *or* (bä′ skĭt-) *n.* **1.** A game played with a large ball by two teams of five players each. The game is played on a rectangular court with a raised basket at each end. Players score by throwing the ball through the basket at the other team's end of the court. **2.** The large, round ball used in this game.

bear·a·ble (bâr′ ə bəl) *adj.* That which can be put up with: *The hot day was bearable because the air conditioner kept us cool.*

beau·ti·ful (byoo′ tə fəl) *adj.* Pleasing to hear or see.

be·fore (bĭ fôr′) *adv.* Earlier; already: *I've read this book before.* —*prep.* Earlier than: *We finished before noon.* —*conj.* Sooner than the time when: *The soup started to boil before I finished making my sandwich.*

be·lieve (bĭ lēv′) *v.* **be·lieved, be·liev·ing. 1.** To think that something is true or real. **2.** To think; suppose: *I believe she went home.*

bench (bĕnch) *n., pl.* **bench·es. 1.** A long seat: *park bench.* **2.** A heavy work table: *the carpenter's bench.* **3.** The seat for judges in a court of law.

be·neath (bĭ nēth′) *prep.* Below; under; underneath.

birth·day (bûrth′ dā′) *n.* **1.** The day on which a person was born. **2.** The anniversary of that day.

blind (blīnd) *adj.* **blind·er, blind·est.** Not able to see: *a blind person.* —*n.* Something that shuts out light or blocks sight, such as a window shade. —*v.* **blind·ed, blind·ing. 1.** To take away sight: *The sun can blind you.* **2.** To take away reason: *Fright blinded him.*

bliss (blǐs) *n.* Great happiness; joy: *Swimming is bliss on a hot day.*

blood (blŭd) *n.* **1.** The red liquid that is pumped through the body by the heart. **2.** Family relationship: *My cousin and I are related by blood.*
  Idioms. **make one's blood boil.** To anger. **make one's blood run cold.** To frighten.

blue·ber·ry (bloo′ bĕr′ ē) *n.,* *pl.* **blue·ber·ries.** A small, round, dark blue, sweet berry that grows on a shrub.

blunt (blŭnt) *adj.* **blunt·er, blunt·est.** Having a dull point or edge; not sharp.

Blvd. Abbreviation of **Boulevard** (bool′ ə värd′) A wide street usually lined with trees.

board (bôrd) *n.* **1.** A flat, thin piece of lumber. **2.** A flat piece of hard material used for a special purpose: *a diving board; a game board.* **3.** A group of people who manage something: *a school board.* —*v.* To get on a plane, train, ship, or bus.

boast (bōst) *v.* **boast·ed, boast·ing.** To brag. —*n.* A bragging statement: *Don't believe his boast that he is the best player on the team.*

boil·er (boi′ lər) *n.* **1.** A large tank for heating water and turning it into steam. **2.** A pot or kettle used for boiling liquids.

bois·ter·ous (boi′ stər əs) *or* (boi′ strəs) *adj.* Noisy and not having discipline; unruly: *The speaker asked the boisterous audience to be quiet.*

bor·row (bŏr′ ō) *v.* **bor·rowed, bor·row·ing.** **1.** To take something from someone with the understanding that it must be given back: *borrow a pencil; borrow a library book.* **2.** To adopt: *The English language borrowed many words from other languages.*
  Idiom. **borrow trouble.** To take on trouble unnecessarily.

both·er (bŏth′ ər) *v.* **both·ered, both·er·ing.** **1.** To trouble; disturb; annoy. **2.** To take the trouble; to be concerned: *Don't bother waiting for me.* —*n.* Something or someone that is annoying: *Washing dishes is a bother.*

bot·tom (bŏt′ əm) *n.* **1.** The lowest part: *the bottom of the well.* **2.** The under or lower part: *The bottom of the boat was covered with barnacles.*

bought Look up **buy.**

bowl¹ (bōl) *n.* **1.** A round dish used to hold things. **2.** Something shaped like a bowl.

bowl² (bōl) *v.* **bowled, bowl·ing.** **1.** To play the game of bowling: *Rita likes to bowl after school.* **2.** To roll a ball in the game of bowling: *Who bowls first?*

bowl·ing (bō′ lĭng) *n.* A game played by rolling a heavy ball down a wooden alley to knock over ten wooden pins at the opposite end.

Pronunciation Key

ă	pat	ŏ	pot	ŭ	cut
ā	pay	ō	toe	ûr	urge
âr	care	ô	paw, for	ə	about,
ä	father	oi	noise		item,
ĕ	pet	o͝o	took		edible,
ē	bee	oō	boot		gallop,
ĭ	pit	ou	out		circus
ī	pie	th	thin	ər	butter
îr	deer	*th*	this		

brain (brān) *n.* **1.** The large mass of nerve tissue inside the skull of a person or animal. **2. brains.** Intelligence: *The pioneers had brains as well as courage.*
  Idiom. **rack one's brain.** To try hard to solve something.

branch (brănch) *or* (bränch) *n., pl.* **branch·es.** **1.** A part of a tree or shrub that grows out from the trunk. **2.** Any part that grows out of a main part: *a branch of the river.* —*v.* **branched, branch·ing.** To divide into branches: *Turn left where the road branches.*

break (brāk) *v.* **broke, break·ing. 1.** To make something come apart by force; smash. **2.** To harm; damage. **3.** To fail to obey: *break the law.* **4.** To change: *break an Olympic record.* —*n.* **1.** A gap; opening: *a break in the fence.* **2.** A beginning: *the break of day.*

break·fast (brĕk′ fəst) *n.* The first meal of the day.

breath (brĕth) *n.* The air inhaled into and exhaled from the lungs.
  Idioms. **out of breath.** Breathing with difficulty. **save one's breath.** To refrain from useless talking: *Save your breath—he won't go.* **under one's breath.** In a whisper.

breathe (brēth) *v.* **breathed, breath·ing. 1.** To inhale and exhale. **2.** To say quietly; whisper: *I won't breathe a word about the surprise party.*

bridge¹ (brĭj) *n.* **1.** Something built over a river, road, or other obstacle so that people can get across. **2.** The top part of a person's nose. —*v.* **bridged, bridg·ing.** To build a bridge over.

bridge² (brĭj) *n.* A card game for four people.

bring (brĭng) *v.* **brought** (brôt), **bring·ing. 1.** To carry along or escort: *Bring your sister to our party.* **2.** To cause to happen: *April showers bring May flowers.*

broad·cast (brôd′ kăst′) *v.* **broad·cast** *or* **broad·cast·ed, broad·cast·ing. 1.** To send out news, music, etc., by radio or television. **2.** To make known: *broadcast gossip.*

broil (broil) *v.* **broiled, broil·ing. 1.** To cook directly over or under heat: *Dad likes to broil steak for dinner.* **2.** To be very hot: *We broiled in the hot sunlight.*

brooch (brōch) *or* (brōōch) *n., pl.* **brooch·es.** A large pin worn for decoration: *The woman wore a diamond brooch on her dress.*

brought Look up **bring.**

budg·et (bŭj′ ĭt) *n.* A plan for using the money that one receives: *We have a budget so that we won't spend more money than we earn.*

build (bĭld) *v.* **built** (bĭlt), **build·ing. 1.** To make by putting parts together. **2.** To make gradually: *built a good business.*

built Look up **build.**

busi·ness (bĭz′ nĭs) *n., pl.* **busi·ness·es. 1.** What one does to earn a living; occupation: *Her family is in the jewelry business.* **2.** Factory, store, or other commercial enterprise: *They sold their business when they retired.* **3.** Concern, affair: *none of your business.*

bus·y (bĭz′ ē) *adj.* **bus·i·er, bus·i·est. 1.** Active: *We are busy getting ready for a vacation.* **2.** Full of activity: *a busy day.* **3.** In use: *The phone has been busy all day.*

buy (bī) *v.* **bought** (bôt), **buy·ing.** To purchase.

by·line (bī′ līn′) *n.* A line at the beginning of a newspaper or magazine article giving the name of the writer.

cal·en·dar (kăl′ ən dər) *n.* **1.** A chart that shows the days, weeks, and months of the year. **2.** A schedule; a list of things to be done arranged in order: *the school calendar.*

calf¹ (kăf) *n., pl.* **calves** (kăvs) **1.** A young cow or bull. **2.** A young whale, elephant, or seal: *The calf was born last summer.* **3.** Leather made from the hide of a calf; calfskin.

calf² (kăf) *n., pl.* **calves** (kăvs) The fleshy back of the human leg below the knee.

cam·er·a (kăm′ ər ə) *or* (kăm′ rə) *n.* **1.** A machine for taking photographs or motion pictures. **2.** The part of a television system that changes an image into electronic signals.

can·did (kăn′ dĭd) *adj.* Honest; frank; open: *a candid answer.*

ca·noe (kə nōō′) *n.* A light, narrow boat with pointed ends that is moved with a paddle. —*v.* **ca·noed, ca·noe·ing.** To paddle or go in a canoe.

can·o·py (kăn′ ə pē) *n., pl.* **can·o·pies.** **1.** A covering made of cloth or other material hung over a bed, throne, or entrance: *The canopy over the bed was made of white lace.* **2.** A rooflike covering: *In the rain forest, a canopy of leaves from the taller trees shades the smaller plants.*

care·ful (kâr′ fəl) *adj.* **1.** Watchful; cautious: *Be careful crossing busy streets.* **2.** Done with care; thorough: *careful handling of the expensive equipment.* —*adv.* **care·ful·ly.**

cart·wheel (kärt′ wēl′) *n.* **1.** The wheel of a cart. **2.** A sideways handspring.

catch (kăch) *v.* **caught** (kôt), **catch·ing. 1.** To get hold of something that is moving; capture. **2.** To become infected: *catch a cold.* —*n.* **1.** The act of grabbing a ball: *The baseball player made a great catch.* **2.** A game in which a ball is thrown back and forth.

caught Look up **catch.**

ce·les·tial (sə lĕs′ chəl) *adj.* **1.** Having to do with the sky: *The moon and stars are celestial bodies.* **2.** Heavenly; divine.

cel·lar (sĕl′ ər) *n.* An underground storage room.

cen·ter (sĕn′ tər) *n.* The middle point of a circle or a ball. **2.** The middle of anything: *the center of the table.* **3.** A place of activity: *a shopping center.*

cen·tu·ry (sĕn′ chə rē) *n., pl.* **cen·tu·ries.** A period of 100 years.

cer·tain (sûr′ tn) *adj.* **1.** Positive; sure: *I'm certain this is the right road.* **2.** Some: *Certain animals hibernate in winter.*

chalk·board (chôk′ bôrd′) *n.* A hard surface used for writing on with chalk; a blackboard.

cham·pi·on (chăm′ pē ən) *n.* A person or animal that wins first place in a contest.

chap·ter (chăp′ tər) *n.* **1.** A main division of a book. **2.** A small division of a club.

char·ac·ter (kăr′ ək tər) *n.* **1.** All the qualities that make a person or thing what it is. **2.** A person in a book, play, or story. **3.** *Informal.* A person who is different or funny.

charge (chärj) *v.* **charged, charg·ing. 1.** To ask as a price. **2.** To delay payment: *He charged his new rug.* **3.** To attack: *charge the fort.* —*n.* **1.** The price asked: *the charge for delivery.* **2.** Responsibility; supervision: *take charge of someone or something.*

check·er (chĕk′ ər) *n.* **1. a. checkers** (*used with a singular verb*). A game played on a checkerboard by two players. **b.** One of the flat, round pieces used in this game. **2.** One square in a pattern of squares. **3.** An employee who checks out purchases in a self-service store.

cheese·burg·er (chēz′ bûr′ gər) *n.* A hamburger sandwich with melted cheese on the meat.

chick·en (chĭk′ ən) *or* (-ĭn) *n.* **1.** A hen or rooster. **2.** The meat of this bird. —*adj. Slang.* Afraid.

chil·i (chĭl′ ē) *n., pl.* **chil·ies. 1.** The pod of a red pepper that is often dried and ground to make a spicy seasoning. **2.** A spicy food made of chili powder, beef, tomatoes, and sometimes beans. *These sound alike:* **chili, chilly.**

chill·y (chĭl′ ē) *adj.* **chill·i·er, chill·i·est. 1.** Cold enough to be somewhat uncomfortable: *Fall days are often chilly.* **2.** Unfriendly: *I was upset by the chilly greeting my friend gave me. These sound alike:* **chilly, chili.**

chim·ney (chĭm′ nē) *n., pl.* **chim·neys.** An upright hollow structure connected to a furnace, fireplace, or stove to carry away smoke.

choice (chois) *n.* **1.** The act of choosing: *make a choice between two things.* **2.** Someone or something that is chosen: *This hat is my choice.* —*adj.* **choic·er, choic·est.** Very good; excellent: *choice fruit.*

choose (chōōz) *v.* **chose** (chōz), **cho·sen, choos·ing. 1.** To pick out: *choose a dessert.* **2.** To decide: *Do as you choose.*

cho·rus (kôr′ əs) *or* (kōr′-) *n., pl.* **cho·rus·es. 1.** A group of people who sing together. **2.** The part of a song that is repeated after each verse.

chose Look up **choose.**

cit·rus (sĭt′ rəs) *adj.* Belonging to orange, lemon, lime, or grapefruit trees.

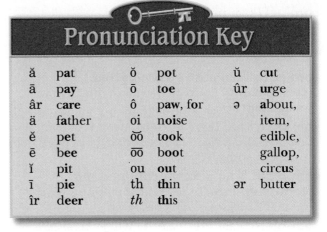

climb (klīm) *v.* **climbed, climb·ing.** To go up or move up. —*n.* **1.** The act of climbing: *the climb up the mountain.* **2.** A place to be climbed: *The rocky path is a difficult climb.*

clos·et (klŏz′ ĭt) *or* (klô′ zĭt) *n.* A small room or cabinet used for hanging or storing things.

cloth·ing (klō′ thĭng) *n.* Coverings worn on the body.

clue (klōō) *n.* Something that helps solve a mystery.

coach (kōch) *n.* **1.** A large carriage pulled by horses. **2.** A train car for passengers. **3.** A low-priced seat on a bus, train, or plane. **4.** A trainer: *a basketball coach; a voice coach.*

coast (kōst) *n.* The edge of land along the sea. —*v.* **coast·ed, coast·ing.** To move without power or effort: *coast down a hill.*

code (kōd) *n.* **1.** A set of signals that stand for letters and numerals: *Morse code.* **2.** Secret writing: *The spy wrote the message in code.* **3.** A set of rules or laws: *a traffic code.*

coin (koin) *n.* A piece of metal issued by a government for use as money.

col·lar (kŏl′ ər) *n.* Something that is worn around the neck: *lace collar; dog collar.*

Pronunciation Key

ă	pat	ŏ	pot	ŭ	cut
ā	pay	ō	toe	ûr	urge
âr	care	ô	paw, for	ə	about,
ä	father	oi	noise		item,
ĕ	pet	ŏŏ	took		edible,
ē	bee	ōō	boot		gallop,
ĭ	pit	ou	out		circus
ī	pie	th	thin	ər	butter
îr	deer	*th*	this		

col·lec·tion (kə lĕk′ shən) *n.* **1.** A group of things gathered and kept together: *a stamp collection.* **2.** Money that is gathered: *We took up a collection to buy him a gift.*

col·um·nist (kŏl′ əm nĭst) *or* (-ə mĭst) *n.* One who writes a newspaper or magazine column.

com·et (kŏm′ ĭt) *n.* A bright heavenly body with a starlike center and a long tail. Comets travel around the sun.

com·fort (kŭm′ fərt) *v.* **com·fort·ed, com·fort·ing.** To ease someone's sorrow. —*n.* **1.** A condition of ease: *They live in comfort.* **2.** A person or thing that gives relief: *He is a comfort to his mother.*

com·ma (kŏm′ ə) *n.* A punctuation mark (,) that separates parts of a sentence, parts of an address, and other series of words and numbers.

com·mer·cial (kə mûr′ shəl) *adj.* Relating to or engaged in business: *a commercial product.* —*n.* A radio or television advertisement.

com·mit (kə mĭt′) *v.* **com·mit·ted, com·mit·ting.** To do, carry out, or be guilty of: *commit a crime.*

com·mon (kŏm′ ən) *adj.* **com·mon·er, com·mon·est. 1.** Shared by all: *common knowledge; common property.* **2.** Occurring often; usual: *Rain is common along the coast.* **3.** Average; ordinary: *common housefly.*
   Idiom. **in common.** Jointly: *interests in common.*

com·pa·ny (kŭm′ pə nē) *n., pl.* **com·pa·nies. 1.** One or more guests. **2.** Companionship. **3.** A business firm.

com·pare (kəm pâr′) *v.* **com·pared, com·par·ing.** To find out or point out how things are alike and how they are different: *Let's compare our answers.*

com·pass (kŭm′ pəs) *or* (kŏm′-) *n.* **1.** An instrument used to show directions. **2.** An instrument used for drawing circles.

com·pel (kəm pĕl´) *v.* **com·pelled, com·pel·ling.** To force or make someone do something: *A big snowstorm might compel schools to close early.*

com·pete (kəm pēt´) *v.* **com·pet·ed, com·pet·ing.** To try hard against others to win something: *compete in a race.*

com·pe·ti·tion (kŏm pĭ tĭsh´ ən) *n.* **1.** A contest: *a diving competition.* **2.** The person or persons one competes with: *Is the competition any good?*

com·plain (kəm plān´) *v.* **com·plained, com·plain·ing.** To say that something is wrong: *complain about a headache.*

com·plete (kəm plēt´) *adj.* **1.** Whole: *a complete set of the encyclopedia.* **2.** Finished; ended: *My report is complete.* **3.** Fully equipped: *a new car complete with power steering.* —*v.* **com·plet·ed, com·plet·ing.** To finish.

con·cept (kŏn´ sĕpt) *n.* A general idea, notion, or understanding: *The concept of equal rights for all is important in the United States.*

con·demn (kən dĕm´) *v.* **con·demned, con·demn·ing.** **1.** To strongly disapprove of: *I condemn cheating on a test.* **2.** To find someone guilty and give a punishment: *The judge condemned the robber to five years in prison.*

con·serve (kən sûrv´) *v.* **con·served, con·serv·ing.** To keep from loss, waste, or harm by using carefully: *conserve the earth's natural resources.*

con·stel·la·tion (kŏn´ stə lā´ shən) *n.* A group of stars, such as the Big Dipper.

con·ster·na·tion (kŏn´ stər nā´ shən) *n.* Great fear, shock, or loss of courage: *Even though there was consternation when the fire alarm sounded, everyone got out safely.*

con·tain·er (kən tā´ nər) *n.* A box, jar, or can used to hold something.

con·trol (kən trōl´) *v.* **con·trolled, con·trol·ling.** To have power over: *control a country; control a car.* —*n.* **1.** Authority or power: *the athlete's control over his body.* **2. controls.** Instruments for operating a machine.

cop·per (kŏp´ ər) *n.* A reddish-brown metal. —*adj.* Reddish brown.

cos·met·ic (kŏz mĕt´ ĭk) *n., pl.* **cos·met·ics.** A preparation, such as powder, lipstick, or skin cream, used to make the face or body more beautiful.

cos·mos (kŏz´ məs) *or* (kŏz´ mōs) *n.* The universe thought of as an orderly and harmonious system.

cot·tage (kŏt´ ĭj) *n.* A small house.

coun·try (kŭn´ trē) *n., pl.* **coun·tries.** **1.** A nation: *Mexico is a country.* **2.** The land outside of towns and cities: *Farms are in the country.*

cou·ple (kŭp´ əl) *n.* **1.** Two things of the same kind; a pair. **2.** A man and a woman who are engaged, married, or partners in a dance. **3.** *Informal.* A few: *a couple of months.* —*v.* **cou·pled, cou·pling.** To join together.

course (kôrs) *or* (kōrs) *n.* **1.** Onward motion; progress: *the course of history.* **2.** Direction; path: *the course of a river.* **3.** A class in a subject. **4.** A piece of land laid out for a sport: *golf course.* **Idiom. of course.** Naturally; certainly.

court (kôrt) *or* (kōrt) *n.* **1.** An open place enclosed by buildings or walls. **2.** A place marked for a game: *tennis court.* **3.** A place for holding legal trials.

cous·in (kŭz´ ən) *n.* The daughter or son of an aunt or uncle.

crack (krăk) *v.* **cracked, crack·ing.** To break with a sharp, snapping sound. —*n.* **1.** A sharp, snapping sound. **2.** A long, narrow opening; a narrow space.

crash (krăsh) *v.* **crashed, crash·ing.** **1.** To fall against or bump into noisily. **2.** To collide. —*n., pl.* **crash·es.** **1.** A loud noise like that made by things falling and breaking. **2.** A violent collision.

crawl (krôl) *v.* **crawled, crawl·ing.** **1.** To move slowly on hands and knees or by dragging the body along the ground. **2.** To move very slowly: *The cars crawled up the crowded street.* —*n.* A slow movement.

crush (krŭsh) *v.* **crushed, crush·ing.** **1.** To press together so as to crumple or injure; squash. **2.** To break into small pieces: *crush ice.*

cy·cling (sī´ klĭng) *n.* The sport of riding a bicycle or motorcycle.

D

dam·age (dăm´ ĭj) *n.* Injury or harm. —*v.* **dam·aged, dam·ag·ing.** To injure; harm; hurt.

dan·ger·ous (dān´ jər əs) *adj.* Unsafe; risky; likely to do harm.

daugh·ter (dô´ tər) *n.* A female child; a girl or woman, when thought of in relation to her parents.

dawn (dôn) *n.* The coming of daylight in the morning. —*v.* **dawned, dawn·ing.** **1.** To begin to grow light in the morning. **2.** To begin to appear or develop: *A new age dawned.*

De·cem·ber (dĭ sĕm´ bər) *n.* The twelfth month of the year.

de·cide (dĭ sīd´) *v.* **de·cid·ed, de·cid·ing.** To make up one's mind; come to a conclusion.

de·clare (dǐ klâr′) *v.* **de·clared, de·clar·ing.**
To make known; announce: *The company declared a new policy.*

ded·i·ca·tion (děd′ ǐ kā′ shən) *n.* The act of giving oneself completely to something; devotion: *She shows her dedication to the violin by practicing two hours every day.*

de·feat (dǐ fēt′) *v.* **de·feat·ed, de·feat·ing.**
To overcome; beat; win a victory over. —*n.* A loss; an overthrow.

de·gree (dǐ grē′) *n., pl.* **de·grees. 1.** A unit for measuring temperature. **2.** A unit used in measuring angles: *a 90-degree angle.* **3.** A title given by a college or university.

de·lay (dǐ lā′) *v.* **de·layed, de·lay·ing.** To put off until later. —*n.* The act of putting off; a wait.

de·liv·er·y (dǐ lǐv′ ə rē) *or* (dǐ lǐv′ rē) *n., pl.* **de·liv·er·ies. 1.** Distribution; handing over: *mail delivery.* **2.** Manner of speaking: *Her forceful delivery made us listen to her speech.*

de·part (dǐ pärt′) *v.* **de·part·ed, de·part·ing.
1.** To go away; leave: *The bus departs in five minutes.* **2.** To change: *The builders departed from the original plan for the house.*

depth (děpth) *n.* **1.** The distance from the top to the bottom: *the depth of the lake.* **2.** Deepness of thought, tone, color, etc.

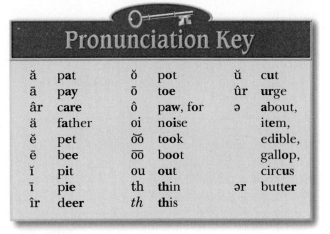

des·ert¹ (děz′ ərt) *n.*
A dry, sandy region.

de·sert² (dǐ zûrt′) *v.* **de·sert·ed, de·sert·ing.** To forsake; abandon: *She did not desert her friends when they needed her.*

de·stroy (dǐ stroi′) *v.* **de·stroyed, de·stroy·ing.** To ruin; make useless; lay waste.

dif·fer·ent (dǐf′ ər ənt) *or* (dǐf′ rənt) *adj.* **1.** Not alike: *Our paintings are different.* **2.** Separate; distinct; not the same: *We saw him three different times today.*

di·rec·tion (dǐ rěk′ shən) *or* (dī) *n.* **1.** Management; guidance. **2.** The point toward which a person or thing faces, points, or moves. **3. directions.** Orders; instructions: *Read the directions before you begin the test.*

di·rec·tor (dǐ rěk′ tər) *or* (dī) *n.* A person who directs or manages something.

dirt·y (dûr′ tē) *adj.* **dirt·i·er, dirt·i·est.
1.** Not clean: *dirty clothes.* **2.** Unfair: *a dirty trick.*

dis·charge (dǐs chärj′) *v.* **dis·charged, dis·charg·ing.** To let go; release.

dis·close (dǐ sklōz′) *v.* **dis·closed, dis·clos·ing.** To reveal or make known: *The teacher will disclose the answer to the puzzle later.*

dis·cov·er (dǐ skŭv′ ər) *v.* **dis·cov·ered, dis·cov·er·ing. 1.** To see or learn for the first time; find out: *They discovered they were late.*

dis·cuss (dǐ skŭs′) *v.* **dis·cussed, dis·cuss·ing.** To talk over thoughtfully; consider.

dis·ease (dǐ zēz′) *n.* Sickness; illness.

dis·lodge (dǐs lǒj′) *v.* **dis·lodged, dis·lodg·ing.** To move out of a place or position: *It is hard to dislodge the big rock from the soil.*

dis·tort (dǐ stôrt′) *v.* **dis·tort·ed, dis·tort·ing.
1.** To twist or bend out of the usual shape: *When I look in the lake, the ripples of the water distort my face.* **2.** To change the facts so that what one says is partly false: *Don't distort what really happened.*

di·vide (dǐ vīd′) *v.* **di·vid·ed, di·vid·ing.** To separate; keep apart.

dol·lar (dǒl′ ər) *n.* The unit of money in the United States and some other countries, equal to 100 cents.

dou·ble (dŭb′ əl) *adj.* **1.** Twice as much. **2.** In pairs: *double doors.* —*v.* **dou·bled, dou·bling.
1.** To make twice as great. **2.** To fold over: *double the blanket.*

dou·bly (dŭb′ lē) *adv.* In twice the amount or degree: *I wanted to win the bicycle race, so I pedaled doubly fast.*

dough (dō) *n.* A thick mixture of flour, water or milk, and other ingredients for baking into bread, cake, etc.

doz·en (dŭz′ ən) *n.* A group of twelve.

ear·ly (ûr′ lē) *adj.* **ear·li·er, ear·li·est. 1.** Near the beginning: *the early evening.* **2.** Before the usual time: *The early bird catches the worm.* —*adv.*
1. At or near the beginning of: *early in the morning.*
2. Before the usual time: *to arrive early.*

earn (ûrn) v. **earned, earn·ing. 1.** To receive as payment in return for work: *earn $10 a week.* **2.** To gain through effort: *He earned good grades.*

ear·phone (îr' fōn') n., pl. **ear·phones.** A telephone, radio, TV, or stereo receiver that is held to the ear.

earth·en·ware (ûr' thən wâr') n. Pots, bowls, dishes, vases, and other like objects made from clay and baked at a low temperature.

ea·sel (ē' zəl) n. A tall stand or frame used to support, hold, or display things, such as artists' paintings, chalkboards, or signs: *The artist put the canvas on the easel and began to paint.*

ech·o (ĕk' ō) n., pl. **ech·oes.** A repetition of sound, caused by the throwing back of sound waves. —v. **ech·oed, ech·o·ing.** To give back or repeat sound.

e·clipse (ĭ klĭps') n. passing from sight because light is cut off: *The sun disappeared during the eclipse.*

ed·i·to·ri·al (ĕd ĭ tôr' ē əl) n. An article in a newspaper or magazine or a comment on a radio or TV station that gives the opinion of the editor, owner, or publisher.

ed·u·ca·tion (ĕj ə kā' shən) n. **1.** Training, schooling: *public school education.* **2.** Knowledge and skill.

el·bow (ĕl' bō) n. The joint in the arm between the wrist and shoulder.

e·lec·tion (ĭ lĕk' shən) n. A choosing or selecting by vote.

el·e·phant (ĕl' ə fənt) n. A very large Asian or African animal with a thick, wrinkled hide, stout legs, long tusks, and a long, flexible trunk.

else (ĕls) adj. **1.** Besides; in addition. **2.** other; different; instead.

em·ploy (ĕm ploi') v. **em·ployed, em·ploy·ing. 1.** To hire; give work to. **2.** To make use of: *Employ your study time to good advantage.*

em·ploy·ee (ĕm ploi' ē) n. A person who is paid to work for someone else: *She is a good employee.*

em·ploy·ment (ĕm ploi' mənt) n. Work; occupation; job.

emp·ty (ĕmp' tē) adj. **1.** Containing nothing. **2.** Without meaning: *empty promises.* —v. **emp·tied, emp·ty·ing, emp·ties.** To remove the contents of.

en·deav·or (ĕn dĕv' ər) n. A serious attempt; effort: *an endeavor to learn Spanish.* —v. To seriously try; attempt: *Let's endeavor to get better grades.*

en·er·gy (ĕn' ər jē) n., pl. **en·er·gies. 1.** The ability to do work. **2.** Force; strength.

en·joy (ĕn joi') v. **en·joyed, en·joy·ing. 1.** To take pleasure in: *enjoy the parade.* **2.** To have or benefit by: *enjoy good health.*

e·nough (ĭ nŭf') adj. As much or as many as necessary or desirable: *There is enough paint for everyone in the art class.* —n. A sufficient amount: *We have had enough to eat.* —adv. Fully; quite: *I felt well enough to go to school.*

e·quip·ment (ĭ kwip' mənt) n. The things needed for a particular purpose: *gardening equipment.*

es·cape (ĭ skāp') v. **es·caped, es·cap·ing. 1.** To break loose; get free; get away: *escape from jail.* **2.** To avoid: *escape a storm.* —n. The act of escaping.

eve·ning (ēv' nĭng) n. The time between sunset and bedtime; early night.

ex·am·ple (ĭg zăm' pəl) or (-zăm'-) n. **1.** Sample. **2.** Someone or something that is a model. **Idiom. set an example.** To be a model worthy of imitation.

ex·cel·lent (ĕk' sə lənt) adj. Extremely good; unusually high in quality.

ex·cept (ĭk sĕpt') prep. Outside of; apart from; but: *everyone except me.*

ex·er·cise (ĕk' sər sīz) n., pl. **ex·er·cis·es.** Physical or mental activity that improves the body or mind. —v. **ex·er·cised, ex·er·cis·ing. 1.** To put into action: *exercise care.* **2.** To do exercise: *exercise your muscles.*

ex·ile (ĕg' zīl) or (ĕk' sīl) n. An enforced living away from one's country, often as punishment: *The spy's exile meant that he couldn't visit his native land.* —v. **ex·iled, ex·il·ing.** To send away from one's native land as punishment.

ex·pect (ĭk spĕkt') v. **ex·pect·ed, ex·pect·ing. 1.** To think that something will probably happen. **2.** To require: *You are expected to do a good job.*

ex·pert (ĕk' spûrt) n. A person who has special skill or knowledge. —adj. **1.** Having special skill or knowledge: *an expert swimmer.* **2.** Given by an expert: *expert advice.*

ex·plain (ĭk splān') v. **ex·plained, ex·plain·ing. 1.** To make plain or clear; tell the meaning of: *explain directions.* **2.** To give the reason for: *explain your mistake.*

ex·ploit (ĕk' sploit') v. **ex·ploit·ed, ex·ploit·ing.** To make the best use of: *Maria wants to exploit her ability to get along with animals by becoming an animal trainer.* —n. A daring act: *The exciting book was about the exploits of the hero.*

ex·port (ĭk spôrt') or (-spōrt') or (ĕk' spôrt') or (-spōrt') v. **ex·port·ed, ex·port·ing.** To send or carry out goods to another country for sale or trade. —n. **1.** The act of exporting. **2.** Goods sold and sent to another country.

ex·tra (ĕk′ strə) *adj.* More than what is usual or expected: *earn extra cash.* —*adv.* Especially: *an extra good dinner.* —*n.* Often **extras.** Something additional: *a car with all the extras.*

fac·to·ry (făk′ tə rē) *n., pl.* **fac·to·ries.** A building or group of buildings where things are made.

fan·cy (făn′ sē) *adj.* **fan·ci·er, fan·ci·est.** Not plain; elaborate: *fancy clothes.* —*n., pl.* **fan·cies. 1.** Imagination. **2.** A whim: *a sudden fancy for ice cream.*

fare (fâr) *n.* The cost of a ride on a plane, bus, train, taxi, etc.

far·ther (fär′ *th*ər) *adv.* To a greater distance: *She hiked farther than I did.* —*adj.* More distant: *the farther road.*

fault (fôlt) *n.* **1.** Blame; responsibility: *It was my fault.* **2.** A weakness; shortcoming. **3.** A mistake.

Feb·ru·ar·y (fĕb′ rōō ĕr′ ē) *or* (fĕb′ yōō-) *n.* The second month of the year.

fe·male (fē′ māl′) *adj.* Having to do with women or girls; a female voice. —*n.* **1.** A girl or woman. **2.** A female animal.

feud (fyōōd) *n.* A very long, unpleasant quarrel between two people, families, groups, or countries: *The feud lasted so long that people forgot why they were angry at each other.* —*v.* **feud·ed, feud·ing.** To carry on a long, bitter quarrel: *Let's not feud with each other.*

fight (fīt) *v.* **fought** (fôt), **fight·ing.** To take part in a struggle or battle: *Doctors fight disease.* —*n.* **1.** A struggle; battle. **2.** A quarrel.

film (fĭlm) *n.* **1.** A thin strip or roll of light-sensitive material for taking photographs. **2.** A motion picture; movie. —*v.* **filmed, film·ing.** To make a movie.

fi·nal (fī′ nəl) *adj.* **1.** Coming at the end; last: *the final act of a play.* **2.** Settling the matter; deciding: *the final words on the subject.* —*n.* Often **finals.** The last game or last examination.

firm¹ (fûrm) *adj.* **firm·er, firm·est. 1.** Solid; not easily moved. **2.** Not changing: *a firm belief.* **3.** Steady: *a firm voice.*

firm² (fûrm) *n.* A group of persons who have joined in a business: *a law firm.*

flash·light (flăsh′ līt′) *n.* A small portable electric light.

float (flōt) *v.* **float·ed, float·ing. 1.** To be held up by liquid or air. **2.** To move or drift freely. —*n.* **1.** Something that floats: *a float on a fishline.* **2.** An exhibit on a platform with wheels, used in a parade.

flood (flŭd) *n.* **1.** A great flow of water over land that is usually dry. **2.** A great outpouring: *a flood of tears; a flood of letters.* —*v.* **flood·ed, flood·ing.** To cover with water.

fol·low (fŏl′ ō) *v.* **fol·lowed, fol·low·ing. 1.** To come after; go after: *follow me.* **2.** To go along: *follow this road.* **3.** To accept as a guide; obey: *follow the rules; follow directions.*

fool·ish (fōō′ lĭsh) *adj.* Without sense; unwise; silly; ridiculous.

foot·ball (fŏŏt′ bôl′) *n.* **1.** A game played by two teams of eleven players each on a long field with a goal at either end. The object is to carry the ball or kick it across the opponent's goal line. **2.** The oval leather ball used in this game.

for·tu·nate (fôr′ chə nĭt) *adj.* Favored; lucky.

fought Look up **fight.**

frac·tion (frăk′ shən) *n.* **1.** One or more of the equal parts of a whole object or number. **2.** A very small part or amount; fragment.

fraud (frôd) *n.* An intentional trick or deception of someone in order to gain an unfair advantage or to cheat: *It is fraud to copy a computer video game and sell it as an original.*

fray (frā) *v.* **frayed, fray·ing.** To wear away and separate into loose threads, especially along an edge: *My favorite shirt began to fray at the collar.*

freeze (frēz) *v.* **froze, froz·en, freez·ing. 1.** To change into ice. **2.** To make or become hard or solid with cold: *freeze meat in the refrigerator.* **3.** To become very cold: *I froze in the cold wind.* **4.** To become motionless: *freeze in terror.* —*n.* A frost; a condition of extreme coldness: *a sudden freeze.*

fric·tion (frĭk′ shən) *n.* The rubbing of one thing or surface against another: *The friction of tires against a road causes them to wear out.*

Fri·day (frī′ dē) *or* (-dā′) *n.* The sixth day of the week.

friend·ly (frĕnd′ lē) *adj.* **friend·li·er, friend·li·est. 1.** Like a friend; kind: *a friendly person.* **2.** Not hostile: *a friendly game.*

fruit (frōōt) *n., pl.* **fruit** *or* **fruits.** A juicy or fleshy plant part that is good to eat.

fur·nish (fûr′ nĭsh) *v.* **fur·nished, fur·nish·ing. 1.** To equip with furniture: *furnish a house.* **2.** To supply; provide: *furnish cookies for the party.*

fur·ni·ture (fûr′ nĭ chər) *n.* Articles, usually movable, to make a room fit for living or working, such as tables, desks, chairs, beds, etc.

fu·ror (fyŏōr′ ôr′) *or* (-ər) *n.* An outburst or noisy commotion; uproar: *The closing of the zoo caused a furor in the town.*

gal·ax·y (găl′ ək sē) *n., pl.* **gal·ax·ies.** A group of billions of stars that form one system.

gar·bage (gär′ bĭj) *n.* **1.** Scraps of food that are thrown away. **2.** Trash.

gath·er (gă*th*′ ər) *v.* **gath·ered, gath·er·ing. 1.** To bring into one place or group; collect: *gather wood for a fire.* **2.** To conclude: *I gather you are excited about your new bike.* **3.** To pull cloth together with a thread: *gather the material.*

gen·er·al (jĕn′ ər əl) *adj.* **1.** For everyone; for the whole: *a general meeting.* **2.** Common to most; widespread: *general interest in sports.* **3.** Not detailed: *Give us a general idea of how your invention works.* —*n.* A high-ranking officer in the Army, Air Force, or Marine Corps.
    Idiom. **in general.** Usually; for the most part.

gen·tle (jĕn′ tl) *adj.* **gen·tler, gen·tlest. 1.** Mild: *a gentle hug.* **2.** Tame: *a gentle donkey.* **3.** Soft; low: *gentle lapping of the waves.*

glue (glōō) *n.* A substance used to stick things together. —*v.* **glued, glu·ing. 1.** To fasten together with glue. **2.** To hold firmly: *My eyes were glued to the clock.*

golf (gŏlf) *or* (gôlf) *n.* A game played outdoors over a large course. The course has 9 or 18 holes into which a player must try to hit a ball with a club.

gov·ern·ment (gŭv′ ərn mənt) *n.* **1.** The group of people who rule a country, state, city, etc.: *We elect our government.* **2.** A way of ruling: *a democratic government.*

graph·ic (grăf′ ĭk) *n., pl.* **graph·ics.** A drawn or photographic image, for example, one that appears on a television or computer screen: *The new video game has great graphics.*

grass·hop·per (grăs′ hŏp′ ər) *or* (grăs′-) *n.* A winged insect with strong back legs for jumping.

greet (grēt) *v.* **greet·ed, greet·ing. 1.** To welcome politely: *greet the guests.* **2.** To receive; to respond to: *Her arrival was greeted with joy.*

grind (grīnd) *v.* **ground, grind·ing. 1.** To crush into fine pieces: *grind wheat into flour.* **2.** To sharpen or smooth: *grind a knife.* **3.** To grate: *grind your teeth.*

groan (grōn) *v.* **groaned, groan·ing.** To make a deep, sad or annoyed sound. —*n.* A moan. *These sound alike:* **groan, grown.**

grow (grō) *v.* **grew, grown** (grōn), **grow·ing. 1.** To become bigger. **2.** To exist: *Moss grows in the shade.* **3.** To raise; produce: *grow vegetables.* **4.** To become: *grow cold.*

grown Look up **grow.** *These sound alike:* **grown, groan.**

guide (gīd) *n.* Someone or something that shows the way or directs: *a museum guide.* —*v.* **guid·ed, guid·ing.** To direct; show the way; lead.

guilt·y (gĭl′ tē) *adj.* **guilt·i·er, guilt·i·est. 1.** Having done wrong; deserving blame or punishment: *guilty of a crime.* **2.** Feeling that one has done wrong: *a guilty conscience.*

gui·tar (gĭ tär′) *n.* A musical instrument that has a long neck and a large sound box. Its six strings are played with the fingers or a pick.

half (hăf) *n., pl.* **halves** (hăvz) *or* (hävz). **1.** One of two equal parts. **2.** One of two equal periods of time in certain games: *the first half of a football game.*
    Idioms. **in half.** Into two equal parts. **not half.** Not at all: *not half bad.*

hall·way (hôl′ wā′) *n.* Corridor; passageway; hall.

hand·made (hănd′ mād′) *adj.* Made by hand rather than by a machine: *a handmade kite.*

har·vest (här′ vĭst) *n.* **1.** The act of gathering in a crop: *Farmers expect an early harvest this year.* **2.** The crop that is gathered: *We store our harvest in large barns.* —*v.* **har·vest·ed, har·vest·ing.** To gather a crop.

head·line (hĕd′ līn′) *n.* Words printed in large, heavy type at the top of a newspaper article telling what the article is about.

health·y (hĕl′ thē) *adj.* **health·i·er, health·i·est.** Having good health: *a healthy body.*

hear (hîr) *v.* **heard** (hûrd), **hear·ing. 1.** To receive sound through one's ears: *hear music.* **2.** To listen to with care: *hear both sides of the argument.*

heard Look up **hear.**

hem·i·sphere (hĕm′ ĭ sfîr′) *n., pl.* **hem·i·spheres.** One half of the earth's surface as divided by either the equator or a meridian. The equator divides the Northern and Southern hemispheres, and a meridian divides the Eastern and Western hemispheres.

he·ro (hîr′ ō) *n., pl.* **he·roes. 1.** A person admired for courage or special achievements. **2.** The main character in a story, play, movie, etc.

hob·by (hŏb′ ē) *n., pl.* **hob·bies.** An activity that a person does for his or her own pleasure.

hock·ey (hŏk′ ē) *n.*
1. Also **ice hockey.** A game played on ice by two teams of six players each. The players wear skates and use sticks to try to hit a puck into the other team's goal.

2. Also **field hockey.** A similar game played on a field with a ball and eleven players on a team.

hole (hōl) *n.* **1.** An opening: *hole in the ground; hole in a sock.* **2.** An animal's burrow: *a fox hole.* These sound alike: *hole, whole.*

hol·i·day (hŏl′ ĭ dā′) *n.* A day when people don't work, such as Thanksgiving or a vacation.

home·work (hōm′ wûrk′) *n.* Schoolwork assigned to be done outside the classroom.

hon·est (on′ ĭst) *adj.* Truthful; fair; sincere.

hon·or (ŏn′ ər) *n.* A sense of what is right and proper; nobility of mind: *He is a man of honor.* —*v.* **hon·ored, hon·or·ing. 1.** To show respect to. **2.** To accept as payment.
Idiom. **on one's honor.** pledged to speak the truth and do what is right.

hos·pi·tal (hŏs′ pĭ tl) *or* (-pĭt′ l) *n.* A place where sick or injured people are cared for.

ho·tel (hō tĕl′) *n.* A house or large building that supplies rooms and food for pay to travelers and others.

hu·mor (hyōō′ mər) *n.* **1.** The quality of being funny: *Clowns provide humor at the circus.* **2.** The ability to enjoy something funny: *a sense of humor.* **3.** State of mind; mood: *in a bad humor.*

hun·dred (hŭn′ drĭd) *n.* Ten times ten; 100.

hurt (hûrt) *v.* **hurt, hurt·ing. 1.** To cause pain to; injure: *hurt your foot.* **2.** To feel pain: *My eyes hurt after a day at the beach.* **3.** To have a bad effect on; harm: *to hurt one's chances.* —*n.* An injury; pain.

hus·band (hŭz′ bənd) *n.* A married man.

Pronunciation Key

ă	pat	ŏ	pot	ŭ	cut
ā	pay	ō	toe	ûr	urge
âr	care	ô	paw, for	ə	about,
ä	father	oi	noise		item,
ĕ	pet	ŏŏ	took		edible,
ē	bee	ōō	boot		gallop,
ĭ	pit	ou	out		circus
ī	pie	th	thin	ər	butter
îr	deer	*th*	*th*is		

I

i·de·a (ī dē′ ə) *n.* **1.** Any result of mental activity or understanding; thought, belief, or opinion. **2.** The point or purpose of something: *The idea of a vacation is to get some rest.*

i·den·ti·cal (ī dĕn′ tĭ kəl) *adj.* Exactly alike: *My sister and I wore identical blouses.*

im·port (ĭm pôrt′) *or* (ĭm′ pôrt′) *or* (-pōrt′) *v.* **im·port·ed, im·port·ing.** To bring in something from another country for sale, trade, or use. —*n.* (ĭm′ pôrt′) *or* (-pōrt′). Something imported from another country.

im·por·tant (ĭm′ pôr′ tnt) *adj.* Having value; significant; worth noticing or considering.

im·prove (ĭm prōōv′) *v.* **im·proved, im·prov·ing.** To make or become better: *improve your golf swing.*

in·crease (ĭn krēs′) *v.* **in·creased, in·creas·ing.** To make or become greater or larger. —*n.* (ĭn′ krēs). The amount by which something is increased: *an increase of 25 percent.*

in·dus·try (ĭn′ də strē) *n., pl.* **in·dus·tries. 1.** Manufacturing, business, and trade: *a center of industry; the steel industry.* **2.** Hard work; steady effort.

in·for·ma·tion (ĭn′ fər mā′ shən) *n.* Facts or knowledge about a subject.

in·sect (ĭn′ sĕkt′) *n.* Any of a group of small animals without backbones, usually having wings, six legs, and a body divided into three parts.

in·sist (ĭn sĭst′) *v.* **in·sist·ed, in·sist·ing.** To demand, or maintain persistently; to take a strong stand.

in·spec·tion (ĭn spĕk′ shən) *n.* **1.** The act of examining. **2.** An official examination: *daily inspection of the soldiers.*

in·stead (ĭn stĕd′) *adv.* In place of someone or something.

in·struct (ĭn strŭkt′) *v.* **in·struct·ed, in·struct·ing. 1.** To teach. **2.** To give orders to: *The crossing guard instructed us to remain on the sidewalk.*

in·struc·tion (ĭn strŭk′ shən) *n.* **1.** Lessons: *music instruction.* **2. instructions.** Directions; orders.

in·tend (ĭn tĕnd′) *v.* **in·tend·ed, in·tend·ing. 1.** To have in mind; plan: *to intend to go somewhere.* **2.** To mean for a particular use or person: *The surprise was intended for you.*

in·vent (ĭn vĕnt′) *v.* **in·vent·ed, in·vent·ing. 1.** To think up and make for the first time: *invent a machine.* **2.** To make up: *invent excuses.*

in·ven·tion (ĭn vĕn′ shən) *n.* **1.** Something invented: *an invention.* **2.** The act of inventing: *the invention of the wheel.* **3.** A false statement: *His story is only an invention.*

in·vite (ĭn vīt′) *v.* **in·vit·ed, in·vit·ing. 1.** To ask someone to go somewhere or to do something: *invite to a party.* **2.** To ask for: *invite questions.*

is·land (ī′ lənd) *n.*

1. A body of land that is surrounded by water. An island is smaller than a continent. **2.** Something that is different or separated from things around it: *There is a traffic island in the middle of the street.*

its (ĭts) *pron.* The possessive of **it**; of or belonging to **it**: *The bird flapped its wings. These sound alike:* **its, it's.**

it's (ĭts). The contraction for "it is" and "it has." *These sound alike:* **it's, its.**

jab·ber (jăb′ ər) *v.* **jab·bered, jab·ber·ing.** To talk in a fast, silly, or mixed-up way; chatter: *Sometimes very young children jabber to themselves.*

Jan·u·ar·y (jăn′ yōō er′ ē) *n.* The first month of the year.

jave·lin (jăv′ lĭn) *or* (jăv′ ə-) *n.* A long, thin, light spear that is thrown for distance in an athletic track and field event.

jos·tle (jŏs′ əl) *v.* **jos·tled, jos·tling.** To bump, shove, and push against one another: *I was jostled by the crowd as I entered the stadium.*

jot (jŏt) *v.* **jot·ted, jot·ting.** To write quickly or briefly: *Please jot down your telephone number so I can call you later.*

jour·nal·ism (jûr′ nə lĭz′ əm) *n.* The gathering, reporting, writing, and publishing of news in newspapers or magazines or on television or radio.

judge (jŭj) *n.* **1.** A public official who decides cases in a law court. **2.** A person who decides the winner in a contest. —*v.* **judged, judg·ing. 1.** To hear and decide a case in a law court. **2.** To form an opinion: *Judge this book for yourself.*

juice (jōōs) *n.* **1.** The liquid in fruit, vegetables, and meats. **2.** *Slang.* Electricity.

Ju·ly (jōō lī′) *n.* The seventh month of the year.

June (jōōn) *n.* The sixth month of the year.

jun·gle (jŭng′ gəl) *n.* **1.** Land in the tropics with a thick growth of trees and plants. **2.** A confused mass of objects.

Ju·pi·ter (jōō′ pĭ tər) *n.* **1.** The largest planet in our solar system and the fifth-closest to the sun. **2.** In ancient Roman mythology, the ruler of the gods.

kan·ga·roo (kăng′ gə rōō) *n.* An animal from Australia and New Guinea that has short forelegs, long and powerful hind legs for leaping, and a long tail. The female carries her young in a pouch in front of her body.

kitch·en (kĭch′ ən) *n.* A room where food is prepared.

knife (nīf) *n., pl.* **knives** (nīvz). A thin blade used for cutting or spreading.

know (nō) *v.* **knew, known** (nōn), **know·ing. 1.** To understand: *know the answers.* **2.** To be acquainted with: *I know her well.* **3.** To have skill in: *know how to ride a bike.*

known Look up **know.**

knuck·le (nŭk′ əl) *n.* A joint of a finger.

land·slide (lănd′ slīd′) *n.* The sliding of rocks and soil down a steep slope: *The landslide covered the town at the foot of the mountain.*

laugh·ter (lăf′ tər) *n.* The act of making sounds to express happiness, amusement, or scorn.

lawn (lôn) *n.* Land covered with grass kept closely cut, especially near or around a house.

learn·ing (lûr′ nĭng) *n.* Knowledge gained by study.

length (lĕngkth) *or* (lĕngth) *n.* **1.** How long something is from one end to another; its measured distance. **2.** How long something lasts from beginning to end: *the length of your visit.*

lib·er·ty (lĭb′ ər tē) *n., pl.* **lib·er·ties. 1.** The state of being able to speak and act freely. **2.** Political freedom.

li·brar·y (lī′ brĕr′ ē) *n.*, *pl.* **li·brar·ies. 1.** A building where books, magazines, and reference material are collected. **2.** Any collection of books: *a library in the living room.*

light-year (līt′ yîr′) *n.* Also **light year.** A measure of distance equal to the distance that light travels in one year through space.

loathe (lō*th*) *v.* **loathed, loath·ing.** To dislike very much; hate: *Readers may loathe the cruel actions of the book's main character.*

lob·ster (lŏb′ stər) *n.* **1.** A large, hard shellfish with five pairs of legs and large claws on the front pair. **2.** The meat of this shellfish, used as food.

lo·ca·tion (lō kā′ shən) *n.* A place where something is positioned: *the location of the restaurant.*

loose (lōōs) *adj.* **loos·er, loos·est. 1.** Not fastened or firmly attached: *a loose cap.* **2.** Not closed in; free: *The dog was loose.* **3.** Not tightly fitted: *a loose pair of jeans.*

lose (lōōz) *v.* **lost, los·ing. 1.** To be without: *Don't lose the keys.* **2.** To be unable to keep: *to lose your temper.* **3.** To fail to win: *I won't lose this race.*

loy·al (loi′ əl) *adj.* True and faithful.

loy·al·ty (loi′ əl tē) *n.* The act of being true and faithful; faithfulness.

lu·nar (lōō′ nər) *adj.* Having to do with the moon.

lyr·ics (lĭr′ ĭks) *pl. n.* The words of a song: *The lyrics of the song came from a poem.*

M

mag·ic (măj′ ĭk) *n.* Mysterious effects produced by tricks, usually as entertainment. —*adj.* Having magic power; done by magic: *a magic wand.*

mag·net (măg′ nĭt) *n.* **1.** A piece of metal or ore that draws iron toward it. **2.** Anything that attracts.

male (māl) *n.* **1.** A man or a boy. **2.** Any animal of the same sex as a man or boy.

mar·ble (mär′ bəl) *n.*, *pl.* **marbles 1.** A smooth, hard stone that is streaked or colored, often used in buildings. **2.** A small ball made of a hard substance such as glass. **3. marbles.** A children's game played with small balls.

March (märch) *n.* The third month of the year.

mar·gin (mär′ jĭn) *n.* **1.** An edge or rim: *Water lilies grew along the margin of the pond.* **2.** A border around print or writing on a page: *Don't write in the margin of the book.*

ma·roon (mə rōōn′) *n.* A very dark brownish red.

mas·ter (măs′ tər) *or* (mä′ stər) *n.* **1.** A person who has control of something: *the dog's master; the ship's master.* **2.** A person who has a great skill or ability: *a master of foreign languages.* —*v.* **mas·tered, mas·ter·ing. 1.** To bring under control: *to master your angry feelings.* **2.** To become skilled: *to master your spelling words.*

mast·head (măst′ hĕd′) *n.* **1.** The top of a ship's mast. **2.** The section in a newspaper or magazine that gives its name, owner, chief editors, address, and other information about the publication.

May (mā) *n.* The fifth month of the year.

mea·ger *also* **mea·gre** (mē′ gər) *adj.* Hardly enough; very little: *The meager amount of water did not satisfy my thirst.*

meas·ure (mĕzh′ ər) *v.* **meas·ured, meas·ur·ing. 1.** To find the length, size, contents, weight, or length of time of anything in standard units: *Let's measure these plants.* **2.** To be of a certain size, weight: *I measure five feet tall.*

med·dle (mĕd′ l) *v.* **med·dled, med·dling.** To busy oneself with other people's things or doings without being asked or needed: *Please do not meddle with my stereo.*

mem·ber (mĕm′ bər) *n.* **1.** A part of the body. **2.** A person or thing belonging to a group, society, etc.: *a club member; a class member.*

Me·mo·ri·al Day (mə môr′ ē əl) *n.* A holiday in the United States that honors members of the armed forces who have died in wars. The official date is May 30, but it is observed on the last Monday in May.

mem·o·ry (mĕm′ ə rē) *n.*, *pl.* **mem·o·ries. 1.** The power of recalling something learned: *I have a poor memory for names.* **2.** A person or thing remembered: *Our old house is only a memory.*

men·tion (mĕn′ shən) *v.* **men·tioned, men·tion·ing.** To speak or write about: *Don't mention our plans.*

mer·ry (mĕr′ ē) *adj.* **mer·ri·er, mer·ri·est.**
Happy and cheerful; full of good spirits; jolly:
a merry twinkle in his eye.

mes·sage (mĕs′ ij) *n.* **1.** Any news or information
sent from one person to another. **2.** A written
statement or speech.

met·al (mĕt′ l) *n.* A chemical element that is shiny
when pure or polished and is a good conductor of
electricity or heat. Gold, silver, copper, tin, iron,
and aluminum are metals.

me·te·or (mē′ tē ər) *or* (-ôr′) *n., pl.* **me·te·ors.**
A shooting star; a piece of matter that falls toward
the earth at great speed from outer space. Meteors
burn with a bright glow when they hit the air
around the earth and usually burn up before they
reach the ground.

met·ric (mĕt′ rĭk) *adj.* Of or relating to the metric
system, a system of weights and measures based on
the meter for length and the gram for weight.

mi·cro·phone (mī′ krə fōn′) *n.* An instrument that
changes sound waves into electrical signals.
Microphones are used to make sound louder,
to broadcast TV and radio shows, and
to record sound for movies and sound
recordings.

mi·cro·scope (mī′ krə skōp′)
n. An instrument that, by an
arrangement of lenses makes tiny
things look large enough to be
seen and studied.

mild (mīld) *adj.* **mild·er, mild·est.**
1. Gentle; kind; calm: *a mild person.*
2. Not extreme, harsh, or severe: *a mild winter.*

mois·ture (mois′ chər) *n.* **1.** Dampness; slight
wetness: *There is still moisture in the ground from the
spring rains.* **2.** Water vapor in the air or condensed
on a surface: *Beads of moisture formed on the outside
of the pitcher.*

Mon·day (mŭn′ dē) *or* (-dā′) *n.* The second day of
the week.

mon·key (mŭng′ kē) *n., pl.* **mon·keys.** An
animal that has hands with thumbs and usually has
a long tail; not a gorilla, chimp, or other large ape.

mos·qui·to (mə skē′ tō) *n., pl.* **mos·qui·toes** or
mos·qui·tos. A slender, long-legged, blood-
sucking insect with wings, the bite of which may
cause swelling and itching. Some kinds carry
yellow fever or malaria germs.

mo·tion (mō′ shən) *n.* **1.** Action or movement; a
changing from one place or position to another:
*The motion of a boat on a rough sea makes some people
ill.* **2.** A gesture: *He made a motion for silence.* —*v.*
mo·tioned, mo·tion·ing. To make a gesture
or movement to express meaning; to signal: *He
motioned to me to be quiet.*

mus·cu·lar (mŭs′ kyə lər) *adj.* **1.** Having muscles
that are strong and well-developed: *a muscular
body.* **2.** Relating to or having to do with muscle.

mu·si·cal (myoo′ zĭ kəl) *adj.* **1.** Having to do with
music: *a musical instrument.* **2.** Pleasing to the ear;
melodious: *the musical song of a bird.* —*n.* A light,
amusing movie or play with songs and dances: *a
musical on Broadway.*

mu·si·cian (myoo zĭsh′ ən) *n.* A person skilled
in music, especially one whose profession is
playing music.

mu·tu·al (myoo′ choo əl) *adj.* **1.** Shared; held in
common: *My friend and I have a mutual love of
shopping.* **2.** Given and received in equal amounts:
Our friendship is mutual.

mys·te·ry (mĭs′ tə rē) *n., pl.* **mys·te·ries.**
1. Something that is secret, strange, or unexplained:
The name of the thief is a mystery. **2.** A story dealing
with secret events.

na·tion (nā′ shən) *n.* An independent country.

nat·u·ral (năch′ ər əl) *or* (năch′ rəl) *adj.*
1. Belonging to by nature; inborn; native: *Tyrel
has a natural singing voice.* **2.** Formed or made
by nature; not artificial: *There is the famous
natural bridge.*

nau·ti·cal (nô′ tĭ kəl) *adj.* Relating to or having to
do with sailors, ships, or navigation: *nautical charts.*

nee·dle (nēd′ l) *n.* **1.** A slender pointed steel
sewing tool with a hole, or "eye," to hold a thread.
2. A plain slender rod or a rod with a small hook
at the end, used in knitting or crocheting. **3.** A
device used by doctors and nurses to give shots.

neigh·bor (nā′ bər) *n., pl.* **neigh·bors. 1.** A
person who lives nearby. **2.** A person, country,
or thing that is near another. **3.** A fellow human
being: *Love your neighbor.*

net·work (nĕt′ wûrk′) *n.* **1.** Any system of lines
that cross: *a network of roads.* **2.** A chain of radio
or television stations that carry the same programs.

news·pa·per (nooz′ pā pər) *or* (nyooz′-) *n.* Sheets
of paper printed daily or weekly, containing news,
pictures, advertisements, etc.

nick·el (nĭk′ əl) *n.* **1.** A hard, silver-colored metal
found in certain rocks; a chemical element.
2. A coin in the U.S. that is worth five cents.

night·mare (nīt′ mâr′) *n.* **1.** A scary or bad
dream. **2.** A scary or bad experience.

ninth (nīnth) *n.* **1.** Next after eighth. **2.** One of
nine parts; 1/9.

noise (noiz) *n.* **1.** An unpleasant sound. **2.** Any kind of sound: *The noise of the machine made study difficult.*

no·mad (nō′ măd′) *n.* **1.** A member of a group of people who move from one place to another, looking for food and water for themselves and their animals. **2.** A person who moves from place to place; a wanderer.

North Pole (nôrth pōl) *n.* The farthest northern point on earth and the northern end of the earth's axis.

note·book (nōt′ bŏŏk′) *n.* A book with blank pages for writing.

no·tice (nō′ tĭs) *v.* **no·ticed, no·tic·ing.** To see; observe: *I notice that you have a new car.* —*n.* **1.** Attention: *He escaped notice.* **2.** Written or printed announcement or description: *There are several notices on the bulletin board.*

No·vem·ber (nō vĕm′ bər) *n.* The eleventh month of the year.

oak (ōk) *n.* **1.** Any acorn-bearing tree. **2.** The wood of these trees.

ob·ject¹ (ŏb′ jĕkt) *n.* **1.** A thing that has shape and can be touched and seen: *The only object rescued when the car sank into the lake was a tire.* **2.** Purpose; goal: *My object in life is to be a surgeon.*

ob·ject² (əb jĕkt′) *v.* **ob·ject·ed, ob·ject·ing. 1.** To be opposed; feel dislike: *Father objects to our walking barefoot in the living room.* **2.** To oppose; give reasons against: *Do you object to our plan?*

o·cean (ō′ shən) *n.* **1.** The vast body of saltwater covering three fourths of the earth's surface. **2.** Any of its main divisions, such as the Atlantic Ocean.

Oc·to·ber (ŏk tō′ bər) *n.* The tenth month of the year.

of·ten (ô′ fən) *or* (ŏf′ ən) *or* (ôf′ tən) *or* (ŏf′-) *adv.* Frequently; many times.

O·lym·pic (ō lĭm′ pĭk) *adj.* Of or relating to the Olympic Games. —*n.* **Olympics. 1.** The Olympic Games, festival of ancient Greece with contests in athletics, music, and poetry. **2.** The modern Olympic Games, a sports competition held every four years in a different country: *Athletes from many countries compete in the Olympics.*

o·men (ō′ mən) *n.* Something that is supposed to be a sign of a good or bad event to come: *When Keesha found a penny, she thought it was an omen of good luck.*

on·ion (ŭn′ yən) *n.* A plant grown as a vegetable having a bulb, a strong odor, and a biting taste.

or·bit (ôr′ bit) *n.* The path in which one heavenly body moves about another. —*v.* **or·bit·ed, or·bit·ing.** To travel in an orbit: *The earth orbits the sun.*

or·chard (ôr′ chərd) *n.* A piece of land where fruit trees are grown.

owe (ō) *v.* **owed, ow·ing. 1.** To have to pay; to be in debt. **2.** To have to do something because of the law, a promise, or a duty: *owe an apology.*

oy·ster (oi′ stər) *n.* A soft-bodied animal that lives inside two rough half-shells: *Many oysters have pearls.*

pack·age (păk′ ĭj) *n.* A container or box that holds something. —*v.* **pack·aged, pack·ag·ing.** To put into a container or box.

paid Look up **pay.**

pa·rade (pə rād′) *n.* A public event for a special occasion: *the Thanksgiving Parade.* —*v.* **pa·rad·ed, pa·rad·ing. 1.** To march. **2.** To walk proudly: *to parade around in new clothes.*

par·ty (pär′ tē) *n., pl.* **par·ties. 1.** An entertainment or social gathering: *a birthday party.* **2.** A group of people acting together: *A search party was sent out to find the missing child.* **3.** A political organization: *In an election, each party has a candidate.*

pay (pā) *v.* **paid** (pād), **pay·ing. 1.** To give money in return for things or work done. **2.** To give or make: *pay attention; pay a visit.*

peace (pēs) *n.* **1.** Freedom from fighting. **2.** Quiet; order.

pearl (pûrl) *n.* A small, round, white or grayish gem that is found inside the shell of certain oysters.

pe·can (pĭ **kän′**) or (-**kăn′**) or (**pē′** kan) n. An edible nut that has a thin, smooth, oval shell and grows on a tree.

ped·es·tal (**pĕd′** ĭ stəl) n. The base or support on which a statue or column stands: *The statue stood on a pedestal made of concrete.*

pen·al·ty (**pĕn′** əl tē) n., pl. **pen·al·ties. 1.** A punishment established by law. **2.** A disadvantage imposed by a referee upon a game player: *One more penalty and he's out of the game.*

pen·du·lum (**pĕn′** jə ləm) or (**pĕn′** dyə-) n. A weight that is hung from a fixed support, so that it can swing back and forth: *Pendulums are used to regulate the actions of some clocks.*

pen·sion (**pĕn′** shən) n. An amount of money that is paid regularly to a person who has retired from work or is disabled: *After teaching thirty years, Mrs. Mays retired and received a pension.*

per·fect (**pûr′** fĭkt) adj. **1.** Without fault; exactly right: *He got a perfect score on the test.* **2.** Complete; whole; thorough. —v. (pər **fĕkt′**). **per·fect·ed, per·fect·ing.** To remove all flaws from.

per·form (pər **fôrm′**) v. **per·formed, per·form·ing. 1.** To do or carry out: *to perform your obligations.* **2.** To act with skill: *She performed in the play.*

per·fume (**pûr′** fyo͞om′) or (pər **fyo͞om′**) n. **1.** A sweet-smelling liquid: *a new perfume.* **2.** A sweet smell; fragrance: *The perfume from the roses is wonderful.*

per·haps (pər **hăps′**) adv. Maybe; possibly: *Perhaps it will rain today.*

pe·ri·od·i·cal (pîr′ ē **ŏd′** ĭ kəl) n. A magazine or other publication that is printed at regular intervals, such as every week, every two weeks, or every month: *I look forward to receiving my favorite periodical every month.*

per·mit (pər **mĭt′**) v. **per·mit·ted, per·mit·ting.** To allow. —n. (**pûr′** mĭt) or (pər **mĭt′**). A written letter, license, or document giving permission.

per·son·al (**pûr′** sə nəl) adj. **1.** Belonging to a person; individual; private. **2.** Done in person. **3.** Of a person's body or physical appearance.

pet·al (**pĕt′** l) n. One of the parts of a flower, usually brightly or lightly colored.

pi·an·o (pē **ăn′** ō) n., pl. **pi·an·os.** A large musical instrument with steel wire strings that sound when struck by felt-covered hammers operated from a keyboard.

pick·le (**pĭk′** əl) n., pl. **pick·les.** A cucumber that has been preserved by soaking in salt water or vinegar.

pic·nic (**pĭk′** nĭk) n. Food that is packed and eaten outdoors; a meal eaten in the open air. —v. **pic·nicked, pic·nick·ing, pic·nics.** To have a picnic.

pin·na·cle (**pĭn′** ə kəl) n. **1.** A tall, pointed peak, as on a mountain. **2.** The highest point: *Being a star in the movie was the pinnacle of his career.*

pi·rate (**pī′** rĭt) n. A person who robs ships at sea.

pitch (pĭch) v. **pitched, pitch·ing. 1.** To throw or toss: *to pitch a baseball.* **2.** To set or put up: *to pitch a tent.* —n. A throw to a batter: *a good pitch right over home plate.*

piz·za (**pēt′** sə) n. An Italian dish made by baking a pie crust covered with tomato sauce, cheese, sausage, mushrooms, etc.

plain (plān) adj. **plain·er, plain·est. 1.** Something that is easy to hear, see, or understand. **2.** Simple; without any decoration. **3.** Not rich or too spicy: *plain food.* —n. Flat, treeless land. *These sound alike:* **plain, plane.**

plane (plān) n. **1.** A flat, level surface. **2.** An aircraft flown by an engine; airplane. *These sound alike:* **plane, plain.**

plan·et (**plăn′** ĭt) n. One of the nine celestial bodies that move in a circular path around the sun: Mercury, Venus, Earth, Mars, Jupiter, Saturn, Uranus, Neptune, and Pluto.

plas·tic (**plăs′** tĭk) n. Any of many chemically made substances that are molded by heat and pressure and then shaped.

pleas·ure (**plĕzh′** ər) n. **1.** A feeling of happiness or enjoyment. **2.** Something that causes a feeling of delight and happiness.

pledge (plĕj) n. A serious promise: *The friends made a pledge to stay together.* —v. **pledged, pledg·ing.** To promise.

po·em (**pō′** əm) n. Writing in verse, often imaginative and in rhyme.

po·lar (**pō′** lər) adj. Anything to do with a region around a geographic pole, such as the North Pole.

po·lite (pə **līt′**) adj. **po·lit·er, po·lit·est.** Having or showing good manners.

pol·lu·tion (pə **lo͞o′** shən) n. Contamination of the environment with waste.

pop·u·la·tion (pŏp′ yə **lā′** shən) n. **1.** The number of people who live in an area. **2.** People as a whole.

pore (pôr) n., pl. **pores.** A tiny opening in the skin of an animal or on the surface of a leaf, through which gases or liquids may pass.

pre·car·i·ous (prĭ **kâr′** ē əs) adj. Dangerous; unstable: *a precarious position.*

pre·pare (prĭ **pâr′**) v. **pre·pared, pre·par·ing.** To get ready; put oneself or things in readiness.

pre·sume (prĭ zōōm′) *v.* **pre·sumed,**
pre·sum·ing. To think to be true, even without
proof; take for granted: *I presume that everyone will
be on time.*

pret·ty (prĭt′ ē) *adj.* **pret·ti·er, pret·ti·est.**
1. Pleasing; attractive. **2.** Appealing; charming.

pri·or (prī′ ər) *adj.* Before or earlier in order, time,
or importance: *Although she is now a nurse, her
prior job was teaching.*

prob·lem (prŏb′ ləm) *n.* A confusing question or
situation; something difficult to figure out: *Finding
a babysitter is a real problem.*

pro·duc·er (prə dōō′ sər) *or* (-dyōō′-) *n.* **1.** The
person, place, or organization responsible for
making something: *Brazil is a producer of coffee
beans.* **2.** A person who manages the making of a
play, movie, or show: *a famous movie producer.*

pro·fes·sion·al (prə fĕsh′ ə nəl) *adj.* **1.** Having a
special knowledge or education for a job: *A doctor
is a professional person.* **2.** Making money by doing
what most people do for fun: *a professional tennis
player.* —*n.* **1.** A person who has special knowledge
or education. **2.** A person who makes money
doing what most people do for fun.

pro·gram (prō′ grăm) *or* (-grəm) *n.* **1.** A list of
what is to be shown or done in a presentation,
ceremony, etc. and who is to take part.
2. The ceremony or presentation itself. —*v.*
pro·grammed, pro·gram·ming. 1. To direct
or control according to a plan. **2.** To prepare
a set of instructions for a computer or other
automatic machine: *program a computer.*

prom·ise (prŏm′ ĭs) *n.* **1.** A statement that one
will or will not do something: *I gave a promise not
to be late again.* **2.** A sign of future success: *She
showed promise of becoming a good astronaut.* —*v.*
prom·ised, prom·is·ing. To make a statement
that one will or will not do something.

proof (prōōf) *n.* Evidence; demonstration of truth.

prove (prōōv) *v.* **proved, proved** *or* **prov·en,**
prov·ing. To show to be true; to demonstrate or
to give evidence: *She proved she knew how to do
long division.*

pump·kin (pŭmp′ kĭn)
or (pŭm′-) *n.* A large,
round, orange-yellow
fruit grown on a vine
and often used in
making pies.

pur·pose (pûr′ pəs)
n. The aim; intention; desired result.
   Idiom. **on purpose.** Not by accident.

puz·zle (pŭz′ əl) *n.* **1.** Something that is confusing;
a problem. **2.** A game or toy: *a crossword puzzle.*
—*v.* **puz·zled, puz·zling.** To confuse: *The magic
trick puzzled them.*

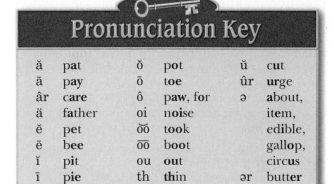

Pronunciation Key

ă	pat	ŏ	pot	ŭ	cut
ā	pay	ō	toe	ûr	urge
âr	care	ô	paw, for	ə	about,
ä	father	oi	noise		item,
ĕ	pet	ōō	took		edible,
ē	bee	ōō	boot		gallop,
ĭ	pit	ou	out		circus
ī	pie	th	thin	ər	butter
îr	deer	*th*	this		

Q

qual·i·fy (kwŏl′ ə fī′) *v.* **qual·i·fied,**
qual·i·fy·ing. 1. To be fit or show ability in skill
or knowledge: *They qualified for the football team.*
2. To limit: *to qualify your comments.*

quan·ti·ty (kwŏn′ tĭ tē) *n., pl.* **quan·ti·ties.** The
number or amount: *Pens and pencils are needed in
equal quantity.*

quar·rel (kwôr′ əl) *or* (kwŏr′-) *n.* A fight with
words; an argument. —*v.* **quar·reled,**
quar·rel·ing. To have a fight with words.

ques·tion (kwĕs′ chən) *n., pl.* **ques·tions.**
1. Something asked in order to find out something.
2. Matter to be discussed; problem or proposal:
The question of the class party was never settled. —*v.*
ques·tioned, ques·tion·ing. To ask in order
to find out something.
   Idiom. **out of the question.** Not to be thought
about; impossible.

quick (kwĭk) *adj.* **quick·er, quick·est.** Fast;
rapid; done with speed. —*adv.* **quick·ly.** Rapidly.

quit (kwĭt) *v.* **quit, quit·ting. 1.** To stop: *quit
work at five o'clock.* **2.** To give up; let go: *quit
college.*

quite (kwīt) *adv.* **1.** Completely; entirely: *You are
quite right.* **2.** To a considerable degree: *It is quite
cold today.*

quiz·zi·cal (kwĭz′ ĭ kəl) *adj.* Showing confusion or
puzzlement: *Because the student hadn't heard the
question, she had a quizzical look on her face.*

R

rab·bit (răb′ ĭt) *n.* A soft, furry animal with long
ears and a short fluffy tail.

rac·coon (ră **kōōn′**) *n.* A grayish-brown animal with black mask-like markings on the face and a long, bushy, black-ringed tail.

raise (rāz) *v.* **raised, rais·ing. 1.** To lift or move to a higher position: *raise your hand.* **2.** To gather together; collect: *to raise money for charity.* **3.** To help grow or rear: *to raise children.* **4.** To bring up or ask: *to raise a question.* —*n.* An increase in amount, price, pay, etc.: *a raise in salary.*

ran·dom (răn′ dəm) *adj.* Made or done without a definite plan or pattern: *I didn't know which package to open first, so I made a random choice.*
   Idiom. at random. With no method, purpose, or pattern.

rap·id (răp′ ĭd) *adj.* Fast; quick.

rath·er (ră*th*′ ər) *adv.* **1.** More willingly; preferably: *I'd rather see a movie.* **2.** Somewhat; to a certain extent: *a rather silly idea.*

raw (rô) *adj.* **raw·er, raw·est. 1.** Not cooked: *a raw potato.* **2.** Not artificially treated or processed; natural: *raw lumber.*

ra·zor (rā′ zər) *n.* An instrument with a sharp blade used to shave or cut hair: *Be careful not to cut yourself with the razor.*

rea·son (rē′ zən) *n.* **1.** A cause or motive for acting or feeling a certain way: *I have a reason for being angry.* **2.** An explanation; an excuse: *Give me one good reason.* **3.** The ability to think logically and clearly: *lost all reason.* —*v.* **rea·soned, rea·son·ing. 1.** To think with a clear mind. **2.** To try to persuade; to attempt to change a person's mind: *I will reason with you.*

re·cede (rĭ sēd′) *v.* **re·ced·ed, re·ced·ing.** To move back or away: *After the flood, the river water began to recede slowly from the field.*

re·cord·er (rĭ kôr′ dər) *n.* **1.** Someone who takes notes. **2.** A machine that keeps sounds on magnetic tape: *a tape recorder*

re·cy·cle (rē sī′ kəl) *v.* **re·cy·cled, re·cy·cling.** To treat or process materials that might be thrown away so that they can be used again: *Our class project was to recycle newspapers.*

ref·e·ree (rĕf′ ə rē′) *n.* An official in certain sports and games who enforces the rules and supervises the play: *The referee ruled that the team had scored a goal.*

re·lax (rĭ lăks′) *v.* **re·laxed, re·lax·ing.** To become less stiff; to loosen up; to be at ease.

re·main (rĭ mān′) *v.* **re·mained, re·main·ing. 1.** To stay behind after others go: *remain after school.* **2.** To be left: *So much remains to be done!* **3.** To continue as before: *She remained my friend.*

re·mem·ber (rĭ mĕm′ bər) *v.* **re·mem·bered, re·mem·ber·ing. 1.** To think of again; to recall or cause to remind: *I can remember my homework from yesterday.* **2.** To keep in mind: *to remember an appointment.* **3.** To present with a gift or reward: *You'll be remembered on your birthday.*

re·mind (rĭ mīnd′) *v.* **re·mind·ed, re·mind·ing.** To cause to remember; to recall to mind.

re·source·ful (rĭ sôrs′ fəl) *adj.* Able to deal with new, difficult, or different situations effectively or imaginatively: *On our picnic we had to be resourceful because we forgot our knives and forks.*

re·view (rĭ vyōō′) *v.* **re·viewed, re·view·ing. 1.** To look back, study, or examine again. **2.** To look back in one's mind. **3.** To write or tell about a book, movie, play, or event: *review a book.* —*n.* **1.** A study of something covered earlier in school. **2.** A report of a book, movie, play, or event: *I read the movie review in the paper.*

re·vise (rĭ vīz′) *v.* **re·vised, re·vis·ing. 1.** To look over and change in order to improve: *revise a story.* **2.** To change or make different: *to revise an opinion.*

rev·o·lu·tion (rĕv′ ə lōō′ shən) *n.* **1.** A complete overthrow of government: *the American Revolution.* **2.** A sudden or dramatic change. **3.** Movement in a circular path: *It takes a year for the earth to make a revolution around the sun.*

re·ward (rĭ wôrd′) *n.* **1.** Something given in return for a service or act. **2.** Money offered for the return of something lost. —*v.* **re·ward·ed, re·ward·ing.** To give something in return for something done.

rid·dle¹ (rĭd′ l) *v.* **rid·dled, rid·dling.** To make many holes in: *Arrows had riddled the walls.*

rid·dle² (rĭd′ l) *n.* A problem or question that is not easy to understand: *Try to answer this riddle.*

ride (rīd) *v.* **rode** (rōd), **rid·den, rid·ing. 1.** To sit on something in order to make it move: *to ride a bicycle.* **2.** To be carried on or by; to travel: *I ride the bus.* —*n.* **1.** A short trip on an animal or vehicle. **2.** A structure at an amusement park, used for pleasure: *The Ferris wheel is my favorite ride.*

right (rīt) *n.* **1.** On the side opposite the left: *Her house is on the right.* **2.** Just; good: *the difference between right and wrong.* —*adv.* **1.** Straight on; directly: *He looked right at the object.* **2.** Correctly: *John guessed right.* These sound alike: **right, write.**
   Idioms. right of way. The right to move first. **right away.** Immediately.

right·ful (rīt′ fəl) *adj.* Having a just or lawful claim: *Arthur was the rightful king.*

road (rōd) *n.* **1.** Pavement or cleared ground used to go from one place to another; a route or path: *Which road goes to town?* **2.** A direction toward something: *your road to success.* These sound alike: **road, rode.**

roar (rôr) *n.* **1.** A loud, deep sound: *a lion's roar.* **2.** A loud laugh. —*v.* **roared, roar·ing.** To make a loud, deep sound: *Please don't roar in my ear.*

roast (rōst) *v.* **roast·ed, roast·ing.** **1.** To cook by dry heat or over an open fire; to bake: *to roast a chicken.* **2.** To be extremely hot; to feel overheated: *You'll roast with your coat on indoors.* —*n.* A large cut of meat suitable for roasting.

rode Look up **ride.** *These sound alike:* **rode, road.**

rook·ie (rŏŏk' ē) *n.* **1.** A person who is a first-year player in a professional sport. **2.** A beginner who lacks training or experience.

room·mate (rōōm' māt') *or* (rōōm'-) *n.* A person who lives with others in a room or apartment: *My sister's roommate at college is from another country.*

roost·er (rōō' stər) *n.* A full-grown male chicken.

ro·ta·tion (rō tā' shən) *n.* Circular turning on an axis: *The rotation of the earth takes 24 hours.*

rough (rŭf) *adj.* **rough·er, rough·est.** **1.** Having an uneven surface; not smooth: *a rough road.* **2.** Violent; severe; not gentle.

roy·al (roi' əl) *adj.* **1.** Anything belonging to or having to do with a king or queen: *a royal palace.* **2.** Made for or acceptable for a king or queen: *a royal welcome.*

rum·mage (rŭm' ĭj) *v.* **rum·maged, rum·mag·ing.** To look for something thoroughly by turning things over or moving them around: *rummage through the closet.*

sa·fa·ri (sə fär' ē) *n., pl.* **sa·fa·ris.** A hunting trip, especially in Africa.

sail·boat (sāl' bōt') *n.* A boat that travels by wind blowing against its sails.

sal·ad (săl' əd) *n.* A combination of vegetables or fruit that is often served with a dressing.

sam·ple (săm' pəl) *or* (săm'-) *n.* A small piece of something that shows what the rest is like. —*v.* **sam·pled, sam·pling.** To try a part; to test.

sand·wich (sănd' wĭch) *or* (săn'-) *n., pl.* **sand·wich·es.** Two or more slices of bread with a filling of jelly, cheese, meat, egg, etc.

sat·el·lite (săt' l īt') *n.* **1.** A heavenly body that travels in orbit around another larger body. **2.** A man-made object that orbits the earth, the moon, or any other body in space.

Pronunciation Key

ă	pat	ŏ	pot	ŭ	cut
ā	pay	ō	toe	ûr	urge
âr	care	ô	paw, for	ə	about,
ä	father	oi	noise		item,
ĕ	pet	ŏŏ	took		edible,
ē	bee	ōō	boot		gallop,
ĭ	pit	ou	out		circus
ī	pie	th	thin	ər	butter
îr	deer	*th*	this		

Sat·ur·day (săt' ər dē) *or* (dā') *n.* The seventh day of the week.

saw·dust (sô' dŭst') *n.* The tiny pieces of wood that fall off during sawing.

scale¹ (skāl) *n.* An instrument used to find out the weight of something.

scale² (skāl) *n.* **1.** Equally spaced marks on a line used to measure: *Your ruler is a scale.* **2.** Musical tones that go up and down in pitch: *to play the scales on the piano.* —*v.* **scaled, scal·ing.** To climb.

scale³ (skāl) *n.* One of the layered plates on the outer covering of a fish, snake, etc.

scarf (skärf) *n., pl.* **scarves** (skärvz) *or* **scarfs** (skärfs). A piece of cloth worn around the head, neck, or shoulders for decoration or warmth: *Scarves are good for keeping your face and neck warm in winter.*

sci·ence (sī' əns) *n.* **1.** Knowledge based on facts about nature and the universe. **2.** Any branch of knowledge about the universe: biology, astronomy, etc.

scold (skōld) *v.* **scold·ed, scold·ing.** To blame with angry words in an angry tone of voice.

score (skôr) *or* (skōr) *n.* **1.** A number of points in a game. **2.** A result on a test. —*v.* **scored, scor·ing.** To make as points in a game, contest, or test.

score·board (skôr' bôrd') *n.* A large board that shows the score and other important game or contest information to spectators.

sea·son (sē' zən) *n.* **1.** One of the four parts of the year: spring, summer, autumn, winter. **2.** A special time of the year: *The holiday season.* —*v.* **sea·soned, sea·son·ing.** To give flavor to: *season food.*

sec·tion (sĕk' shən) *n.* A separated part; a cut-off area of a whole. —*v.* **sec·tioned, sec·tion·ing.** To separate or cut into sections.

se·lec·tion (sĭ lĕk' shən) *n.* The act of selecting or choosing.

self (sĕlf) *n., pl.* **selves** (sĕlvz). One's own person separate from any other.

self·ish (sĕl′ fĭsh) *adj.* Caring too much for oneself and not for others.

sen·tence (sĕn′ təns) *n.* **1.** A group of words that expresses a complete thought. **2.** A decision by a judge in a court of law; a verdict.

Sep·tem·ber (sĕp tĕm′ bər) *n.* The ninth month of the year.

serv·ice (sûr′ vĭs) *n.* A useful act. —*v.* **serv·iced, serv·ic·ing.** To provide or make ready for use: *I'll service your car.*

sew (sō) *v.* **sewed, sewn** *or* **sewed, sew·ing.** To attach or fasten with a needle and thread.

shad·y (shā′ dē) *adj.* **shad·i·er, shad·i·est. 1.** Sheltered from sun or light. **2.** Of questionable honesty or character: *a shady person.*

sham·poo (shăm pōō′) *n.* A preparation for cleaning. —*v.* **sham·pooed, sham·poo·ing.** To wash and clean with soap or detergent.

share (shâr) *v.* **shared, shar·ing. 1.** To take part; join: *to share in the happiness.* **2.** To use, enjoy, or have in common: *to share the same room.* **3.** To divide or portion: *to share your lunch.* —*n.* Portion or part of something received, done, or enjoyed by a number of persons: *He took his share of the profits.*

sheet (shēt) *n.* **1.** Cloth used to cover a bed: *Fresh sheets are on the bed.* **2.** A thin, large piece of something: *A sheet of ice is slippery.* **3.** A piece of paper: *Take out a new sheet of paper.*

shock (shŏk) *n.* **1.** A sudden or violent blow: *the shock of an explosion.* **2.** A sudden upset of the mind or emotions: *The bad news was a terrible shock to them.* **3.** Effect of electric current on the body: *a shock from a wire.* —*v.* **shocked, shock·ing.** To surprise, horrify, or disgust.

shoe (shōō) *n.* An outer covering for the foot, often made of leather.

shore (shôr) *or* (shōr) *n.* The land at the edge of an ocean, sea, river, or lake.

shut·tle (shŭt′ l) *n.* **1.** The thread holder used in weaving to carry the threads back and forth through the yarn. **2.** A train, plane, bus, etc., that goes only between two places on a frequent and regular schedule. **3.** A spacecraft capable of carrying astronauts back and forth for short distances in space: *The astronauts took the shuttle from their spaceship to Earth and back again.* —*v.* **shut·tled, shut·tling.** To move back and forth.

siege (sēj) *n.* The surrounding of an enemy town or fort and cutting off supplies to it for a long time in order to force a surrender.

sig·nal (sĭg′ nəl) *n.* **1.** A sign that warns, gives notice, or points out something: *a railroad signal.* **2.** An action that is used to start something: *a referee's signal to start the game.* —*v.* **sig·naled, sig·nal·ing.** To warn or point out.

sil·ver (sĭl′ vər) *n.* **1.** A soft, shiny metal that is easily shaped into jewelry, coins, etc. **2.** Coins; change: *to carry silver.* **3.** Forks, knives, and other tableware made with this metal; silverware. —*adj.* Having the color of silver.

sim·i·lar (sĭm′ ə lər) *adj.* Alike somehow but not the same.

sim·ple (sĭm′ pəl) *adj.* **sim·pler, sim·plest. 1.** easy to understand or to do: *a simple test.* **2.** plain; not fancy: *a simple white shirt.*

since (sĭns) *prep.* **1.** From a certain time in the past until now: *I have been ready since noon.* **2.** At any time between some past time or event and the present: *I have not seen him since yesterday.* —*conj.* **1.** Because. **2.** After: *She has changed her clothes since I saw her last.*

sixth (sĭksth) *n.* **1.** Next after fifth. **2.** One of six equal parts; 1/6.

skate (skāt) *n.* A boot or shoe made with a blade or wheels on the bottom, used for moving on the ice, street, floor, etc.: *roller skate.* —*v.* **skat·ed, skat·ing.** To move by using a blade or wheels on the foot: *to skate home.*

ski (skē) *n., pl.* **skis** *or* **ski.** A long, thin piece of wood, plastic, or metal attached to a boot to glide on snow. —*v.* **skied, ski·ing, skis.** To travel on skis.

skill (skĭl) *n.* Knowledge or ability to do something well: *It takes skill to build a house.*

skin div·ing (skĭn′ dī′ vĭng) *n.* Swimming underwater for a long time by using a face mask, rubber flippers, and a snorkel.

skirt (skûrt) *n.* Clothing worn by girls and women, which hangs from the waist down. —*v.* **skirt·ed, skirt·ing.** To travel along the edge of: *The car skirted the puddle.*

smol·der *also* **smoul·der** (smōl′ dər) *v.* **smol·dered, smol·der·ing. 1.** To burn slowly with little smoke and no flame: *The coals will smolder for hours.* **2.** To continue in a hidden manner.

snack (snăk) *n.* A small amount of food eaten between meals; a light meal.

snake (snāk) *n.* A long, scaly, crawling animal without legs; serpent.

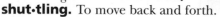

soc·cer (sŏk′ ər) *n.* A game in which two teams of 11 players each try to kick a round ball into the other team's goal. The arms and hands cannot be used for hitting the ball or stopping an opponent.

so·lar (sō′ lər) *adj.* Of or having to do with the sun: *solar energy.*

sol·id (sŏl′ ĭd) *adj.* **1.** Having a definite size and shape, not a liquid or a gas. **2.** Hard; firm; able to support weight: *solid ground.* **3.** Having a sound character; trustworthy: *a solid person.*

sol·i·tude (sŏl′ ĭ tōōd′) or (sŏl′ ĭ tyōōd′) *n.* **1.** The state of being alone: *The author needed solitude in order to write the book.* **2.** A place away from people: *the solitude of the mountain cabin.*

span·iel (spăn′ yəl) *n.* A small- to medium-sized dog with drooping ears, short legs, and silky, wavy hair.

sparse (spärs) *adj.* Not crowded; widely scattered: *Plants are sparse in the desert.*

spe·cial (spĕsh′ əl) *adj.* Uncommon, unusual; that which is different from others: *a special day.*

speech (spēch) *n., pl.* **speech·es. 1.** The act of speaking: *to burst into speech.* **2.** Words; remarks: *Her speech is full of slang.* **3.** A formal talk delivered in public: *a graduation speech.*

square (skwâr) *n.* **1.** A figure with four equal sides and four right angles. **2.** Anything that has this shape. **3.** An open space in a town or city surrounded on all sides by streets: *Trees were planted in the city square.* —*adj.* **squar·er, squar·est. 1.** Having four equal sides. **2.** Measure of a surface area: *a square foot.* **3.** Honest, direct, or fair: *a square deal.*

St. Abbreviation of **Street** and **Saint.**

stare (stâr) *v.* **stared, star·ing.** To look with open eyes for a long time. —*n.* A wide-eyed, fixed look held for some time.

starve (stärv) *v.* **starved, starv·ing. 1.** To become very ill or to die from extreme hunger. **2.** To be hungry: *I'm starving for chocolate chip cookies.*

sta·tion (stā′ shən) *n.* **1.** A regularly scheduled stop on a train or bus route. **2.** A building used for such a stop: *a train station.* **3.** A place that is used to send or receive radio or television programs: *How many television stations do you get?* —*v.* **sta·tioned, sta·tion·ing.** To put oneself at an appointed place: *The detective stationed himself nearby.*

steep (stēp) *adj.* **steep·er, steep·est. 1.** Having a sharp slope; almost straight up and down: *a steep cliff.* **2.** Very high: *steep prices.*

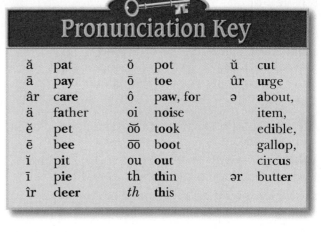

stom·ach·ache (stŭm′ ək āk′) *n.* A pain in the stomach or abdomen.

sto·ry[1] (stôr′ ē) *n., pl.* **sto·ries. 1.** An account, oral or written, of something that has happened: *a newspaper story.* **2.** A tale of fiction. **3.** A lie: *Tell the truth, not a story.*

sto·ry[2] (stôr′ ē) or (stōr′ ē) *n., pl.* **sto·ries.** Any level or floor of a building.

stow·a·way (stō′ ə wā′) *n.* A person who hides in a ship, airplane, or other vehicle in order to travel without paying for the trip: *The stowaway was found by the captain of the ship.*

straw (strô) *n.* **1.** A narrow tube made of plastic or waxed paper used for drinking a liquid: *a soda straw.* **2.** Stems or stalks of grain that have been seeded and dried: *The animals in the barn sleep on straw.*

straw·ber·ry (strô′ bĕr′ ē) *n., pl.* **straw·ber·ries.** A sweet, red fruit with many small seeds on its surface: *Strawberries grow close to the ground.*

stu·di·o (stōō′ dē ō′) or (styōō′-) *n.* **1.** An artist's workroom. **2.** A place where a film, TV, or radio program is made.

sug·ar (shŏŏg′ ər) *n.* A sweet substance obtained from sugar beets, sugar cane, maple trees, fruits, etc.

suit·case (sōōt′ kās′) *n.* A flat, rectangular traveling bag.

Sun·day (sŭn′ dē) or (-dā′) *n.* The first day of the week.

sup·pose (sə pōz′) *v.* **sup·posed, sup·pos·ing. 1.** To assume; expect; take for granted: *I suppose I'll see you at the party.* **2.** To imagine; pretend: *Let's suppose you won the lottery.*

sur·prise (sər prīz′) *v.* **sur·prised, sur·pris·ing. 1.** To take someone unawares; to come upon unexpectedy: *He surprised me with a visit.* **2.** To cause to feel wonder or astonishment: *The mild man's fury surprised us.* —*n.* **1.** A catching unawares: *to be caught by surprise.* **2.** Something sudden or unexpected. **3.** A feeling caused by something sudden or unexpected; astonishment: *Imagine our surprise when we saw our new bikes!*

sur·vey·or (sər vā′ ər) *n.* A person whose job is to measure land: *The surveyor will tell us exactly how big our property is.*

swal·low¹ (swŏl′ ō) *v.* **swal·lowed, swal·low·ing. 1.** To transfer food or drink from the mouth to the stomach through the throat: *to swallow cake.* **2.** To engulf; destroy. **3.** To believe easily: *They'll swallow anything you tell them.* —*n.* **1.** The act of swallowing. **2.** The amount swallowed at one time.

swal·low² (swŏl′ ō) *n.* A slender fork-tailed bird with pointed wings and swift, graceful flight.

sweat·er (swĕt′ ər) *n.* A knitted or crocheted garment, with or without sleeves, for the upper part of the body.

sweat·shirt (swĕt′ shûrt′) *n.* A heavy long-sleeved pullover shirt usually made of cotton jersey knit.

swim (swĭm) *v.* **swam, swum, swim·ming. 1.** To pass through water by moving legs, arms, fins, etc. **2.** To cross by swimming: *The team swam the English Channel.* **3.** To be immersed in or covered by a liquid: *Their eyes began to swim with tears.* —*n.* The act or sport of swimming.

symp·tom (sĭm′ təm) *or* (sĭmp′-) *n.* **1.** A sign in the body that is an indication of a disease or illness: *My cough was the first symptom that I had the flu.* **2.** A sign or indication of something.

sys·tem (sĭs′ təm) *n.* **1.** A group of things that go together to make up a whole: *The trains, the tracks, the schedule, and the engineer are all parts of a railroad system.* **2.** A combination of parts of the body that work together and are dependent on one another: *the circulatory system.* **3.** Orderly method of doing things; routine: *Hugh has a system for his day's work.*

ta·ble·spoon (tā′ bəl spoon′) *n.* **1.** A measuring spoon equal to three teaspoons that is used for cooking. **2.** A large serving spoon.

tar·dy (tär′ dē) *adj.* **tar·di·er, tar·di·est. 1.** Not on time; late: *We were all tardy because of the storm.* **2.** Slow: *a tardy growth of plants.*

taught Look up **teach.**

teach (tēch) *v.* **taught** (tôt), **teach·ing.** To give lessons; to help someone or something to learn.

teach·er (tē′ chər) *n.* A person who teaches.

tear¹ (târ) *v.* **tore** (tôr) *or* (tōr), **torn, tear·ing.** To pull apart.

tear² (tîr) *n.* A drop of water from the eyes.

tel·e·phone (tĕl′ ə fōn′) *n.* An instrument or system for sending and receiving speech and other sounds over electric wires. —*v.* **tel·e·phoned, tel·e·phon·ing.** To use this instrument to speak with someone; call: *Please telephone me.*

tel·e·scope (tĕl′ ə skōp′) *n.* An instrument for making distant things appear larger, especially a large instrument of this kind for studying heavenly bodies. —*v.* **tel·e·scoped, tel·e·scop·ing.** To fit a smaller object into a larger similar object; nest: *Let's telescope these boxes to save space.*

tel·e·vi·sion (tĕl′ ə vĭzh′ ən) *n.* **1.** A system for sending and receiving moving pictures and sound. **2.** A machine that receives these pictures and sounds and presents them to a viewer.

ten·nis (tĕn′ ĭs) *n.* A game for two players or two pairs of players who use rackets to hit a ball back and forth across a net.

their (thâr) *pron.* The possessive of **they.** Of or belonging to them: *Their float won first prize.* These sound alike: **their, there, they're.**

theme (thēm) *n.* **1.** A subject written or talked about; topic: *the theme of the discussion; the theme of a party.* **2.** Short essay: *Students write themes.*

there (thâr) *adv.* **1.** In or at that place: *Put it there, not here.* **2.** To or toward that place: *I can walk there in an hour.* —*n.* That place: *We came from there an hour ago.* These sound alike: **there, their, they're.**

they're (thâr). The contraction for "they are." These sound alike: **they're, their, there.**

think (thĭngk) *v.* **thought** (thôt), **think·ing.** To use the mind to form ideas, opinions, beliefs, decisions, etc.

third (thûrd) *adj.* **1.** Next after second. **2.** One of three equal parts; 1/3: *He ate a third of the pie.*

thir·teen (thûr′ tēn′) *n.* Amount or quantity that is one greater than twelve.

though (thō) *conj.* **1.** In spite of the fact that; although: *We kept on working, though it was very late.* **2.** Even if: *Start the job now, though you cannot finish it.*

thought Look up **think.**

thread (thrĕd) *n.* A fine cord of twisted silk, cotton, wool, or similar fibers from which cloth is woven or with which things are sewed. —*v.* **thread·ed, thread·ing.** To make one's way through obstacles: *We threaded our way through the crowd.*

threw Look up **throw.** These sound alike: **threw, through.**

throat (thrōt) *n.* **1.** The passage running from the back of the mouth to the lungs and stomach: *a sore throat.* **2.** A narrow entrance or passage: *the throat of a cave.*

through (thrōō) *prep.* From one end to the other: *to go through a tunnel.* —*adj.* **1.** Going or extending from one end to another: *a through street.* **2.** Finished: *I'm through with this work. These sound alike:* **through, threw.**

throw (thrō) *v.* **threw** (thrōō) **thrown, throw·ing. 1.** To fling with a motion of the arm; hurl: *to throw a ball.* **2.** To cause to fall; cause to lose balance: *One wrestler threw the other.* **3.** To cast; project: *The lamp throws a shadow on the wall.* —*n.* A flinging; a casting: *a throw of the ball.*
   Idiom. **a stone's throw.** Short distance.

thun·der·storm (thŭn′ dər stôrm′) *n.* A storm of lightning and thunder, usually with a downpour of rain.

Thurs·day (thûrz′ dē) *or* (-dā′) *n.* The fifth day of the week.

tim·id (tĭm′ ĭd) *adj.* Lacking in courage; shy; easily frightened: *Tandalyn was too timid to give her speech.*

to (tōō) *or* (tə *when unstressed*) *prep.* **1.** Toward; in the direction of: *on my way to school.* **2.** As far as: *going to Boston.* **3.** For the purpose of; for: *built to last; a key to the door.* **4.** Opposite: *face to face.* **5.** On; upon; against: *There is a sign tacked to the door.* **6.** Until; till: *The play lasts to 10:30.* **7.** Before: *five minutes to six. These sound alike:* **to, too, two.**
   Idiom. **to and fro.** Back and forth.

toast·er (tō′ stər) *n.* An electrical device for browning and heating bread and rolls.

to·ken (tō′ kən) *n.* **1.** Something that represents something else, such as an event, special occasion, fact, object, or feeling; symbol: *The postcard is a token of our trip.* **2.** A piece of metal that looks like a coin and is used in place of money, as in paying the fares on buses or subways.

to·mor·row (tə mŏr′ ō) *or* (-môr′ ō) *n.* **1.** The day after today: *Is tomorrow a holiday?* **2.** The near future: *the world of tomorrow.* —*adv.* On the day after today: *I will give this to you tomorrow.*

tongue (tŭng) *n.* **1.** The muscular, movable organ in the mouth used in tasting and also, in human beings, for talking. **2.** A language: *Her native tongue is Spanish.* **3.** A manner of speaking: *to have a sharp tongue.* **4.** Anything like a tongue in shape or use, such as leaping flame or the piece of leather under the laces of a shoe.

too (tōō) *adv.* **1.** Also; in addition; besides: *You are invited to the graduation ceremony and the party, too.* **2.** More than enough: *There was too much food. These sound alike:* **too, to, two.**

tore Look up **tear.**

tor·na·do (tôr nā′ dō) *n.,* *pl.* **tor·na·does** *or* **tor·na·dos.** Violent, whirling wind that travels rapidly in a narrow path. It is seen as a twisting, dark cloud shaped like a funnel.

touch (tŭch) *v.* **touched, touch·ing. 1.** To be in contact: *Their heads touched as they whispered.* **2.** To feel with the fingers: *She touched the paint.*

to·ward (tôrd) *or* (tə wôrd′) *prep.* **1.** In the direction of: *We sailed toward Hawaii.* **2.** Close upon; near: *We camped toward sundown.* **3.** About; regarding: *What is your attitude toward the candidates?*

track (trăk) *n.* **1.** A mark left by something moving: *The animal left its tracks.* **2.** A path or trail: *The track is two miles long.* **3.** The rails on which a train moves. **4.** A racetrack. —*v.* **tracked, track·ing.** To follow by sight or scent.

traf·fic (trăf′ ĭk) *n.* **1.** The movement of people, automobiles, planes, ships, etc.: *There was much traffic on the road.* **2.** The exchange of goods; buying and selling. —*v.* **traf·ficked, traf·fick·ing, traf·fics.** To buy or sell.

trans·por·ta·tion (trăns′ pər tā′ shən) *n.* The means of moving anything from one place to another.

tra·peze (tră pēz′) *n.* A short bar placed between two hanging ropes, used by gymnasts and circus acrobats.

treas·ure (trĕzh′ ər) *n.* Valuable thing or things such as jewels, gold, money, etc. —*v.* **treas·ured, treas·ur·ing.** To value; to think of very highly.

trem·ble (trĕm′ bəl) *v.* **trem·bled, trem·bling. 1.** To shake from fright, cold, anger, etc.: *Your hand is trembling.* **2.** To move or quake: *I think the building is trembling.* —*n.* A shudder.

tried Look up **try.**

trou·ble (trŭb′ əl) *n.* **1.** A dangerous situation: *The police rushed to the scene of trouble.* **2.** Extra effort or bother: *Please don't go to any trouble for me.* —*v.* **trou·bled, trou·bling. 1.** To disturb or cause worry: *His fever troubles me.* **2.** To bother: *May I trouble you for a minute?*

truth (trōōth) *n., pl.* **truths** (trōōthz) *or* (trōōths). **1.** Something that is true; fact. **2.** Honesty or sincerity of speech and action.

try (trī) *v.* **tried** (trīd), **try·ing. 1.** To make an effort: *I tried to finish in time.* **2.** To test or experiment: *Try out your new skates.* **3.** To examine or investigate in a court of law: *The case will be tried in court.* —*n.* An effort.

Tues·day (tōōz′ dē) *or* (-dā′) *or* (tyōōz′-) *n.* The third day of the week.

tum·ble (tŭm′ bəl) *v.* **tum·bled, tum·bling. 1.** To fall or roll over. **2.** To perform acrobatics such as leaps, headstands, etc. —*n.* A fall.

tu·tor (tōō′ tər) *or* (tyōō′-) *n.* A teacher who gives private instruction to a student: *My English tutor helped me three times a week.* —*v.* **tu·tored, tu·tor·ing.** To teach privately.

tweed (twēd) *n.* A rough woolen fabric made with two or more colors of yarn that is often used to make coats and casual suits.

two (tōō) *n.* A number written 2, meaning one more than one. *These sound alike:* **two, to, too.**

ty·rant (tī′ rənt) *n.* A person or ruler who uses power in a cruel and unjust way: *The people were very upset because the king had become a tyrant.*

ug·ly (ŭg′ lē) *adj.* **ug·li·er, ug·li·est. 1.** Unpleasant to look at: *ugly wallpaper.* **2.** Mean and disagreeable: *an ugly temper.*

ul·ti·mate (ŭl′ tə mĭt) *adj.* **1.** Last; final: *Her ultimate goal is to be President of the United States.* **2.** Basic: *The ultimate cause of the accident was carelessness.*

um·pire (ŭm′ pīr′) *n.* A person whose job is to rule on plays in sports, especially in baseball: *The umpire called the pitch a strike.* —*v.* **um·pired, um·pir·ing.** To act as an umpire for: *Ling umpired the game.*

u·ni·verse (yōō′ nə vûrs′) *n.* Everything in existence: the earth, the heavens, and all of space.

up·roar (ŭp′ rôr′) *or* (-rōr′) *n.* A loud noise caused by excitement or confusion.

up·set (ŭp sĕt′) *v.* **up·set, up·set·ting. 1.** To overturn or knock over: *The kitten upset the fishbowl.* **2.** To interfere or cause disorder: *The holiday crowds upset the train schedule.* **3.** To disturb or worry: *Did I upset you?* **4.** To unexpectedly defeat in a contest: *Our soccer team upset the champions.* —*n.* (ŭp′ sĕt′). The act of overturning or causing a disturbance. —*adj.* (ŭp sĕt′). **1.** Overturned: *an upset boat.* **2.** Disturbed; sick: *an upset stomach.*

u·til·i·ty (yōō tĭl′ ĭ tē) *n., pl.* **u·til·i·ties. 1.** A company that supplies a service to the public: *The company that provides electricity is a utility.* **2.** Usefulness: *The utility of computers is well known.* —*adj.* Of or relating to a company that provides a service to the public.

va·ca·tion (vā kā′ shən) *n.* Time of rest from a regular routine; freedom from school or work: *a summer vacation.*

veg·e·ta·ble (vĕj′ tə bəl) *or* (vĕj′ ĭ tə-) *n., pl.* **veg·e·ta·bles.** A plant whose seeds, leaves, or roots may be used as food: *Carrots are my favorite vegetables.*

ve·loc·i·ty (və lŏs′ ĭ tē) *n., pl.* **ve·loc·i·ties.** The rate at which something moves in a particular direction; speed: *the velocity of sound.*

vid·e·o (vĭd′ ē ō′) *n., pl.* **vid·e·os. 1.** The picture on a television or computer screen. **2.** A videocassette or videotape. —*adj.* Having to do with what is seen on a television or computer screen: *video equipment.*

vil·lage (vĭl′ ĭj) *n.* A group of houses and businesses forming a small community, usually smaller than a town.

vir·tu·al (vûr′ chōō əl) *adj.* Being so for all practical purposes, though not in fact or name: *Kendall was the virtual star of the play even though she didn't have the biggest part.*

vo·cal (vō′ kəl) *adj.* **1.** Relating to or made by the voice: *vocal chords.* **2.** Relating to or made by singing: *I enjoyed the vocal music performed by the school choir.* **3.** Expressing opinions freely and often; outspoken: *He was vocal in his support of the new school building, making long speeches at every town meeting.*

voice (vois) *n.* A sound coming from the mouth made by speaking, shouting, singing, etc. —*v.* **voiced, voic·ing.** To give expression to: *He voiced his opinions.*

void (void) *n.* Empty space: *There was a void in the stadium after the teams and fans went home.* —*adj.* **1.** Empty. **2.** Worth nothing.

vol·ley·ball (vŏl′ ē bôl′) *n.* **1.** A game in which two teams try to bat a large ball back and forth across a net with their hands without letting the ball touch the ground. **2.** The ball used in this game.

vote (vōt) *n.* **1.** A formal expression of a choice: *a vote for student government.* **2.** The right or opportunity to express a choice: *I am too young to have a vote.* —*v.* **vot·ed, vot·ing.** To express a choice in an election.

voy·age (voi′ ĭj) *n.* A long journey to a faraway place made by water or through space.

waist (wāst) *n.* **1.** The narrow part of the body between the ribs and the hips. **2.** Part of an object that is narrower than the rest of it: *the waist of a violin. These sound alike:* **waist, waste.**

wal·low (wŏl′ ō) *v.* **wal·lowed, wal·low·ing.** To roll about in something such as mud or water: *Sometimes pigs will wallow in mud.*

wan·der (wŏn′ dər) *v.* **wan·dered, wan·der·ing. 1.** To roam without a particular purpose: *I wandered through the old gardens.* **2.** To get lost: *A search party was sent after the child who wandered from camp.* **3.** To ramble in speech or thought: *The speaker began to wander from the subject.*

warn (wôrn) *v.* **warned, warn·ing. 1.** To put on guard against danger; alert; caution: *The coast guard warned all ships of the hurricane.* **2.** To notify, signal: *Her look warned us it was time to leave.*

waste (wāst) *v.* **wast·ed, wast·ing. 1.** To squander; use without profit: *I am afraid that my brother wasted his allowance.* **2.** To destroy; spoil; ruin: *The forest was wasted by fire.* —*n.* **1.** Useless expenditure; profitless use: *a waste of opportunity.* **2.** Discarded material; refuse; something left over: *Factory waste pollutes our river. These sound alike:* **waste, waist.**

watch (wŏch) *v.* **watched, watch·ing. 1.** To look carefully; be attentive; be on the lookout: *If you watch, you may see how I do this trick.* **2.** To see; look at: *to watch a parade.* —*n.* **1.** Close observation: *Keep careful watch, and you'll see a falling star.* **2.** Wakefulness for the purpose of guarding or tending to: *a mother's watch over her sick child.* **3.** A small timepiece, usually worn on the wrist.

weak (wēk) *adj.* **weak·er, weak·est. 1.** Lacking physical strength: *to be weak from hunger.* **2.** Likely to fail or break if placed under pressure, stress or strain: *a weak bridge.* **3.** Lacking in ability: *weak in math.*

wealth (wĕlth) *n.* **1.** A large quantity of money or possessions; riches. **2.** An abundance: *a wealth of ideas.*

wear (wâr) *v.* **wore** (wôr) **worn, wear·ing. 1.** To have on the body: *wear clothes; wear a smile.* **2.** To cause damage by long use: *wear a hole in a sock.*

weath·er (wĕ*th*′ ər) *n.* The atmospheric conditions at any place at a particular time: *The weather is beautiful today.* —*v.* **weath·ered. weath·er·ing. 1.** To come through safely or successfully: *to weather a storm.* **2.** To become bleached, dried, etc., by the action of the sun, wind, rain, etc.: *The shingles of the old house had weathered to a beautiful silver gray.*
   Idiom. **under the weather.** Not feeling well; ill. *These sound alike:* **weather, whether.**

Wednes·day (wĕnz′ dē) *or* (-dā′) *n.* The fourth day of the week.

week·end (wēk′ ĕnd′) *n.* The end of the week, especially the time from Friday night to Sunday night.

weigh (wā) *v.* **weighed. weigh·ing. 1.** To find out the heaviness of something by means of a scale or balance: *to weigh a parcel.* **2.** To have a certain weight: *He weighs 90 pounds.* **3.** To turn over in the mind; ponder: *He weighed another plan.*

weight (wāt) *n.* **1.** The amount a thing weighs: *the weight of a feather.* **2.** An object, usually metal, of specific heaviness used to balance a scale: *a set of weights from one ounce to five pounds.*
   Idiom. **pull one's weight.** To do one's part.

weight·less (wāt′ lĭs) *adj.* **1.** Having very little or no weight. **2.** Not affected by the pull of gravity: *The astronaut had to get used to being weightless in space.*

wheat (wēt) *n.* **1.** A kind of grain. **2.** The seeds of this plant used to make flour.

wheth·er (wĕ*th*′ ər) *conj.* **1.** If: *I don't know whether you're telling the truth or not.* **2.** No matter if: *The race is beginning whether or not you are ready.* These sound alike: **whether, weather.**

whis·tle (wĭs′ əl) *v.* **whis·tled, whis·tling. 1.** To make a shrill, piercing sound: *The train whistled.* **2.** To make a shrill sound with puckered lips or between the teeth: *We whistled for a taxicab.* **3.** To move with a speed fast enough to make a sharp, shrill, or piercing sound: *The wind whistled in the storm.* —*n.* **1.** A sharp, shrill, piercing sound: *the whistle of a quail.* **2.** A sound made by forcing air through puckered lips. **3.** A device used to make a whistle: *The traffic officer blew her whistle loud enough for everyone to hear.*

whole (hōl) *adj.* **1.** Not broken; having all parts: *The vase was dropped, but it is still whole.* **2.** The entire amount or extent: *We had trouble with the car the whole way home.* —*n.* **1.** Entire amount with all pieces; sum: *The whole is equal to the sum of its parts.* **2.** A complete system; unity: *The organs of the body work together as a whole.* These sound alike: **whole, hole.**

whom (hōōm) *pron.* **1.** What person: *To whom am I speaking?* **2.** That (person): *This is the man whom I mentioned yesterday.*

whose (hōōz) *adj.* Possessive form of **who:** *the man whose painting we bought.*

wife (wīf) *n., pl.* **wives** (wīvz). A married woman.

wish (wĭsh) *n., pl.* **wish·es.** Something desired, needed, or wanted. —*v.* **wished, wish·ing. 1.** To crave; to want or feel a desire for. **2.** To express a hope for another: *I wish only the best for you.*

won·der·ful (wŭn′ dər fəl) *adj.* **1.** Extraordinary; remarkable; causing wonder: *a wonderful trip.* **2.** Admirable; excellent: *a wonderful idea.*

wore Look up **wear.**

wreck (rĕk) *v.* **wrecked, wreck·ing.** To destroy or to take apart: *The building was wrecked because it was a fire hazard.* —*n.* **1.** Damage or destruction caused by wind, an accident, etc. **2.** Remains of anything ruined or destroyed: *The wreck was hauled away.*

wrin·kle (rĭng′ kəl) *n.* A fold or ridge on a surface; crease: *a shirt full of wrinkles.* —*v.* **wrin·kled, wrin·kling.** To make a fold or to become creased.

wrist (rĭst) *n.* The joint connecting the hand and forearm.

write (rīt) *v.* **wrote, writ·ten, writ·ing. 1.** To shape letters or words with a pencil or pen: *Write so that I can read.* **2.** To make up stories, poems, or books: *She writes stories.* **3.** To send a note or letter: *Write a thank-you letter.* These sound alike: **write, right.**

wrong (rông) *or* (rŏng) *adj.* **1.** Incorrect; false: *a wrong answer.* **2.** Not right; bad, wicked: *It is wrong to steal.* **3.** Unsuitable; inappropriate: *to do or say the wrong thing.* **4.** Out of order; amiss: *There is something wrong with my watch.* —*v.* **wronged, wrong·ing.** To treat unfairly.

yolk (yōk) *n.* The yellow part of an egg.

zone (zōn) *n.* Any area that is set off from others. —*v.* **zoned, zon·ing.** To divide into special areas.